ADVANCING BLACK MALE STUDENT
SUCCESS FROM PRESCHOOL
THROUGH PH.D.

ADVANCING BLACK MALE STUDENT SUCCESS FROM PRESCHOOL THROUGH PH.D.

EDITED BY

Shaun R. Harper and J. Luke Wood

STERLING, VIRGINIA

Sty/us

Published by Stylus Publishing, LLC
22883 Quicksilver Drive
Sterling, Virginia 20166-2102

Library of Congress Cataloging-in-Publication Data
Harper, Shaun R., 1975-
  Advancing black male student success from preschool through
Ph.D. / edited by Shaun R. Harper and J. Luke Wood.
    pages cm
Includes bibliographical references and index.
ISBN 978-1-62036-184-9 (pbk. : alk. paper)
ISBN 978-1-62036-183-2 (cloth : alk. paper)
ISBN 978-1-62036-185-6 (library networkable e-edition)
ISBN 978-1-62036-186-3 (consumer e-edition)
1. African American young men–Education. 2. African American
men–Education. 3. African American men–Education (Higher)
4. African American young men–Social conditions. 5. African
American men–Social conditions. I. Wood, J. Luke, 1982- II. Title.
LC2731.H36 2015
371.829'96073–dc23
                                                                    2014038098
13-digit ISBN: 978-1-62036-183-2 (cloth)
13-digit ISBN: 978-1-62036-184-9 (paperback)
13-digit ISBN: 978-1-62036-185-6 (library networkable e-edition)
13-digit ISBN: 978-1-62036-186-3 (consumer e-edition)

Printed in the United States of America

All first editions printed on acid-free paper
that meets the American National Standards Institute
Z39-48 Standard.

Bulk Purchases

Quantity discounts are available for use in workshops and for
staff development.
Call 1-800-232-0223

First Edition, 2016

10 9 8 7 6 5 4 3 2 1

*To Barack Obama, Our Brothers' Keeper and 44th President of the
United States of America*

CONTENTS

LIST OF TABLES AND FIGURES

Tables

Figures

Long before the highly publicized murders of Trayvon Martin, Jordan Davis, Tamir Rice, and Michael Brown, the world learned much about young Black men through alarming newspaper headlines and one-sided portrayals of them in televised news programs. Consumers of this media, as well as those who read about Black boys and men in academic publications (books, peer-reviewed journal articles, and research reports), have likely come to know this population as endangered, chronically low performing, at risk, deviant, and hopeless. A nation and a world that hears nothing but deficit perspectives about a group understandably comes to expect little that is good of its members. This situation has persistently disadvantaged Black male Americans across all age groups. In his 1933 book, *The Mis-Education of the Negro*, Carter G. Woodson famously observed that a young Black boy is repeatedly reminded of his inferiority in every class he takes and every book he reads. The same is certainly true for anyone else who reads much of what is written about Black boys in academic literature and the popular press. This book contributes nothing to the long-standing narrative of social and educational hopelessness concerning those who are Black, male, and American. Instead, its focus is on advancing their success through educational attainment.

In the East Room of the White House on February 27, 2014, U.S. president Barack Obama announced the launch of My Brother's Keeper, a national initiative created to improve the lives and outcomes of boys and men of color. In that speech, President Obama noted the following: "In the aftermath of the Trayvon Martin verdict, with all the emotions and controversy that it sparked, I spoke about the need to bolster and reinforce our young men, and give them the sense that their country cares about them and values them and is willing to invest in them." This book contributes to the My Brother's Keeper imperative by offering teachers, educational leaders, and policymakers a comprehensive resource that, if taken seriously and used effectively, will help them show Black males that their schools care about their individual and collective potential, value their personhood, and are authentically invested in their success. While challenges confronting this population are acknowledged in each chapter, ours is not a book of problems. Instead, we offer much guidance to the nation on ways to actually advance Black male student success at every juncture in the educational pipeline through hopeful, sensible, and forward-thinking practices and policies.

Ninety days after the launch of the initiative, the My Brother's Keeper task force submitted its first progress report to President Obama. The report prioritized six focal areas for young men of color: (1) entering school ready to learn; (2) reading at grade level by third grade; (3) graduating from high school ready for college and career; (4) completing postsecondary education or training; (5) successfully entering the workforce; and (6) reducing violence and providing a second chance. Many of these same priorities are advanced in this book. Schooling and educational attainment affect each of them. Also prioritized herein is the role and importance of scholarship. Three days after the release of the My Brother's Keeper task force report, the research institutes we direct at the University of Pennsylvania (Center for the Study of Race and Equity in Education) and San Diego State University (Minority Male Community College Collaborative) joined five other education research centers in crafting a joint statement in which we applauded the presidential initiative. We also called for programs, policies, and services that are guided by research and documented effectiveness. That statement is included in the appendix of this book. *Advancing Black Male Student Success From Preschool Through Ph.D.* synthesizes research about the lives, status, needs, experiences, and outcomes of Black male students across all levels and sectors of education; recommendations offered in each chapter were informed by published evidence.

Organization of This Book: From Preschool Through Ph.D.

This book is organized by education level. Specifically, each chapter is about a different juncture in the U.S. educational pipeline. We identified and invited leading scholars who have written about Blacks in education and young men of color to author chapters for this text. Their expertise is reflected in what they have written. In Chapter 1, David J. Johns, whom President Obama appointed executive director of the White House Initiative on Educational Excellence for African Americans, writes about the role of child care and preschool, Head Start and Early Head Start, and kindergarten in shaping Black boys' educational trajectories. He also highlights efforts to support learning and development from birth. In Chapter 2, Chezare A. Warren writes about the role of stakeholder relationships in the success of Black boys in elementary schools. He calls for research and practice to consider the roles all adults (families, community agents, teachers, students, and school and district leaders) play in shaping Black male students' educational outcomes.

In Chapter 3, Dorinda Carter Andrews discusses three prominent themes in the education literature regarding Black adolescent male students' experiences in middle school: (1) developing positive Black male identities; (2) the overrepresentation of Black adolescent boys in special education and their underrepresentation in gifted education programs; and (3) the disproportionate number of Black male students who are suspended and expelled from middle school. Carter Andrews uses Critical Race Theory to examine these issues and concludes the chapter with several recommendations that she believes will confer first-class citizenship onto Black adolescent males. Chapter 4 focuses on Black male high school students' academic performance, graduation rates, and college readiness. Despite the challenges he documents, Terry K. Flennaugh cautions against hopelessly one-sided perspectives on Black male high schoolers, what he calls "the danger of a single story." In light of this, Professor Flennaugh highlights promising practices across the United States and concludes with guidelines for evaluating emerging interventions that are intended to improve Black male student achievement in high school.

J. Luke Wood, Edward Bush, Terence Hicks, and Hassiem A. Kambui write about community college contexts in Chapter 5. Specifically, they explain the undercurrents of statistical trends that point to Black male student underperformance, and juxtapose those challenges with empirically proven insights into factors that enable Black male community college students to succeed. In Chapter 6, Mauriell Amechi, Jonathan Berhanu, Jonathan M. Cox, Keon M. McGuire, Demetri L. Morgan, Collin D. Williams Jr., and Michael Steven Williams call for educators to understand and more effectively respond to within-group diversity among Black undergraduate men at four-year colleges and universities. They synthesize literature on six Black male subgroups: (1) gay and bisexual men; (2) men in historically Black fraternities; (3) male student-athletes; (4) undergraduate men at historically Black colleges and universities; (5) underprepared, disengaged low performers; and (6) academic achievers and student leaders. They show how these and other Black men experience college in markedly different ways. Ultimately, the authors argue that advancing success for Black male collegians requires a sophisticated set of policies and practices that appeal to the unique experiences of diverse groups of Black undergraduate men in four-year postsecondary contexts.

In Chapter 7, Terrell L. Strayhorn writes about Black male students in master's programs. He uses national statistics to highlight their enrollment, status, distribution, and achievement. Additionally, Professor Strayhorn presents new findings from a multi-institutional survey of 306 Black men in master's degree programs, one of the largest studies of this particular subpopulation to date. The chapter is framed around theories on graduate student persistence and socialization, and concludes with recommendations for enhancing the success of Black men in master's degree programs. In the final chapter, Shaun R. Harper and Robert T. Palmer write about the persistent underrepresentation of Black men among doctoral degree–seeking students and doctoral degree recipients, a range of racialized experiences in Ph.D. programs at predominantly White universities, and the underproduction of Black male professors. At the beginning of the chapter, Drs. Harper and Palmer introduce Ian, a Black man who succeeded in a Ph.D. program and subsequently transitioned to a successful career in academia. Their chapter concludes with recommendations for replicating the best of Ian's experience among Black men in doctoral programs at universities across the United States.

ACKNOWLEDGMENTS

W e first acknowledge President Barack Obama for his willingness to make young men of color a national priority. While My Brother's Keeper has been criticized for its exclusion of girls and women of color, we salute our nation's leader for being willing to do something meaningful. We also thank the 10 foundations that generously supported the launch of My Brother's Keeper: the Annie E. Casey Foundation, Atlantic Philanthropies, Bloomberg Philanthropies, the California Endowment, Ford Foundation, John and James L. Knight Foundation, Open Society Foundations, Robert Wood Johnson Foundation, W. K. Kellogg Foundation, and the Kapor Center for Social Impact. We also applaud the other 28 foundations that are part of the Executives' Alliance to Expand Opportunities for Boys and Men of Color. Special thanks to Tina Gridiron, Sam Cargile, and their colleagues at Lumina Foundation for their financial support of the National Black Male College Achievement Study and the Institutional Responsibility for Black Male Student Success Project. Indeed, many ideas put forth in this book were made possible through grants from these and other foundations that have invested richly in the pursuit of scholarly projects aimed at advancing Black male student success from preschool through Ph.D.

We thank our spouses, Shawn and Idara, for their support of us and the important work to which we routinely overcommit ourselves. Our gratitude is also extended to Frank Harris III, a dear friend and intellectual companion to us both. This book would not have been possible without the excellent contributions of the 16 scholar friends who joined us in authoring the chapters that follow. We thank them, along with Sarah Burrows and John von Knorring at Stylus Publishing, for partnering with us to produce an important book that will hopefully inspire, instruct, and greatly impact our nation. Emily Wood assisted us with copyediting early drafts of this manuscript; we appreciate her excellent work. Last, but certainly not least, we express our sincerest gratitude to the parents, families, educators, mentors, community members, and countless others who every day do much to advance Black male student success. Their work signals to young men that someone in their country cares about and is willing to invest in them. As Black men ourselves, we both will forever appreciate those who were willing to care for us, value our humanity, and invest in our futures.

AN IMPERATIVE FOR READERS

We appreciate everyone who purchases, reads, and adopts this book, as well as those who feel compelled to recommend it to others. We would be most grateful to those who *actually* do something substantive and sustainable with the research and ideas presented in the pages that follow. The future of our nation depends in part on what various stakeholders do to support the most underserved among us. Black males, regardless of age, are incontestably among the most underserved Americans. This book provides guidance to people who are serious about advancing Black male student success, not bandwagoners in search of quick fixes, silver bullets, professional profits, or public praise. We hope you will use the evidence and suggestions offered in each chapter to make a strong case for authentic care, meaningful action, and the strategic investment of time and resources in your respective spheres of influence. However, we respectfully ask that you not do so at the expense of other underserved populations.

As previously noted, the My Brother's Keeper initiative has been critiqued for its exclusion of girls and women of color. As several concerned gender-equity advocates have rightly noted, Black girls have gender-specific needs and issues that, too, are in need of presidential validation, philanthropic investment, and national attention. The same is also true for Latina/o, Asian American, Pacific Islander, and Native American girls and boys. We hope our book is not misused in ways that harm, deprive, or further marginalize them and others. Readers are urged to reject the zero-sum game mentality that leads many to erroneously believe that civil rights and racial equity wins for one group must result in losses for other groups. Instead, we envision *Advancing Black Male Student Success From Preschool Through Ph.D.* becoming a blueprint for educators who seriously commit themselves to proving to the most underserved Americans that their nation's educational system cares about them, values them, and is willing to invest in them. For reasons that are profoundly personal to us as Black men, we chose to commit this project to young Black men; we encourage other scholars to do the same on behalf of other racialized gender groups about whom they most care.

Shaun R. Harper, Ph.D.
Philadelphia, Pennsylvania

J. Luke Wood, Ph.D.
San Diego, California

EXPANDING HIGH-QUALITY EARLY CARE AND EDUCATION FOR BLACK BOYS

David J. Johns

The nearly 20 million young Americans under the age of five have their entire lives before them. They have opportunities to be whatever their hearts desire and the chance to influence the world in unknown ways. But by the time they have entered kindergarten, for many, this opportunity has already been stymied. In the United States, low-income and minority children begin kindergarten at an academic disadvantage. In 2006, only 28% of Black 4-year-olds were proficient at letter recognition and 55% were proficient at number and shape recognition, compared with 37% and 73%, respectively, for White 4-year-olds (Aud, Fox, & KewalRamani, 2010). That these gaps are present so early in life indicates that providing high-quality, early learning opportunities in kindergarten may be too late to equitably benefit to these children.

During the critical first years of a child's life, nature and nurture contribute to the cognitive, social, and emotional foundation upon which all future learning and development will be built. This highly complex process—in which a child's experiences at home, in child care, and other early care and education settings, along with his or her interactions with other caring adults, communities, and society more generally—shapes how that child comes to understand his or her place within the world. For low-income Black boys in particular, we must optimize opportunities early on to close achievement gaps and to ensure that they are prepared to begin elementary school ready to learn.

Students who begin elementary school without access to high-quality early learning programs and support services have a tendency to remain behind throughout their academic careers. This gap has significant implications for the life trajectory of so many low-income and minority students. The groundwork for high school completion, postsecondary success, career success, viable employment, and positive contributions to society is laid in the earliest years of a child's life. Access to high-quality early learning opportunities, for Black boys especially, can be the difference between a pathway that leads to the White House and one that leads to the jailhouse. Beyond the moral imperative to provide all children with the skills needed to be successful in school and in life, research shows that investments in high-quality early learning programs for children from birth through age five include a return of $2.50 to $17.00 for every $1.00 invested. Children who receive quality early learning services are less likely to become adults who live in poverty, require social services, or spend time incarcerated. Quality early learning investments are an economically sound choice for our nation.

For no other community of individuals is the importance of access to high-quality early childhood education and child care opportunities more essential than for Black boys. Nobel laureate economist James Heckman underscores the importance of ensuring that Black boys, especially low-income Black boys, have access to quality early learning opportunities. He states,

> Because of the dynamic nature of the skill formation process, remediating the effects of early disadvantages at later ages is often prohibitively costly. Skill begets skill; learning begets learning. Early disadvantage, if left untreated, leads to academic and social difficulties in later years. Advantages accumulate; so do disadvantages. (Heckman & Masterov, 2007, p. 447)

Additionally, Rashid writes, "It should also be noted that many low-income African American children are enrolled in preschool settings that are less likely to expose them to practices associated with social, emotional, and academic gains. Indeed as it currently exists, the education of young Black children, boys in particular, is largely a national disgrace" (Rashid, 2013, p. 30). To be sure, there is much work to be done to ensure that many more Black boys have access to high-quality early education programs and related support services for children and families.

For generations, Black boys and men have occupied the lowest rungs of almost any quality-of-life indicator used to assess health, well-being, and success across myriad sectors. For example, Black males have extremely high rates of homicide and rising rates of suicide. They are also less likely to have health care coverage. Black men have the lowest rates of employment of any racial group in the United States. In the education realm, nearly 80% or more of Black public school students in the fourth, eighth, and 12th grades are unable to read or do math at grade level (Children's Defense Fund, 2011), and according to the *2012 Schott 50-State Report on Black Males in Public Education*, the overall 2009–2010 graduation rate for young Black men in the United States was only 52%. The graduation rate for young Black men in 14 states is below the national average (Schott, 2012). These enduring and unnerving trends begin during the early years, when Black boys are unable to take full advantage of quality early care and education programs and services. Without such early interventions, we should expect young boys of color, who have not had access to high-quality, early learning opportunities, to continue to face education and employment challenges (U.S. Department of Health and Human Services, 2010; U.S. Department of Health and Human Services, Administration for Children and Families, 2010). We will not solve the employment and educational crises facing Black boys and men until we ensure that all Black boys have access to high-quality early care and education programs and services.

Because too many Black boys are denied access to the types of experiences that lead to good schools; accredited colleges and universities; and high-skill, high-wage employment opportunities, it should come as no surprise that Black boys are underrepresented in these spaces. Here, I discuss the opportunities that high-quality early care and education programs provide for children and the challenges that parents and families of Black boys face in attempting to access such programs and services.

Early Education and Care Programs and Support

Unlike the "public education system"—a phrase commonly used to refer to state systems of coordinated federal- and state-funded kindergarten through 12th-grade programs and activities—there is no single system for "early learning." *Early care and education* is an umbrella term frequently applied to the range of primarily community-based programs and supports that prepare expectant parents to care for themselves and their young children; provide child care opportunities that enable parents to work; provide children with the skills, experiences, and relationships needed to be successful in elementary school and later in life; and provide preschool opportunities that focus on cognitive, physical, social, and emotional development to ensure that young children successfully transition into kindergarten.

Two overriding factors affecting early learning opportunities are cost and availability. To be sure, high-quality early care and education opportunities are expensive. Consider, for example, the cost of having the necessary number of qualified adults to ensure a low adult-to-child ratio in center-based child care programs. When children are newborns and infants, more care is required. Retaining professional early care and education practitioners and providing them with professional development is costly. In too many communities where there are significant concentrations of low-income Black boys, these costs can be prohibitive, forcing program operators to neglect professional development or close the program altogether. In addition to the cost associated with a skilled workforce (primarily indicated by experience, credentials, and training) are the expenses associated with ensuring healthy and safe environments, small class sizes, and low adult-to-child ratios, each of which has been linked to improved learning and development outcomes. Likewise, implementing early learning standards that are developmentally and linguistically appropriate (ideally aligned with the curriculum that students will encounter as they continue along the educational continuum); providing screening, referral, and support services for children with developmental delays or disabilities; and providing other supports for children and families add to program costs as well. In addition to these central costs are the costs associated with providing nutritious meals and providing full-day, full-year care. In what follows, I explore cost and availability as they relate specifically to child care, Head Start, and prekindergarten programs and services. We must take advantage of opportunities to improve access and reduce costs in ways that will increase the educational and life choices and chances for young Black boys.

Child Care

In the United States, more than 11 million children under the age of five are in some type of child care arrangement each week (Laughlin, 2010). On average, children of working mothers spend 35 hours a week in child care, many with multiple care arrangements to enable parents to work during both traditional and nontraditional working hours (National Association of Child Care Resource and Referral Agencies, 2006). These facts become important when one considers that less than 40% of Black children live with two parents and nearly one in two Black children live solely with their mother, compared with fewer than one in five White children (Children's Defense Fund, 2011). Thus, child care becomes an essential work support for the parents, and it also provides opportunities for young children to develop foundational skills in the areas of vocabulary, letter-word recognition, spelling, and pattern and color identification. For parents, particularly single parents who need a place for their children while they work to support the family, child care is critical.

The work of Jack Shonkoff at the Harvard Center on Developing Children and others underscores the belief that quality child care provides children with early opportunities to develop and sharpen foundational skills (Vandell et al., 2010). High-quality care provides opportunities for children to be screened for developmental delays or disabilities. Developmentally appropriate instruction can bolster intellectual, linguistic, social, and emotional skills and behaviors, including positive health and development more generally. This point is especially true for low-income, disadvantaged students. However, too few boys of color have access to the types of programs and providers who have the skill and experience to assist in the development of preliteracy and prenumeracy skills. The implications for these missed early opportunities are significant. Consider, for example, that Black babies at 24 months old scored significantly lower than White babies on the cognitive assessment administered as part of the Early Childhood Longitudinal Study (Halle et al., 2009). These gaps are only widened when Black boys miss out on quality early learning opportunities. Moreover, failed opportunities to develop foundational skills or to be identified for needed supports contribute to statistics such as the following: Black and Hispanic males constitute almost 80% of children and youth in special education programs, and Black male students are 2.5 times less likely to be enrolled in gifted and talented programs, even if their prior achievement reflects the ability to succeed (National Education Association, 2011). Black male students compose 20% of all students in the United States classified as mentally retarded, despite representing only 9% of the total student population (Codrington & Fairchild, 2012). These challenges could be mitigated if we ensure that all Black and Latino boys, in particular, have access to high-quality early learning and development opportunities.

Unlike K–12 public education, which is largely financed by federal, state, and local governments, the cost for child care is largely borne by parents and families; for too many low-income, minority families, the cost of high-quality care is simply beyond reach.[1] The recent economic crisis, coupled with the high cost of child care and variance in state investments in programs and subsidies, has left many parents unable to pursue center-based care, using, instead, informal care (such as leaving children with grandparents or in multiple arrangements with friends and other caring adults). For those who do pursue center-based facilities, the costs can be an extreme burden. According

---

[1] The federal government supports child care by providing grants to states primarily through the Child Care Development Block Grant (CCDBG). States use these funds to subsidize the cost of child care for low-income families. Additional federal support is provided through the Temporary Assistance for Needy Families (TANF) program, the Social Services Block Grant (SSBG), or state funds.

to the Government Accountability Office, the number of children receiving child care assistance between fiscal years 2006 and 2008 declined by 170,000 children (10%) (United States Government Accountability Office, 2010). The U.S. Department of Health and Human Services estimates that only 17% of eligible children receive assistance (U.S. Department of Health & Human Services, 2010). For too many parents, especially those of Black boys, the inability to afford and access high-quality child care results in the loss of opportunities to develop foundational skills to ensure that children start kindergarten ready to learn.

In 2010, the average annual cost of full-time, center-based child care for an infant ranged from $4,650 in Mississippi to more than $18,200 in Washington DC, and the average cost of center-based care for a preschool-age child ranged from $2,450 in Louisiana to $10,400 in New York (National Association of Child Care Resource and Referral Agencies, 2006). Compare these figures with the average yearly tuition and fees for public higher education, which is $7,600 (College Board, 2010). The average cost of infant care in a licensed center exceeds the cost of public college tuition and related fees in 36 states. Nationally, the cost for full-time care for an infant ranges from 7% to 16% of the median income for married-couple families with children; for single parents, the cost of center-based infant care exceeds 10% of median income in every state. For too many parents of young Black boys, the cost of a quality early learning opportunity is simply too high.

In addition to the cost of quality child care, availability is also a significant hurdle. A study of child care in 13 economically disadvantaged communities found that the supply of child care falls short of the demand. Among other things, the study found that, in the communities studied, nearly half of the children under age 6 who needed care had no access to licensed or regulated child care; parents in these communities paid as much as 70% of their total income for full-time child care of infants and toddlers (with some parents paying more than two thirds of their income for full-time care for preschool-age children; National Association of Child Care Resource and Referral Agencies, 2006). The communities in the study, which included Atlanta, Denver, Des Moines, Oakland, and Providence, highlight the significance of poverty in the lives of the children and parents. The study draws direct connections between the overrepresentation of young children raised by single parents, who need support to work, and the lack of access that such families have to high-quality care that is affordable or supplemented by state support or subsidy. The study also underscores the fact that the cost of high-quality child care is often prohibitive for those who would benefit the most from early care and education programs and supports (National Association of Child Care Resource and Referral Agencies, 2006).

In addition to cost and accessibility, the following issues must also be addressed:

- Improved safety in and of the child care centers, including required background checks for caregivers, unannounced site visits by licensed and authorized inspectors, and increased health and safety standards.
- Increased parent and family engagement to ensure that parents (especially young, single, or first-time parents) have the information and tools needed to maximize their children's learning and development in the early years of life and to ensure that they are viewed and treated by practitioners as valued partners in the education and development of their children.
- Adjustment of reimbursement rates at the federal and state levels to account for actual costs for care.
- Federal, state, and local support for child care more generally should be adjusted to help many more Black boys gain access to quality child care programs that will ensure they begin school ready to learn, which can be accomplished by prioritizing children and families with the most significant need.

Head Start and Early Head Start

Head Start and Early Head Start circumvent the high cost of quality early care and education programs by providing federal support to programs that agree to serve low-income, disadvantaged children and families. In this regard, the program addresses access and affordability by covering the costs for families that meet certain income eligibility criteria, mainly families that would otherwise fail to enroll children in center-based programs.

The Head Start program was created in 1965, during President Lyndon Johnson's War on Poverty and the implementation of Great Society programs, to address challenges faced by students entering kindergarten who did not have the skills and experiences necessary for success. Conceived initially as a summer program to close gaps between low-income children and their more affluent peers, the program proved to be what many parents and educators knew to be the case: While helpful, six weeks of summer school could not overcome five years of poverty and a lack of access to high-quality early childhood education and care programs. In 1981 the program was codified in federal law, asserting a national interest in expanding access for disadvantaged children and families.

Head Start participants must meet income-based eligibility criteria; families must earn less than 130% of poverty-level income, although providers have flexibility to enroll students from higher-income families up to 10% of the total program enrollment.[2] Additional requirements designed to ensure that the program provides disadvantaged children and families with high-quality service include requiring that, as of 2013, half of all teachers and paraprofessionals (i.e., trained teaching assistants) possess bachelor's degrees, and all program staff possess at least an associate's degree. Recent reauthorization of the Head Start Act also includes program performance standards that govern health, safety, and curricular goals and objectives.[3]

A recent impact study of the Head Start program compared the cognitive development, social and emotional development, and physical health outcomes of Head Start program participants to a control group of students who were attending private preschool programs or who were not enrolled in any formal program. The study explored the impact of the program for 3-year-olds who spent two years in the program and 4-year-olds who spent one year in the program before starting kindergarten. The study found that access to Head Start has a positive, statistically significant impact on children's preschool experiences, school readiness, language and vocabulary skills, and socio-emotional development, including more positive relationships with parents. Specific to Black children, the report found that 4-year-olds experienced "favorable impacts in the social-emotional domain at the end of kindergarten as reported by teachers. Black children in the Head Start group were reported to have reduced inattentiveness; fewer problems with structured learning, peer interactions, or teacher interactions; and better relationships with teachers" (U.S. Department of Health and Human Services, Administration for Children and Families, 2010, p. xxvii). While the long-term effects of Head Start require additional research, the program's ability to close gaps and prepare low-income and minority children for kindergarten is difficult to deny. For decades now, the program has improved life opportunities for Black boys as well as other low-income, minority, and otherwise disadvantaged children and families.

We can celebrate the success of Head Start, but more Black boys should have access to the program. Currently, according to the U.S. Department of Health and Human Services, a total of 965,196 children are served in Head Start and Early Head Start programs. Less than 40% of the eligible 3- and 4-year-olds below the poverty line are currently served by Head Start. Even more disappointing, Early Head Start programs are serving less than 4% of children under the age of 3 who are living below the poverty line. Much more

---

[2] For example, to be eligible for Head Start under 2013 federal poverty guidelines, a family of two would need to earn less than $20,163 and a family of four less than $30,612.
[3] For additional information see the Improving Head Start for School Readiness Act of 2007.

needs to be done to increase access to these programs while continuing to ensure that the gains made during these early years are sustained in elementary school. Existing investments can be strengthened if elementary schools (preschool through third-grade teachers and school leaders in particular) and Head Start programs collaborated to provide joint development for students and to ensure their successful and seamless transition into elementary school.

Preschool Education

Prekindergarten (pre-K) programs are an essential component of the early care and education continuum; however, too many Black children do not have access to quality pre-K programs. While provided in myriad forms and for different reasons, pre-K programs are primarily initiatives that are funded, controlled, and directed by a state, city, or other locality, and designed to serve 3- and 4-year-old children in a group setting for a minimum of two times each week. Most quality programs focus on closing existing gaps and preparing children for a successful transition into elementary school.

The NIEER 2010 *State of Preschool Yearbook* includes an analysis of nine studies from 10 states, adding to the research that underscores the short- and long-term effects of state pre-K programs on children's learning and development (Barnett, Carolan, Fitzgerald, & Squires, 2012). The analysis demonstrates the ability of quality pre-K programs to produce significant learning gains in language, literacy, mathematics, and socio-emotional development, as well as reductions in grade repetition and special education participation. More than 1 million children today have access to pre-K programs, and research shows that these children do better in school from their first day of kindergarten through their postsecondary years. Compared with peers who did not attend a pre-K program, students who did attend pre-K programs have higher achievement test scores, repeat fewer grades, need less special education, graduate from high school at substantially higher rates, and are more likely to attend college (Barnett, 2008; Barnett & Masse, 2007; Lynch, 2007; Schweinhart et al., 2005; Temple & Reynolds, 2007). Additionally, also consistent with research on quality child care programs and services, a study of a pre-K program in Tulsa, Oklahoma, found positive learning and socio-emotional outcomes for all children, with particular emphasis on the most disadvantaged.

For poor Black boys, pre-K programs can provide one final opportunity to close or overcome gaps resulting from missed early learning opportunities. Prior to the Great Recession, many states committed resources and passed legislation to support the expansion of pre-K programs. Pre-K access increased from 700,000 in 2001 to more than 1 million in 2013, reflecting the fact that six states expanded pre-K programs for 4-year-olds and that other states worked to supplement their existing investments in those programs. However, tough fiscal and political climates have resulted in several states reducing investments in their pre-K programs and services, which has compromised their quality.

Much more research is needed to identify specific relationships between Black boys and pre-K programs. Anecdotally, we know that Black boys are more likely to be located in states where pre-K programs and services are available (e.g., urban localities in the Northeast and Southeast); however, Black boys are also likely to be in places where the quality of such programs is questionable. For example, Florida invests less than $2,500 per child in pre-K and requires that educators possess only a Child Development Associate (CDA) credential—the minimum requirement for early childhood education professionals. For Black boys in low-income families, Head Start programs in places such as Florida are likely to be of higher quality than state pre-K programs.

In addition to increasing access to pre-K programs, much work must be done to improve existing program quality. There are several ways to measure the quality of pre-K programs. The National Association for the Education of Young Children (NAEYC) uses early learning program quality standards, which include looking for credentialed and experienced educators; opportunities for educators to participate in meaningful professional development; small class size and low teacher-to-student ratios; and screenings for and referrals to health, developmental, and other support services, including nutritious meals—each of which is critical to ensuring that students are healthy and able to focus on learning and development. Also important is considering the ways in which resources (provided by participating parents and families or through state subsidies) affect a program's ability to "purchase quality." For example, state investments in pre-K range from less than $1 million in Arizona to more than $790 million in California and Texas. The average state spends $4,831 per child enrolled in pre-K, almost half the amount spent per child in Head Start ($9,198), and a third of the amount spent per child in kindergarten through grade 12 ($12,404). Accounting for the variance in investments across states, average per-child spending now is almost $700 below the level of spending in 2000–2001. This decline in investment has only been exacerbated by the recent economic crisis, further constricting the ability of low-income minority families to access quality pre-K programs.

To contextualize the importance of this point, consider the availability of quality pre-K programs in the five states with the highest number of Black children under 6 years old—in order, they are Georgia, Florida, Texas, New York, and California.

- In 2010 nearly 37% of 4-year-olds and 90% of 3-year-olds in Georgia were not enrolled in a state pre-K, Head Start, or special education program. State spending in Georgia has decreased steadily since 2001, with an average of $4,206 per child in 2010.
- In Florida, 22% of 4-year-olds and 91% of 3-year-olds were not enrolled in a state pre-K, Head Start, or special education program. State investments have fluctuated since the program was first established in 2005.
- In Texas, 43% of 4-year-olds and 86% of 3-year-olds were not enrolled in a quality pre-K program. The program began in 2005 to provide a half-day preschool education to Texas's at-risk 4-year-olds. Texas spent an average of $3,686 per child enrolled.
- New York's universal pre-K program was established in 1998 to provide all 4-year-olds in the state with pre-K education; however, inadequate funding has prohibited the program from achieving the goal of serving all eligible children. The program was flat funded in 2010, with the state expending an average of $3,503 per child enrolled.
- California was among the earliest states to fund preschool education, beginning in 1965. In 2010 California did not provide preschool services to 69% of eligible 4-year-olds and more than 80% of eligible 3-year-olds. During the same time, the state invested an average of $5,571 per child enrolled.

In each of these states, the number of eligible children who are not served is too high.

Efforts to Support Black Male Learning and Development From Birth

America needs a highly skilled workforce and cannot afford to have a group as large as the current generation of Black boys fall by the wayside because they miss early opportunities to develop critical language, literacy, numeracy, and socio-emotional skills. While such high-quality early learning opportunities face many challenges, some policies, programs, and people are getting it done—"it" being supporting the academic, social, and emotional development of Black boys at the earliest stages possible. Three issues are critical to educating and supporting Black boys to succeed academically and beyond. First, strong direct service program models that employ a holistic strategy are needed in low-income minority communities. Second, more skilled teachers that understand Black culture and learning styles are needed; educators in early education must be trained to understand and support the cognitive, social, and emotional needs of young Black boys. Their early education would likely be greatly strengthened if more Black males were to enter the profession in the early years and throughout the teaching continuum. Third, early childhood and elementary school leaders need to be connected to one another to provide support, professional development, and peer learning.

Here I discuss three programs that encompass these key components: the Harlem Children's Zone, the Call Me MISTER (Mentors Instructing Students Toward Effective Role Models) program, and the Coalition of Schools Educating Boys of Color (COSEBOC).

Harlem Children's Zone

The Harlem Children's Zone (HCZ) is the brainchild of educator Geoffrey Canada. HCZ has become a national model for providing high-quality wraparound supports to ensure that children and families, beginning before birth, have the services and supports needed to begin kindergarten ready to learn, and to ensure that these children graduate from high school ready for college and beyond. The cognitive, physical, social, and emotional supports that HCZ provides often supplement the resources that are missing in economically depressed communities (e.g., parks and recreational facilities and access to quality before-school, after-school, and summer learning programs). The ambitious project began in the 1990s as a one-block pilot. It now encompasses 100 blocks of Central Harlem, in which Black boys constitute 45% of those served. The cornerstones of HCZ are the baby college, workshops for expectant and first-time parents; a full-day pre-K program; Promise Academy, an extended-day charter school; health clinics and community centers that are accessible to students, family, and community members; and social service and other supports that specifically address the challenges plaguing students and families in Harlem. For example, TRUTH is a youth violence prevention program that employs the arts, technology, physical activity, and other innovative methods to engage and enrich the lives of its youth participants. HCZ is anchored by an intentional commitment to supporting children and their families as early as possible. By providing parents with the information and resources they need to be successful, HCZ works to disrupt the cycle of poverty in Harlem, creating a cadre of adults who understand all that is required to ensure their children's academic and life success.

The Obama administration and Congress, through the appropriations process, have provided support for replicating the HCZ strategy. In 2012 the U.S. Department of Education awarded $10 million in federal funds to assist in the development of promise planning grant applications from more than 300 communities across the country. This commitment was reinforced when Congress most recently provided another $20 million to spur further investment in such initiatives.

Call Me MISTER

The Call Me MISTER program works to increase the number of prepared and committed educators from among underserved, socioeconomically disadvantaged, and educationally at-risk communities—principally Black men. Activist and scholar Jawanza Kunjufu frequently writes about the specific challenges facing Black boys in education. The author of works such as *Countering the Conspiracy to Destroy Black Boys* and *Black Students. Middle-Class Teachers*, Kunjufu discusses the fact that White female teachers constitute 83% of the U.S. elementary teaching force while Black educators make up less than 6% of teachers, and less than 2% of that 6% are Black men. Citing correlations between the attitudes and expectations that White teachers bring with them to public schools where Black boys are overrepresented and these boys' academic performance, Kunjufu calls for recruiting and retaining more Black male educators.

While additional research is needed on the exact benefits of having Black male teachers teaching Black boys, my own experience as a Black male kindergarten teacher has led me to believe that there is value in children seeing Black men in a space in which we rarely work. Kunjufu (2002) cites research that finds a 4% increase in student test scores when the teacher is of the same race, suggesting that there are possibly statistically significant implications of more minority teachers entering into and remaining in the (early learning) workforce. Too many schools throughout the country fail to employ Black men as educators or school leaders, instead providing opportunities for these men to clean the schools, drive school buses, work security, or teach physical education.

The Call Me MISTER program is designed to overcome these challenges. Housed at Clemson University, the program provides academic support services and uses incentives such as loan- and debt-forgiveness programs to attract participants. It also leverages the collective resources of historically Black colleges and universities (HBCUs) in South Carolina, including Benedict College, Claflin University, Morris College, and South Carolina State University. Each of these institutions supports the program.

The Coalition of Schools Educating Boys of Color

The Coalition of Schools Educating Boys of Color (COSEBOC) is a network of schools committed to increasing access to and improving the quality of educational opportunities available to boys of color. Founded by educator

Ron Walker, COSEBOC has been successful at bringing educators together with school and community leaders and providing professional development to increase a school's capacity to support the positive development of low-income and minority males. In 2012 COSEBOC launched a partnership with McComb Public Schools in Mississippi to provide culturally relevant professional development services for pre-K and elementary school teachers and leaders. More than half of the kindergarteners served by Kennedy Early Childhood Center in the McComb school are Black boys. To support Black male students, Kennedy is working to recruit more male educators; has established a "boys of distinction" program that provides students with a mentor to ensure that their social and emotional development is supported; and is providing staff with professional development, including a study of behavioral and academic opportunities that support Black boys. While just beginning to address early care and education, the program is positioned to play a critical role in identifying and disseminating promising practices to further support Black boys early on. COSEBOC has an annual conference.

Advancing Success in Preschool and Early Childhood Education

Federal, state, and local policymakers each have a role to play in assisting states, schools, and communities as they increase access to early learning programs while improving the quality of existing programs. These goals require that elected officials, parents, families, communities, and other stakeholders work better together on the following issues:

1. Coordinate the work of existing programs, which includes strengthening collaboration among early care and education programs and elementary schools.
2. Provide funding for programmatic enhancements, including creating, renovating, or modernizing classrooms and centers and improving standards, curricula, assessments, and related professional development.
3. Recruit, provide professional development for, and retain qualified and committed educators—teachers and leaders—especially Black male early-learning educators.
4. Educate the public so that more people understand the importance of early learning. Parent, family, and community engagement is especially important. More low-income, minority, young, and single parents must be educated about the critical importance of high-quality early formal care and education. To be effective, this awareness must be accompanied with resources and support so that parents and families know what is expected

of them and can overcome any barriers preventing them from being active and engaged partners in their child's learning and development.

Politically, work must also be done to improve access to affordable, quality child care and Head Start and pre-K programs and services.

Child Care

To strengthen and improve the child care system, Congress should reauthorize the Child Care Development Block Grant (CCDBG). Established in 1996 as part of the welfare reform legislation, the block grant provides child care subsidies to low-income families that meet eligibility requirements tied to state-determined income thresholds. Through reauthorization of this important bill, Congress would ensure that high-quality child care is affordable and attainable for low-income, disadvantaged families. Specific policy reforms that should be included in this reauthorization are as follows:

1. **Ensuring that all child care programs meet reasonable health, safety, and child development standards**, including making sure that all personnel are trained to provide first aid and cardiopulmonary resuscitation and in how to prevent sudden infant death syndrome. Background checks should be mandatory to ensure that adults who work with children have not or will not cause them harm.

2. **Providing incentives and resources so that programs participate in Quality Rating and Improvement Systems (QRIS)**. These programs are designed to identify and monitor programs as they take steps toward improving quality, such as increasing the number of certified providers, reducing adult-to-child ratios and class size, and converting from half-day to full-day care.

3. **Supporting state efforts to increase the supply of care in particular areas of the state**—for example, those areas with significant concentrations of low-income children and families, or with high school dropouts and un- or underemployed youth and adults. Such efforts would include higher subsidy reimbursement rates, bonuses for educators and other financial incentives for providers, or collaboration grants to fund collective community efforts to provide high-quality child care programs and services.

4. **Expanding research and technical assistance in the classroom.** Classrooms should incorporate trends in educational practice, and providers must have the support they need to meet the demands of young children and their families.

While many of these recommendations require funding, which would be difficult to attain given the present national economic and political environment, several steps that do not require new funds can be taken to improve child care. Among the most significant is increasing coordination among child care programs, other early care and education programs, and elementary schools. Providers, educators and school leaders, and parents and families should be aware of the opportunities available to them, and of the expectations for them. This approach can mitigate many of the existing challenges facing young Black boys before they begin elementary school. For example, joint professional development in which child care providers learn alongside pre-K through third-grade teachers may enable teachers and child care providers to better support children as they mature and matriculate. Similarly, parents, guardians, and caretakers who are informed about their options can make thoughtful decisions about their child's learning, including how to be an effective partner in supporting achievement and positive development. Collaboration can provide new ways to leverage resources, improve quality, and increase access.

Head Start

The U.S. Department of Health and Human Services has continued to implement changes that were included in the 2007 reauthorization of Head Start—chiefly, designing a process through which grant recipients demonstrate their ability to improve achievement; close opportunity gaps for low-income, disadvantaged children and families; and increase school readiness. In addition to these efforts to improve program quality, more funding is needed to increase access. Nonprofit and for-profit entities, including colleges and universities, should consider the merits of operating Head Start programs in collaboration with experts who are skilled in responding to the challenges facing the populations that the Head Start program serves. For example, HBCUs and community colleges can operate Head Start programs that provide students who would like to enter education and related fields with practical opportunities to understand and intervene in the lives of disadvantaged students and families.

Pre-K Programs and Services

Recent advocacy efforts have pushed for the federal government to authorize grants to support the expansion of pre-K. The recent fiscal crisis makes this request seemingly implausible; however, in the absence of new federal funds, state and local governments can take steps to improve the quality of existing pre-K programs while increasing state funding to expand access as well. To improve quality, for example, states can implement new or improve existing early learning standards to be developmentally and linguistically appropriate and to align with K–12 standards and related professional development systems. Over time, work must be done to thoughtfully and appropriately align these learning standards with assessment systems; however, this action must not be done in ways that push down the expectations or practices currently undergirding many K–12 assessment systems or that unfairly penalize early educators or children themselves.

States can also work with institutions of higher education to increase the number of individuals who are certified and trained to work in early childhood education and care programs—by providing scholarships, providing loan- and debt-forgiveness incentives to potential participants, and working to ensure credit transferability within and across the postsecondary education system. Additionally, federal, state, and local leaders must continue to face tough challenges head on in the years ahead, and they must resist the urge to scale back early care and education programs.

Conclusion

We cannot afford to wait for policies to be developed, codified, and funded before addressing the challenges or taking advantage of the opportunities outlined previously. Each of us is morally responsible for investing the time and resources required to change the life of a single child by ensuring that he or she has every opportunity to gain the skills and experiences needed for success. Sometimes this step is as simple as showing up and serving as a positive and stable presence in the life of a child. By investing in the early years—ensuring that young Black boys optimize opportunities and are supported as they transition through school—we can disrupt generations of poverty and improve families, communities, and our country. These investments will ensure success for Black boys and men; they will also have a profound, immutable, and positive impact on our national economy. We owe it to our children, and we owe it to ourselves, to teach the babies, including our boys of color.

References

Aud, S., Fox, M. A., & KewalRamani, A. (2010). *Status and trends in the education of racial and ethnic groups.* (NCES 2010-015). Washington, DC: U.S. Department of Education, National Center for Education Statistics, Institute of Education Sciences.

Barnett, W. S. (2008). *Preschool education and its lasting effects: Research and policy implications.* Boulder, CO: Education and the Public Interest Center & Education Policy Research Unit.

Barnett, W. S., Carolan, M. E., Fitzgerald, J., & Squires, J. H. (2012). *The state of preschool 2012: State preschool yearbook.* New Brunswick, NJ: National Institute for Early Education Research.

Barnett, W. S., & Masse, L. N. (2007). Comparative benefit–cost analysis of the abecedarian program and its policy implications. *Economics of Education Review, 26,* 113–125.

Children's Defense Fund. (2011). *The state of America's children, 2011.* Washington, DC: Author.

Codrington, J., & Fairchild, H. H. (2012). *Special education and the mis-education of African American children: A call to action.* Fort Washington, MD: The Association of Black Psychologists.

College Board. (2010). *Trends in college pricing, 2010.* New York: Author.

Halle, T., Forry, N., Hair, E., Perper, K., Wandner, L., Wessel, J., & Vick, J. (2009). *Disparities in early learning and development: Lessons from the Early Childhood Longitudinal Study—Birth Cohort (ECLS-B).* Washington, DC: The Council of Chief State School Officers.

Heckman, J. J., & Masterov, D. V. (2007). The productivity argument for investing in young children. *Review of Agricultural Economics, 29*(3), 446–493.

Kunjufu, J. (2002). *Black students. Middle-class teachers.* Sauk Village, IL: African American Images.

Laughlin, L. (2010). *Who's minding the kids? Child care arrangements: Spring 2005 / Summer 2006.* Washington, DC: U.S. Department of Commerce, Economics and Statistics Administration.

Lynch, R. G. (2007). *Enriching children, enriching the nation: Public investment in high-quality prekindergarten.* Washington, DC: Economic Policy Institute.

National Association of Child Care Resource and Referral Agencies. (2006). *Child care in thirteen economically disadvantaged communities.* Arlington, VA: Author.

National Education Association. (2011). *Race against time: Educating Black boys.* Washington, DC: Author.

National Scientific Council on the Developing Child. (2007). *The science of early childhood development: Closing the gap between what we know and what we do.* Cambridge, MA: Harvard University, Center on the Developing Child.

Rashid, H. M. (2013). Significant—but not sufficient: Quality early education and the development of young African American boys. In National Black Child Development Institute, *Being Black is not a risk factor: A strengths-based look at the state of the Black child* (pp. 28–31). Washington, DC: National Black Child Development Institute.

Schott Foundation for Public Education. (2012). *The urgency of now: The Schott 50-state report on Black males and public education.* Cambridge, MA: Author.

Schweinhart, L. J., Montie, J., Xiang, Z., Barnett, W. S., Belfield, C. R., & Nores, M. (2005). *The High/Scope Perry Preschool Study through age 40: Summary, con-*

clusions and frequently asked questions. Ypsilanti, MI: High/Scope Educational Research Foundation.

Temple, J. A., & Reynolds, A. J. (2007). Benefits and costs of investments in preschool education: Evidence from the child-parent centers and related programs. *Economics of Education Review, 26,* 126–144.

United States Government Accountability Office. (2010). *Child care: Multiple factors could have contributed to the recent decline in the number of children whose families receive subsidies.* Washington, DC: Author.

U.S. Chamber of Commerce. (2010). *Why business should support early childhood education.* Washington, DC: Institute for a Competitive Workforce.

U.S. Department of Health and Human Services. (2010). *Estimates of child care eligibility and receipt for fiscal year 2006.* Washington, DC: Office of Planning, Research and Evaluation, Office of Human Services Policy.

U.S. Department of Health and Human Services, Administration for Children and Families. (2010). *Head Start impact study final report.* Washington, DC: Office of Planning, Research and Evaluation, Office of Human Services Policy.

Vandell, D. L., Beksky, J., Burchinal, M., Steinberg, L., Vandergift, N., & NICD Early Child Care Research Network. (2010). Do effects of early child care extend to age 15 years? Results from the NICHD study of early child care and youth development. *Child Development, 81*(3), 737–756.

2

MAKING RELATIONSHIPS WORK

Elementary-Age Black Boys and the Schools That Serve Them

Chezare A. Warren

The "conspiracy to destroy Black boys" (Kunjufu, 2005) suggests that school failure among young Black men may have very little to do with these students' actual behavior or the cultural capital that they possess: the knowledge and cultural referents important and valuable for helping them negotiate the communities where they live. Kunjufu implicates other social factors—including interactions among adults responsible for shaping students' learning experiences—as variables worth considering to fully understand the academic vulnerability of young Black boys and men. He concedes, "Before we look at the boys, we have to look at *educators* and the school environment" (Kunjufu, 2005, p. 23, emphasis added). To focus only on students, their families, and their communities as the culprits of elementary-age Black boys' educational underachievement is irresponsible and incomplete. We need to widen the lenses of analysis to include and account for the actions of other stakeholder groups such as teachers, school administrators, and district leaders. Tending to stakeholder relationships may be key to developing empirically supported, asset-based, anti-deficit interventions that enable the academic success of Black boys.

In this chapter, my aim is to spotlight the benefits of productive *stakeholder relationships* for effectively responding to American public schools' failure to effectively educate elementary-age Black boys. The view expressed here considers Black men's success as early as elementary school to be primarily affected by the actions (and interactions) of multiple individuals in a school, not just the actions of students and teachers. Schools fall short when the "village" responsible for educating its young fails to leverage personal and professional relationships to appropriately respond to sudents' needs. Understanding how various human relationships are negotiated to produce favorable outcomes for students is the starting point for my recommendations in this chapter.

In the pages that follow, I explore the nature, consequences, and utility of stakeholder relationships in elementary schools. Although these reflections could be applied to stakeholders in any P–20 educational setting, the focus here is on K–5 students explicitly. I include an examination of factors, such as power and privilege, mediating the quality of those stakeholder relationships. I also discuss how the intentions of different stakeholders cooperate or conflict with each other as well as how those intentions turn into policies and practices that can either privilege or oppress Black boys. Hence, I argue that there must be more attention in the literature, and among school practitioners, to the importance and value of quality stakeholder relationships. Doing so provides a more complicated, robust understanding of Black boys' academic underpreparedness. I call for research and practice related to school relationships to look beyond the traditional student-teacher binary. Instead, more work must explore the contribution of all stakeholders—families, communities, teachers, students, and school and district leaders—to minimize adverse educational outcomes for Black boys. Each adult interaction in a school matters and to some degree may help to prevent Black boys' academic failure in elementary school and beyond.

What Are Stakeholder Relationships, and Why Do They Matter?

A *relationship* is defined as "the way in which two or more people or things are connected" (Relationship, n.d.). The nature and quality of interactions between adults and youth determine the relative strength of stakeholder relationships to produce favorable educational outcomes for students. These outcomes say a lot about the efficacy of students' learning experiences. Moreover, these outcomes are heavily influenced by innumerable human variables, such as mood or personality; life experience; prior knowledge about social context; and the realities of students' home lives, including the types of lessons or messages about school they receive from their parents. Harvey (2004) defines a *stakeholder* as any individual or set of individuals who have a vested interest in the events or activities of an institution. This interest also includes a concern about the products or outputs of that institution or organization. School stakeholders, then, may include any person who works inside the school building or people who are in any way affiliated with the school's operation and success.

In addition to teachers, students, and school administrators, stakeholders may include police officers, community residents, neighborhood merchants, or school custodial staff. To some degree, each has a stake in how well the school runs and functions. Each stakeholder supports the fulfillment of the school's mission and vision, even though he or she may not be the educational professional charged with maintaining pedagogical excellence and integrity.

Black Male Student Outcomes and Stakeholder Relationships

Kunjufu terms the turning point in elementary-age Black boys' school engagement and academic motivation as the *fourth grade syndrome* (Kunjufu, 2005). It has been argued that the trend of academic underachievement for Black boys surfaces at about the fourth grade as they begin to demonstrate a decline in creativity, instructional attentiveness, test scores, and academic investment (Harmon & Stokes-Jones, 2005). Harmon and Ford (2010) attest that this decline begins prior to the fourth grade for a disproportionate number of Black boys. Blame for this decline does not rest solely on the shoulders of students or the many middle- to upper-class White women who teach them (see Toldson, 2013). An analysis of the inhibitors and enablers of their school success should include a thoughtful examination of the many human relationships required to make a school function.

Several issues potentially inhibit the ability of stakeholders to work together in productive relationships. The first issue is the implementation of school reform efforts that fail to account for the unique needs of Black male students. The second issue is the relative isolation of stakeholders who do their jobs with little meaningful interaction with other stakeholders; this isolation contributes to a passing of blame as opposed to a collective sense of responsibility for student outcomes. The third issue is the gross miscommunication among stakeholders.

Repositioning School Reform Efforts

Black boys are likely to attend failing elementary schools in high-poverty communities (Lewis et al., 2010). Still, Payne (2008) insists that school reform has been much more successful in elementary school than in high school. In 2001 President George W. Bush signed into law No Child Left Behind, in an attempt to address the prevailing inequities of America's schools. But the act did not account for the many different human variables influencing the reach or overall effectiveness of any one school's reform efforts. Real school change requires an "ethos of empowerment and collegiality" (Evans, 1996, p. 229). Adults embrace and respond to change differently as they assess their level of investment in that change or reform. Undoubtedly, the way adults support each other affects the material product(s) of that change, particularly for the school's must vulnerable student populations.

Developing systems that improve student outcomes is a primary function of school reform. Reports such as those from Lewis et al. (2010) and the Schott Foundation (2010) suggest that school reform needs to make the effective, appropriate education of Black men a priority as early as elementary school up through high school and beyond. The climate of present-day school reform, particularly as it relates to Black boys, appears more reactionary than proactive. Scholars agree that contemporary school reform efforts are too often disconnected from the individuals most affected by the reform, including teachers, students, and school leaders (Goodlad, 2004; Lewis et al., 2010). Payne (2008) argues that school reform fails to account for the "social infrastructure" of a school. That is, improving student outcomes does not begin with the policy but rather with understanding how the policy fits within the cultural milieu of the school and assessing the implications of that policy on the persons most affected by it. Good reform focuses on fixing the broken structures responsible for student failure in the first place, which starts with unpacking how the individuals responsible for maintaining and improving that structure interpret the needs of those likely to suffer most from the failure to meet the reform effort's intended goal(s).

Stakeholders Assuming Greater Responsibility for Student Outcomes

Duncan-Andrade and Morrell (2008) argue that schools are doing exactly what they were designed to do: subordinate people of color into positions of inferiority and subservience. Who, then, is culpable for disrupting these trends to create equitable schooling and educational outcomes for young Black boys, who eventually become adult Black men? School stakeholders must work together to prevent the deleterious academic outcomes for young Black boys in far too many U.S. public schools. Their school failure has become normal in the American psyche, as evidenced by what can be perceived as a lackadaisical approach to developing aggressive policies, social service programs, and legislation that directly responds to the unique intellectual, emotional, career, educational, and health needs of Black men in the United States. School-age Black boys' disproportionate school attrition, their overrepresentation in special education, and their excessive out-of-school suspension might be easily avoided if more attention was given to early prevention measures—such as the ability of school stakeholders to negotiate their measure of power and influence in the best interest of youth, rather than the adults. Schools are social institutions marked by the regular interaction of human beings with varying degrees of power and influence (Stevenson, 2004). With this assumption, one can assume that each interaction hurts or helps, impedes or improves, the capacity of the school to serve every student exceptionally well. Each adult, teacher, principal, counselor, parent, and community member has some agency to advocate for and negotiate interactions that produce better student outcomes. Stakeholder relationships become most productive when the balance of power is maintained and families as well as the boys, regardless of age, are treated as partners in their school success.

Black teachers in Foster's (1997) study emphasize caring for the whole child, which includes negotiating relationships that form a continuous band of communication and concern among professional educators, the students, their families, and the community. Too little research exists that examines the utility of such relationships. My own professional K–12 teaching experience is absent of many examples of schoolwide efforts that focus intently on improving the quality of teacher-administrator, teacher-student, teacher-family, and family-administrator interactions. Contemporary research must be more explicit and intentional than past research about extending the conversation about school relationships beyond just teachers and students. Some empirical research hints at the theoretical and pragmatic benefits of studying a school's human "moving parts" (Goodlad, 2004)—that is, examining how adults and students interact with each other for the purpose of leveraging their relationships to improve the school's performance.

Roland Barth (1990) laments in his book, *Improving Schools from Within: Teachers, Parents, and Principals Can Make the Difference,* that adult relationships are key to any effort to improve schools. Barth insists that establishing and regularly attending to the maintenance of strong stakeholder relationships is key to making school a place where all students experience success. He calls for school stakeholders to be more collegial. *Collegiality,* defined as "the power of cooperative behavior in the service of a common purpose" (Barth, 1990, p. 30), leads school stakeholders to work together for the professional benefit of students. This cooperative behavior includes making students and parents a priority by including them in the school's decision-making mechanisms. Barth contrasts collegiality with congeniality to say that maintaining positive stakeholder relationships is not limited to nice or friendly interactions. Rather, he finds that collegiality strengthens practices and creates productive learning communities. Sometimes these interactions must necessarily be contentious and confrontational.

The consequence of a lack of positive relations among stakeholders or the absence of collegiality is an inefficiently run school. "School boards infantilize superintendents; superintendents, principals; principals, teachers; teachers, children" (Barth, 1990, p. 36). Most schools have a clear power hierarchy. When the interactions or relationships are volatile or unaccommodating to the persons involved, the consequences create a trickle-down effect that ultimately hurts children, their families, and the community. Barth's research suggests that the absence of a service-minded orientation and humility among stakeholders creates oppressive schooling conditions for youth.

Each individual stakeholder, including students and families, possesses a degree of power valuable for ensuring positive interactions among all stakeholders. The cultural and political expertise or knowledge that each stakeholder possesses is valuable. *Power* carries specific meanings and varying influences, depending on the sociocultural and environmental context. Knowledge has historically been assigned value by the educational institution. Hence, for example, privileged groups had access to specific types of knowledge, such as the classical curriculum (humanities, arithmetic, astronomy, arts, etc.) while subordinated groups were trained for agricultural and mechanical work (Anderson, 1988; Spring, 2004). Those groups and people who possess certain types of knowledge maintain power, privilege, and influence in the school, while others are silenced and subordinated. Teachers regularly assimilate young Black men toward "standard" norms for learning while inculcating them with "curricula" that esteem the social and cultural perspectives of the dominant group. This act, done without consideration of students' personal experiences or cultural expertise, is oppressive, and teachers may significantly impair students' creativity and their healthy racial identity development. A balance of power is possible when different stakeholders choose how to manipulate their positions of authority to negotiate mutually beneficial interactions.

Opening Lines of Communication

In this section I underscore the importance of communication for bolstering collegial stakeholder interactions. Efforts to improve access to high-quality schooling have always been an imperative for people of African descent (Foster, 1997; Siddle Walker, 1996; Watkins, 2001). Learning to read and write has always been a priority for African Americans, as evidenced by the examples of slaves who yearned to be literate at any cost and the formerly enslaved community's insistence on starting their own schools immediately following emancipation (Anderson, 1988). The abundance of literature documenting Black males' persistent academic underachievement could give the perception that Black boys and Black families do not care about school, which is simply not true (Brown, 2011; Harper & Davis, 2012; Howard, 2008, 2014; Howard & Flennaugh, 2010; Howard, Flennaugh, & Terry, 2012; Noguera, 2005).

Deficit perspectives of Black or poor people shade the interactions that teachers have with parents and the ways families perceive the actions of school leadership and personnel. If the teacher believes that his or her students' parents are lazy or uninvolved, the teacher is apt to act negatively in interactions with them. However, a parent's absence from a school meeting may be due to simply a work schedule conflicting with the meeting, for example. Black parents want their boys to do well in school even when the parents do not have formal access to the knowledge or skills needed to help facilitate their child's academic and intellectual development (Halle, Kurtz-Costes, & Mahoney, 1997; Sampson, 2002). Research does suggest that parents' beliefs and expectations contribute to how their children approach and perform in school. Schools must make diligent efforts to partner with families, and that partnership begins by opening up the lines of communication.

Goodlad (2004) found a disturbing trend related to how well stakeholders communicate concerns in interactions with each other about their school. His analysis includes a sample size of more than 27,000 parents, school leaders, administrators, and teachers. Three of the schools in the study had a complete "shakedown," as he calls it. In other words, he performed an exhaustive investigation of the school's operations, policy, curriculum, and culture. He says of his findings,

> We found little evidence to suggest any open meeting of the minds on the part of principals, teachers, students, and parents regarding school weaknesses, problems, and strengths. Yet our data usually revealed for each school some problems perceived by all of these groups to be serious. . . . It came as a surprise to the teachers, for example, to learn that they, the students, and the parents selected many of the same problems as being most serious. (p. 31)

Goodlad's work implies that stakeholders in these schools operate in relative isolation. There can be any number of reasons why teachers are not talking to principals, why parents are not voicing their concerns, or why students do not go to their teachers about troubling issues. The lack of communication may be partly structural, but other social aspects of relationship and coalition building that impinge on the effective communication among stakeholders may be very personal—and avoidable, with simple modifications in how each individual engages and perceives the other.

Lynn et al. (2010) had similar findings in their study of teacher beliefs about African American male high school students. School personnel overwhelmingly blamed students, their families, and the community for the school's failure to educate its students, while students had a completely different view. Lynn and his colleagues also found that the school was not a collegial environment; teachers who did make efforts to communicate their concerns with administrators were met with hostility and unhelpful responses. The communication in this particular school was accusatory and laden with an ideology of hopelessness and defeat. Talking out the problems in a learning community where each voice clearly matters is central to any effort to improve student outcomes for youth of color—in this case, Black boys.

Goodlad goes on to emphasize that efforts to improve a school have to "encompass the school as a system of interacting parts, each affecting the other" (2004, p. 31). His point is particularly important for schools failing to meet the academic needs of their entire student population. Open and honest conversations can only improve stakeholders' interactions. Without such conversations, individuals are left to their own devices, which likely perpetuate misleading stereotypes and deficit perspectives of Black boys and their families.

Cultivating Positive, Productive Stakeholder Relationships

Stakeholder relationships can be positive or negative, volatile or civil, just or oppressive. I have argued here that the academic failure of Black male students in elementary school and thereafter may largely be due to the unexamined nature of stakeholder relationships in schools beyond the teacher-student binary. As previously discussed, each stakeholder in a school is important for making the school function. The miscommunication of expectations, personal circumstances, and preferences for social interaction also add significantly to school dysfunction. Barth (1990) concludes, "The biggest problem besetting schools is the primitive quality of human relationships among children, parents, teachers, and administrators" (p. 36). "Making relationships work" implies leveraging stakeholders' interactions with each other to ensure that educational institutions live up to their full potential in meeting the unique needs of Black children—in this case, elementary-age Black boys.

Using actual examples from my own professional experience, the research literature, and contemporary education-related conflicts covered in popular media, the following section further explores why stakeholder relationships matter. Implications for student outcomes that result from stakeholder interactions are also discussed.

Three Key School Stakeholder Groups

In the following sections I discuss three particular stakeholder group relationships.

- The first group is *students, their families, and their communities*—the individuals whom schools are meant to serve. This group is typically not included in the primary decision-making processes of the school, but they are undoubtedly affected by most decisions.
- The second stakeholder group—*school administrators*—broadly includes principals, assistant/associate/vice principals, program directors, deans, and case managers. Individuals in this group are directly responsible for leading, creating, and implementing school policy. They oversee and cultivate the ethos of a school and ensure that teachers and students are making adequate progress in meeting school and district goals. These individuals also act as agents for the district, carrying out tasks assigned by central office leadership.
- The third, and arguably most important, group of this triad is the *teachers*. Persons in this group stand on the front lines every day, transmitting information and supervising student progress. Teachers are directly responsible for creating a classroom conducive to *every* student's learning.

These three groups each contribute to student outcomes. What one does requires the cooperation and collaboration of the others. The research and stories that follow illustrate how their relationships with each other ultimately influence student outcomes. I close the chapter with recommendations for the reconciliation of mismatched power influence among groups.

Students, Families, and Communities

Students are a school's most precious resource, and their parents pay many of the school employees' salaries. It seems almost commonsensical that schools should adopt the values and cultural ethos of the community to adequately respond to the needs, concerns, and priorities of their constituencies. These stakeholder relationships are valuable, and any district's administrators should account for them in the decision-making processes. The Oakland Ebonics resolution of 1996 is a relevant example of how stakeholder power relations can be leveraged to negotiate policy and the consequences for those decisions on practice.

Perry and Delpit (1998) chronicle the late 1990s policy controversy surrounding the Oakland School District in *The Real Ebonics Debate*. The district's school board passed a resolution recognizing "Ebonics" or "African American vernacular English" (AAVE) as a legitimate language worthy of mainstream instruction for the purpose of improving the district's African American Ebonics-speaking students' access to standard English. The intention of legitimizing AAVE was not so that it could be taught exclusively as an isolated content area by the school. Rather, proponents of the Ebonics resolution believed that by appreciating the home language of African American children, teachers would be better positioned to reframe their approach to teaching standard English. Their intention was to help educators consider pedagogical strategies to better build on the innate linguistic, writing, and speaking skills that Black children bring to school. This decision ignited a polarizing debate nationally about the legitimacy of "Black English," its origin, and its worth as an instructional tool for Black students.

The Oakland School District resolution is an example of a school district attempting to respond thoughtfully to its students' and families' needs. The consequences of its decisions and the hundreds of decisions that school leaders and officials make add to the significance of this particular issue. The Ebonics debate comes down to individual stakeholders' language ideologies. Wolfram (1998) confirms, "Language ideology is unquestioned and appears to make 'common sense' so that no specialized knowledge or information is required to understand fundamental 'facts' about language and its role in society" (p. 110). Every stakeholder has some ideology or set of beliefs about language, its purpose in schools and society, and the methods for transmission. The Oakland task force—comprising district leadership, school administrators, and parents—identified a problem and a solution. The risk they took to develop a plan to address illiteracy among Blacks in the district should be applauded. Even more remarkable is that the resolution had the potential to set the precedent for educating Black children nationally. Unfortunately, many district outsiders—including Black leaders, linguists, teachers, parents, and intellectuals—did not support the resolution and ultimately forced a repeal and revision of the decision.

The Oakland resolution was eventually revised. The revision held that instead of legitimizing AAVE as the primary language of the district's African American student population, it should be used as an "instructional assistant" to help youth acquire standard English. A corollary decision for Spanish-speaking children would be to delegitimize their first language and completely insist that they only speak English without regard to the significance of Spanish as a cultural asset and source of cultural identity development and expression. As Carrie Secret, a teacher and member of the task force responsible for the resolution, asserted,

Our mission was and continues to be: embrace and respect Ebonics, the home language of many of our students, and use strategies that will move them to a competency level in English. We never had, nor do we now have, any intention of teaching the home language to students. They *come to us* speaking the language. (as cited in Perry & Delpit, 1998, p. 81; emphasis in original)

Secret and other proponents for AAVE's utility for bolstering African American student achievement are in somewhat of a power struggle with individuals who have an opinion but do not really have a stake. Their goal is to improve student outcomes, but in doing so they realize that they must surrender approaches considered "normal" or "standard" in mainstream U.S. education. The power of the school board's decision, the power of third-party critics of their decision, and the power of Black families and communities collided in this conflict.

School and district administrators are responsible for responding appropriately to the challenges inhibiting their students' success. The Oakland case is a good example of how one school district courageously identified what it thought to be a solution for improving students' academic outcomes. District leadership in Oakland used data to identify and then respond to student needs by building on the community's cultural strengths. It takes considerable risk sometimes for school leaders and district officials to respond to the needs of children and families.

Unfortunately, school districts are too often entangled in managing the politics of certain decisions, and the districts never get around to actually doing what matters most for the students they serve. Black professionals', thinkers', leaders', and activists' criticisms are peripheral to the district's responsibility to educate. Those individuals are not on the ground with, for example, Oakland's Black youth; therefore, they cannot be fully aware of the complexity and difficulty of organizing culturally responsive learning conditions for each student. What is admirable about the Oakland school board is that they used their power to validate and account for the cultural strengths of students, families, and community stakeholders.

School and District Administrators

Early in my teaching career in the Chicago Public Schools system, I had an interesting interaction with the principal of a school where I taught. The principal, a Harvard-educated older Black woman, perused my resume, nodded in approval of my professional experiences to date, affirmed her recognition of my strong undergraduate work, and sternly asked within the first 60 seconds of our meeting, "Can you teach?" The question jarred me. I was a first-year teacher. I had just been honorably discharged from a very negative teaching experience the Friday prior to our meeting, and the fact was that I did not know if I could really teach. After thinking about it for a moment, I replied, "Yes, I think so."

After I began work at this school, I realized that it was in dire straits. In early December I came on board as the fifth teacher in one school year for about 18 eighth-graders. I had three months to prepare this group of kids to be successful on the state's standardized exams. These students had been passed along with little accountability—socially promoted with little evidence of significant academic growth in three years of schooling. It was an overwhelming task.

My initial interaction that first day with Dr. Rogers (a pseudonym) set the tone for the relationship that she and I would develop during my tenure at the school. She ardently communicated her expectation: If I took the job, I had to teach. With a straight face she would make her intention very clear that there were consequences if I was not successful. In other words, students had to demonstrate evidence of learning and academic growth according to my district's metrics and the state's standardized tests.

Every interaction I had with Dr. Rogers and other administrators in the school communicated a quiet trust in my ability to perform as a professional educator. They believed in my capacity to produce instructional excellence. The administration did everything possible to facilitate that excellence from outside the classroom. Their support included sending me to professional development courses, maintaining an open-door policy, ensuring that I used every prep period effectively, providing hands-on mentoring according to my needs, and advocating for me with parents and colleagues who may not have agreed with my methods. Dr. Rogers leveraged her influence as the principal to support my initiatives rather than micromanaging my classroom. She asked tough questions of me and required results.

The most profound aspect differentiating my experiences with Dr. Rogers from my prior teaching experience was her willingness to let me make my own decisions. Before meeting Dr. Rogers and teaching in her school, I taught seventh grade at another school nearby. The principal, a White man, took every opportunity he could to communicate his distrust in my ability to teach. He offered no support. He would sit in the back of my classroom taking copious notes of my teaching and then call me into disciplinary meetings to discuss how badly I was doing. He eventually demoted me to a teacher's aide without ever warning or consulting me about the consequences of my new position. The key difference between this principal and Dr. Rogers was that Dr. Rogers provided feedback without squelching my creativity or trumping my decisions about how to best manage my classroom. In contrast, my previous principal had micromanaged every aspect of my classroom, which significantly impacted my confidence and professional development as a competent classroom teacher.

I share this story to give a real-life example of how important school leaders are for enabling or limiting a teacher's capacity to succeed at the job. Scholars conclude that the single most cost-effective lever for school improvement is quality school leadership (Branch, Hanushek, & Rivkin, 2012; Cosner, Tozer, & Smylie, 2012; Shelton, 2010). Many Black male students attend schools where the stakes for their academic achievement are high, for both the school's future and the child's life trajectory. Teachers likely perform at maximum capacity when they feel supported and cared for by school and district administration. Consider recent negotiations in the Chicago Public Schools about teacher salary increases (see Ahmed-Ullah, Hood, & Mack, 2012). A clear message about worth is sent when teachers are asked to work longer hours but are not compensated for the extra time (Rossi & Spielman, 2012). School and district administration can make a tremendous difference in the climate and productivity of a school. Progress happens when both stakeholder groups have interactions that respect the other's professional duties to improve the schooling experiences of youth.

Teachers

Research suggests that good teachers are tremendously important to student outcomes (Porter & Brophy, 1988; Wright, Horn, & Sanders, 1997). For Black male students, teacher quality is important, particularly as it relates to the teacher's ability to build strong, productive personal relationships with students (Gay, 2010; Irvine, 1990; Ladson-Billings, 1994; Polite & Davis, 1999; Zamani-Gallaher & Polite, 2010). Teachers who have positive relationships with students have successfully communicated their care for students to the degree that students believe them and reciprocate that care. In other words, a caring teacher cannot be considered caring unless the student perceives the teacher's actions as such (Valenzuela, 1999; Warren, 2012). One way teachers do this is by tailoring their interactions with each child around more than the student's content knowledge. The adoption of students' social and cultural perspectives is important for building and maintaining trusting relationships between students and teachers (Warren, 2014). Effective teachers of Black children build relationships with students by concerning themselves with developing the whole child (Irvine, 1990; Murrell, 2002).

Consider Foster's (1997) important research using oral history in *Black Teachers on Teaching*. These teachers reveal that prior to the *Brown v. Board of Education* decision of 1954, teachers were important role models in the community. They lived among their students and promoted cultural pride in their classrooms. Though the material conditions of those classrooms were less than acceptable, the students were successful because teachers were an extension of each child's parents when the children came to school.

One of the greatest lessons to be learned from Foster's work is that teachers saw themselves as integrated with students, families, and community life. Their work in schools was not separate from the efforts of Black parents to provide high-quality education to their children. Teachers advocated for and supported children from *within* the community, not as outsiders or third parties. Not every Black teacher lived in the communities where their schools were located or among their students' families, but serving from within the community suggests that teachers envisioned themselves as complicit in their students' rise or fall. The reality of the teachers' own professional success was not detached from the success of the entire community of children they served. This perception and the subsequent actions taken to live out this vision earned the trust of students and families. Teachers were committed to building young citizens, which they did by forming active partnerships with parents. Research suggests that these teachers were successful because they positioned themselves as equals to the parents and children they served. Teachers emphasized their concern through the many nonacademic interactions they had with students and families.

Anderson (1988), in his historical study of the education of Blacks in the South after slavery, found that families and communities swiftly partnered to form schools that would equip youth with the literacy skills needed to become informed contributors to society. Schooling and education have traditionally been communal acts in the African American community. When one became learned, other individuals in that person's sphere of influence also benefitted. The dichotomy of teachers and communities was not present. Teachers were important, valued members *of* the community, and the fruits of their labor translated into strong student outcomes, even for the poorest Black children (Siddle Walker, 1996). Clear continuity between home and school was valued and supported by the educational institution, largely because the community built the institution.

Black parents have played and continue to play a significant role in Black boys' racial and academic socialization (Reynolds, 2010). This act alone does not produce the types of outcomes that will shift the pervasive, mainstream narrative of Black boys' academic underachievement. Whose job is it to make school accessible to parents, ensuring that it is a space organized to respond to the needs of families and communities? I contend that it is the job of teachers with the help of their administrators. In addition, Barton et al. (2004) and Reynolds (2010) argue that parents indeed have agency for insisting that schools respond to their sons' unique needs. Parents' engagement must include maintaining regular communication with the school: "question[ing], critiqu[ing], and challeng[ing]" school systems, and insisting on collaborating with school personnel (Howard & Reynolds, 2008). Both stakeholder groups—parents and school administrators—are responsible. A lack of communication or infrequent positive interactions may result in a disproportionate distribution of responsibility and assumptions about whose job is whose, with few willing to take blame when these young men fail.

The vitality of this home/school connection has in too many cases been misplaced. The answer is not as simple as getting more parents into the school, as some literature suggests (e.g., Yan, 1999). Without advocacy from and regular interaction between parents and teachers, Black boys fall prey to a predatory school system that disregards them altogether. Simply inviting parents and families into the building is not enough. Parents in Mapp's (2003) study were most engaged in schools when teachers and school leaders initiated and created opportunities that welcomed parents into the building—opportunities that honored their contributions and connected them in meaningful ways with the school community. This approach assumes that parents are worth being honored and celebrated. Too many poor schools, from my experience, do not take this position. Parents must be agents of the change they want to see, and teachers must be intentional about carving out space for parents' active participation in all matters—from curriculum design to school improvement planning.

Reconciling Power Differentials in Relationships to Advance Black Male Student Success

I have argued here for the importance of strong, productive relationships among teachers, school and district administrators, and families for the overall outcomes of Black children. According to the large body of literature documenting their academic underachievement, Black boys can suffer significantly when stakeholder relationships are volatile or do not function at maximum capacity. The degree of power that each stakeholder brings to these relationships matters for how individuals approach each other. In this final section I include a brief discussion of the consequences that can occur when stakeholders abuse or misappropriate their power. I conclude by making recommendations for how to reconcile the power differential to ensure that schools are maximizing stakeholder relationships.

Pedagogy of the Oppressed Reloaded

> In the banking concept of education, knowledge is a gift bestowed by those who consider themselves knowledgeable upon those whom they con-

sider to know nothing. . . . Education must begin with the solution of the teacher-student contradiction, by reconciling the poles of the contradiction so that both are simultaneously teachers *and* students. (Freire, 2000, p. 72)

Freire's contention can easily be extended to school and district administration. The "knowledge" exchanged between each stakeholder group is essential to a school's effective operation. The power relations among stakeholders determine what gets done on behalf of students. Teachers, students, families, communities, school leaders, and district administrators each bring a specific and valuable expertise to the school building. Consequently, administrators may easily oppress teachers when teachers' knowledge of their day-to-day work with children or what they perceive to be best for youth comes into conflict with directives from their superiors, or when the challenges faced daily in the classroom are not considered in school- or districtwide decision making.

Likewise, students are subordinated when teachers fail to consider the knowledge students possess or refuse to incorporate into daily learning experiences what matters most important to students. Delpit (1995) admonishes teachers to be aware of the consequences when the "language of power" silences "other people's children." This effect occurs when teachers do not take into account the child's family, community, and life experiences or cultural expertise when planning and organizing learning experiences for that child. I found examples of this in my own research on White teachers' empathy for Black boys and their families (Warren, 2012). Many conflicts may arise when teachers fail to account for the unique social and cultural perspectives of individual students and families. Stakeholder groups' failure to capitalize on the reflexivity of knowledge points to a misuse—and, in some cases, an abuse—of power among them.

Proponents of critical pedagogy recognize that schools operate according to a dominant narrative or a mainstream discourse that frames what good teaching practice looks like and what good schools are able to accomplish (McLaren & Kincheloe, 2007). Scholars argue that truth needs to be co-constructed through the interaction of multiple voices around issues relevant to the education of traditionally marginalized groups of students (Giroux, 2005; McLaren, 1998). Power has everything to do with whose truth gains traction in the institution, which leads to the establishment of school policies, professional practice and norms, and the institutional ethos ultimately shaping the child's schooling experience. These experiences either liberate or oppress students of color.

Using a critical pedagogical lens, I find that improving Black male student outcomes as early as elementary school begins with acknowledging that their lived experiences are relevant to the teaching and learning process. The meaningful interactions among the three stakeholder groups discussed in this chapter are shaped by the degree of power accorded to each individual's position in the school building, but also to one's race, social class, or gender group affiliation. Scholars hold that "schooling [is] a resolutely political and cultural enterprise" and that "knowledge (truth) is socially constructed, culturally mediated, and historically situated" (McLaren, 1998, pp. 164, 185). What happens in a school is shaped by the political will, historical context, and cultural hegemony of its agents.

When attempting to ascertain the source of Black boys' academic underachievement, one should look at adults' actions. Adults need to be held accountable for the types of relationships they have with each other and how their interactions influence what decisions are made in schools. Each stakeholder is responsible to partner as well as to take agency when determining what is best for students. Each member's feedback may also point to the structural inequity of K–12 institutions. Traditionally, individuals who have been oppressed, such as Black Americans, are most apt to point out inequity in schools (McLaren, 1998). This agency makes their voice particularly important when schools consider how they might improve the quality of the education being offered to Black students.

Conclusion

In this chapter I addressed one aspect related to elementary-age Black male student success: the interpersonal and professional relationships among school stakeholders. Black boys, their families, and their communities are too often silenced in schools. Students' real desires to be recognized as intellectually capable often go unaddressed when teachers, school leaders, and researchers alike meet with each other to figure out why students are not performing; these stakeholders often do not listen to students' stories or their parents' concerns to better discern the source of the school's failure. This silencing limits the ability of practitioners and concerned citizens alike to identify the source of student disinterest in school that begins as early as third or fourth grade.

The current-day education climate of high-stakes testing and teacher accountability smothers the good sense of education professionals who know better. Individuals in power determine the terms for "equitable" education norms in the United States. As a consequence, the humanist dialogue that Freire (2000) advocates—that schools need to liberate young people—is eliminated. In the middle of all this are Black boys whose creative, energetic, and artistic imagination becomes suppressed. Moving forward, we need to wrestle with how adults can build on what these students bring to school, as early as primary and elementary school, to avoid the fourth-grade decline from ever happening. This approach will take partnership and collaboration among all stakeholders. No one person has all the answers.

The following is a short list of recommendations for improving the quality of stakeholder relationships:

- **Care.** Teachers as well as students and families need to feel heard and seen by those in authority. Because school and district leaders typically have the most decision-making power in a school, their perspectives of care must be congruent with the notions of care that their constituents hold. This may significantly improve the efficacy of teachers and other school personnel. Students should reciprocate the cycle of care for teachers, and teachers for school and district superiors. The higher up the ladder of authority, the greater the obligation one has to serve others. Nonetheless, service to those under one's supervision must come with the expectation that care might not be reciprocated.

- **Patience.** A truly democratic school considers the needs and concerns of all its stakeholders tantamount to the demands of the district. Allowing each person to contribute to a conversation that affects school functioning is time-consuming and requires investment, yet a patient stakeholder is willing to be inconvenienced for the sake of others. *Patience* in this context means making decisions that are uncomfortable. It means trying out multiple strategies, seeing the ideas fail, and then trying again. Not every opinion for doing what is best for kids is realistic, given the constraints of present-day policy mandates. Still, stakeholders have a responsibility to take their time, effectively communicate their intentions, and be open to dissenting opinions.

- **Increased vulnerability.** Improving the nature of stakeholder relationships requires a significant degree of open-mindedness and transparency. The lines of communication need to be open and fluid. Knowledge should be regularly transferred between teachers and students; students, families, and school administration; and school administration, teachers, and community members. Becoming vulnerable is not synonymous with becoming weak or surrendering agency. On the contrary, vulnerability is the willingness of all stakeholders to be flexible. This approach has to be modeled for youth, as Black children, families, and communities have endured generations of abject subordination. Black Americans and other marginalized groups (e.g., women, members of the LGBT community, and Latinos) have had to fight for equal representation in a society that has covertly created systems, policies, and laws that persistently lock them out of opportunity. If schools are to change in a way that better serves Black children, namely Black boys, education institutions and their stakeholders have to be more vulnerable or open to "doing" school differently. Such change begins and ends with the quality of the interactions that stakeholders have with each other. In these interactions, power is used in the best interest of others and not as a conflation of one's ego and hidden agenda.

The effective education of elementary-age Black boys is subject to any number of variables, which may include the school's access to material resources, the overall quality and rigor of instruction, the priorities of school and district administration, and the condition of each student's home life and community. Research and practice must turn a more critical eye to the functionality and efficacy of stakeholder groups' interactions. At the core of a school's effective operation are adults' interactions with each other and with students.

Quality stakeholder relationships are important at every stage of a Black male's school career. The literature suggests that elementary school is the stage where things begin to change in terms of Black boys' academic motivation and investment. Every adult in those children's lives is in some way connected to schooling outcomes. This chapter offers a clarion call to put aside titles and positions so that a stakeholder group's experience, expertise, and collective action improve student outcomes. Change is within reach when compromise becomes a priority rather than a last option. Our boys are depending on the adults to get it right. Studying the interactions and relationships among these stakeholder groups is necessary for placing Black male student achievement in its proper perspective, as well as for avoiding deficit-laden viewpoints of Black men and boys.

References

Ahmed-Ullah, N. S., Hood, J., & Mack, K. (2012). Picket lines up after CPS, teachers fail to prevent strike. *Chicago Tribune*. September 10, 2012. Retrieved from http://articles.chicagotribune.com/2012-09-10/news/chi-chicago-public-schools-chicago-teachers-union-contract-talks-strike_1_picket-lines-teachers-strike-president-david-vitale

Anderson, J. (1988). *The education of blacks in the South, 1860–1935.* Chapel Hill: University of North Carolina Press.

Barth, R. (1990). *Improving schools from within: Teachers, parents, and principals can make the difference.* San Francisco: Jossey-Bass.

Barton, A. C., Drake, C., Perez, J. G., St. Louis, K., & George, M. (2004). Ecologies of parental engagement in urban education. *Educational Researcher, 33,* 3–12.

Branch, G. F., Hanushek, E. A., & Rivkin S. G. (2012). *Estimating the effect of leaders on public sector productivity: The case of school principals.* Retrieved from http://worldclasseducationillinois.org/assets/images/content/NBER_Principal_Effects_in_Hi_Pov_Schls_20122.pdf

Brown, A. L. (2011). "Same old stories": The Black male in social science and educational literature, 1930s to the present. *Teachers College Record, 113*(9), 2047–2079.

Cosner, S., Tozer, S., & Smylie, M. (2012). The Ed.D. program at the University of Illinois at Chicago: Using continuous improvement to promote school leadership preparation. *Planning and Changing, 43*(1/2), 127–148.

Delpit, L. (1995). *Other people's children.* New York: New Press.

Duncan-Andrade, J. M. R., & Morrell, E. (2008). *The art of critical pedagogy: Possibilities for moving from theory to practice in urban schools.* New York: Peter Lang.

Evans, R. (1996). *The human side of school change: Reform, resistance, and the real-life problems of innovation.* San Francisco: Jossey-Bass.

Foster, M. (1997). *Black teachers on teaching.* New York: New Press.

Freire, P. (2000). *Pedagogy of the oppressed* (30th anniversary ed.). New York: Continuum.

Gay, G. (2010). *Culturally responsive teaching: Theory, research, and practice* (2nd ed.). New York: Teachers College Press.

Giroux, H. (2005). *Schooling and the struggle for public life: Democracy's promise and education's challenge* (2nd ed.). Boulder, CO: Paradigm Publishers.

Goodlad, J. I. (2004). *A place called school* (2nd ed.). New York: McGraw-Hill.

Halle, T. G., Kurtz-Costes, B., & Mahoney, J. L. (1997). Family influences on school achievement in low-income, African American children. *Journal of Educational Psychology, 89*(3), 527–537.

Harmon, D. A., & Ford, D. (2010). The underachievement of African-American males in K–12 education. In E. M. Zamani-Gallaher & V. C. Polite (Eds.), *The state of the African-American male* (pp. 3–17). East Lansing: Michigan State University.

Harmon, D. A., & Stokes-Jones, T. (2005). Elementary education: A reference handbook. In D. Weil (Ed.), *Contemporary education issues* (pp. 89–112). Santa Barbara, CA: ABC-CLIO.

Harper, S. R., & Davis, C. H. F., III. (2012). They (don't) care about education: A counternarrative on Black male students' responses to inequitable schooling. *Educational Foundations, 26*(1), 103–120.

Harvey, L. (2004). *Analytic quality glossary.* Quality Research International. Retrieved from http://www.qualityresearchinternational.com/glossary/

Howard, T. C. (2008). Who really cares? The disenfranchisement of African American males in PreK–12 schools: A critical race theory perspective. *Teachers College Record, 110*(5), 954–985.

Howard, T. C. (2014). *Black male(d): Peril and promise in the education of African American males*. New York: Teachers College Press.

Howard, T. C., & Flennaugh, T. (2010). Research concerns, cautions & considerations on Black males in a "post racial" society. *Race, Ethnicity & Education, 14*(1), 105–120.

Howard, T. C., Flennaugh, T. K., & Terry, C. L. (2012). Black males, social imagery, and the disruption of pathological identities: Implications for research and teaching. *Educational Foundations, 26*(1–2), 85–102.

Howard, T. C., & Reynolds, R. (2008). Examining parent involvement in reversing the underachievement of African American students in middle-class schools. *Educational Foundations, 22*(1/2), 79–98.

Irvine, J. J. (1990). *Black students and school failure: Policies, practices, and prescriptions*. New York: Praeger.

Kunjufu, J. (2005). *Countering the conspiracy to destroy Black boys* (2nd ed.). Chicago: African American Images.

Ladson-Billings, G. (1994). *The dreamkeepers: Successful teachers of African American children*. San Francisco: Jossey-Bass.

Lewis, S., Simon, C., Uzzell, R., Horwitz, A., & Casserly, M. (2010). *A call for chance: Social and educational factors contributing to the outcomes of Black males in urban schools*. Retrieved from http://cgcs.schoolwires.net/cms/lib/DC00001581/Centricity/Domain/35/Publication%20Docs/callforchange.pdf

Lynn, M., Bacon, J. N., Totten, T. L., Bridges, T. L., & Jennings, M. E. (2010). Examining teacher beliefs about African American male students in a low-performing high school in an African American school district. *Teachers College Record, 112*(1), 289–330.

Mapp, K. (2003). Having their say: Parents describe why and how they are engaged in their children's learning. *Community School Journal, 13*(1), 35–64.

McLaren, P. (1998). *Life in schools: An introduction to critical pedagogy in the foundations of education*. New York: Addison Wesley Longman.

McLaren, P., & Kincheloe, J. L. (Eds.) (2007). *Critical pedagogy: Where are we now?* New York: Peter Lang.

Murrell, P. C. (2002). *African-centered pedagogy: Developing schools of achievement for African American children*. Albany: State University of New York Press.

Noguera, P. A. (2005). The trouble with Black boys: The role and influence of environmental and cultural factors on the academic performance of African American males. In O. S. Fashola (Ed.), *Educating African-American males: Voices from the field* (pp. 51–78). Thousand Oaks, CA: Corwin.

Payne, C. (2008). *So much reform, so little change: The persistence of failure in urban schools*. Cambridge, MA: Harvard Education Press.

Perry, T., & Delpit, L. (1998). *The real Ebonics debate: Power, language, and the education of African American children*. Boston: Beacon Press.

Polite, V., & Davis, J. E. (Eds.) (1999). *African-American males in school and society: Practices and policies for effective education*. New York: Teachers College Press.

Porter, A. C., & Brophy, J. (1988). Synthesis of research on good teaching: Insights from the work of the Institute for Research on Teaching. *Educational Leadership*, *45*(8), 74–85.

Relationship. (n.d.). In *Merriam-Webster's online dictionary* (11th ed.). Retrieved from http://www.merriam-webster.com/dictionary/relationship

Reynolds, R. (2010). "They think you're lazy," and other messages Black parents send their Black sons: An exploration of critical race theory in the examination of educational outcomes for Black males. *Journal of African American Males in Education*, *1*(2), 144–163.

Rossi, R., & Spielman, F. (2012, September 9). Chicago teachers set Sept. 10th strike date; CPS to open half-day schools. *Chicago-Sun Times*. Retrieved from http://www.suntimes.com/news/metro/14825405-418/cps-to-open125-schools-for-half-days-if-teachers-strike.html

Sampson, W. A. (2002). *Black student achievement: How much do family and school really matter?* Lanham, MD: ScareCrow Education.

Schott Foundation for Public Education. (2010). *Yes We Can: The Schott 50-state report on public education and Black males*. Cambridge, MA: Schott Foundation for Public Education.

Shelton, S. (2010). *Strong leaders, strong schools: 2010 school leadership laws*. Retrieved from http://www.wallacefoundation.org/knowledge-center/school-leadership/state-policy/Documents/2010-Strong-Leaders-Strong-Schools.pdf

Siddle Walker, V. (1996). *Their highest potential: An African-American school community in the South*. Chapel Hill: University of North Carolina Press.

Spring, J. (2004). *American education* (11th ed.). New York: McGraw-Hill.

Stevenson, H. (2004). Boys in men's clothing: Racial socialization and neighborhood safety as buffers to hypervulnerability in African American adolescent males. In N. Way & J. Y. Chu (Eds.), *Adolescent boys: Exploring diverse cultures of boyhood* (pp. 59–77). New York: New York University Press.

Toldson, I. A. (2013). Race matters in the classroom. In C. W. Lewis & I. A. Toldson (Eds.), *Black male teachers: Diversifying the United States' teacher workforce* (pp. 15–21). United Kingdom: Emerald Group Publishing Limited.

Valenzuela, A. (1999). *Subtractive schooling: U.S.-Mexican youth and the politics of caring*. Albany: State University of New York Press.

Warren, C. A. (2012). *Empathic interaction: White female teachers and their Black male students* (Unpublished doctoral dissertation). University of Illinois at Chicago, Chicago.

Warren, C. A. (2014). Towards a pedagogy for the application of empathy in culturally diverse classrooms. *Urban Review*, *46*(3), 395–415.

Watkins, W. H. (2001). *The white architects of Black education: Ideology and power in America, 1865–1954*. New York: Teachers College Press.

Wolfram, W. (1998). Language ideology and dialect: Understanding the Oakland Ebonics controversy. *Journal of English Linguistics*, *26*(2), 108–121.

Wright, S. P., Horn, S. P., & Sanders, W. L. (1997). Teacher and classroom context effects on student achievement: Implication for teacher evaluation. *Journal of Personnel Evaluation in Education*, *11*, 57–67.

Yan, W. (1999). Successful African American students: The role of parental involve-ment. *Journal of Negro Education, 68*(1), 5–22.

Zamani-Gallaher, E. M., & Polite, V. C. (Eds.) (2010). *The state of the African-American male.* East Lansing: Michigan State University Press.

3

BLACK BOYS IN MIDDLE SCHOOL

Toward First-Class Citizenship in a First-Class Society

Dorinda Carter Andrews

In the executive summary of its 2010 report *The Educational Crisis Facing Young Men of Color: Reflections on Four Days of Dialogue on the Educational Challenges of Minority Males*, the College Board Advocacy and Policy Center discussed the economic dichotomy that exists in our society as the "Two Americas"—one characterized by economic wealth and the other characterized by severe economic hardship. The report mapped this analogy onto the nation's public school system, arguing that one system prepares some students to attend and excel in college and another system holds no expectations that many students will even complete high school. Further, the report argued, a third system includes students that mainstream America practically ignores. This system is described as representing a "Third America":

> This is an America that is almost totally ignored by mainstream society. This America is often captured in popular television documentaries and newspaper stories and includes frightening statistics about unemployment, poverty and high rates of incarceration. The citizens of this Third America are primarily men, and mostly men of color. These men now live *outside* the margins of our economic, social and cultural systems. They are the byproduct of many societal failures—*including the failure of our nation's schools*. (p. 2, emphasis added)

The men of color in this Third America were once boys of color in the nation's public schools. What debt do they owe America for their imposed status as third-class citizens in a first-class society? Black men represent a large segment of this third-class citizenry, and I believe that we have a moral and ethical obligation to restore their first-class citizen status so as to fully humanize and liberate them from the oppressive racialized gender politics that they have struggled to negotiate in mainstream U.S. society and schools. Given that most Black boys spend their formative years in public education, schools may be the primary institution where this restoration can occur. Schools can serve as a venue where adults and Black male students work together to construct Black male identities that encompass healthy racial, gender, and achievement self-conceptions.

My nephew, Tariq, entered sixth grade in August 2012. He is a young Black boy growing up in a two-parent household in a low-income suburban neighborhood. From pre-K to fourth grade he attended a private, predominantly Black, Christian academy where all his teachers were Black and held him and his peers to high standards. As a current seventh grader, he is an A/B student and has consistently scored in the higher percentiles on standardized tests. Recently Tariq was invited to participate in the Duke University Talent Identification Program (TIP). Duke TIP identifies academically gifted students nationally and abroad and provides them with services and programs beyond what is offered in the classroom to support their academic and overall development. In Tariq's home state of Georgia, less than 50% of young Black men graduated from high school in 2009–2010. The statistics were not much higher for Black boys at the national level. They are citizens of the Third America. Additionally, the National Assessment of Educational Progress's (NAEP) eighth-grade reading results from 2011 in Georgia indicated that only 10% of Black boys, compared to 33% of their White male counterparts, were reading at or above the proficient level; only 10% of eighth-grade Black boys in Georgia, compared to 41% of eighth-grade White boys, were at or above the proficient level in math in that same year (Schott Foundation for Public Education, 2012). Although Tariq has been identified as academically gifted, he has entered a period of his schooling, the middle school years, where he will have to navigate and negotiate his academic, racial, and gender identities within and outside of school. Simultaneously, he may feel pressured to gain the social acceptance of his peers and will have to develop strategies to resist the negative societal stereotypes that exist about adolescent Black boys. By state and national statistics, Tariq is at risk of becoming a citizen of the Third America.

In my own state, Michigan, only 54% of Black young men graduated from high school in 2009–2010. Ninety-three percent of Black male students in eighth grade read below the basic level and are less than proficient in math (Schott Foundation for Public Education, 2012). In some of my most recent research with East Lansing Public Schools—a high-performing school district with a Black student population of approximately 17%—the 2009–2010 grade point average (GPA) data for East Lansing High School indicated that, when examining GPAs by race, gender, and socioeconomic status, Black males living in poverty had on average the lowest GPAs of all students in the high school (Carter Andrews, 2012).

These data paint a grim portrait for Black boys like Tariq—regardless of the educational context—who enter middle school having been academically supported, still excited about learning, and eager to perform well academically. What should we predict for Tariq's educational and life trajectory? What are the necessary individual, institutional, and communal support structures that need to exist inside and beyond school walls to help him develop and maintain a positive racial identity, a positive gender identity, and a positive achievement self-concept—all parts of his overall self-perception? What role, if any, will experiences with racial discrimination play in Tariq's identity development, and how will they shape his achievement attitudes and academic engagement? Answering these questions in depth is beyond the scope of this chapter; however, they are critical for supporting the academic achievement of Tariq and other adolescent Black boys who are nearing, entering, and attempting to remain in the educational system through the middle grades of school.

In this chapter I provide a brief discussion of three prominent themes in the educational literature regarding young Black males' experiences in middle school. I begin with a discussion of the challenging nature of developing a positive Black male identity at this particular point in the academic journey. Next, I review literature that examines the overrepresentation of adolescent Black boys in special education and underrepresentation in gifted education programs. I then provide a discussion of what we know regarding the overrepresentation of adolescent Black males in school suspension. These thematic issues are salient in the experiences of Black boys across the elementary, middle, and high school years; however, for the purposes of this chapter I focus on the middle school years. I conclude the chapter with specific recommendations for how families and schools can nurture the healthy identity development of adolescent Black boys and ensure their academic success.

Critical race theory is an appropriate theoretical lens through which to examine the three topics I discuss in this chapter, because it posits that racism is a permanent feature of and is endemic to U.S. society (Delgado & Stefancic, 2001). Applying this argument to the functioning of educational institutions in this country allows one to argue that schools have overtly and covertly operated in ways to racially oppress Black boys in middle school, thus gravely impacting their life trajectories. Furthermore, with middle school serving as a critical juncture for many young males of color for either progressing through school or exiting the system (Davis & Jordan, 1994; Mickelson & Greene, 2006; Polite & Davis, 1999), I argue that the permanence of racism and Black male adolescents' experiences with racism inform their identity development, academic engagement, and school behaviors in ways that have been adaptive and maladaptive for schooling.

At the school level, the overrepresentation of Black boys in special education is deplorable and functions as a new type of school segregation that is larger than tracking. Black boys in middle schools are also subject to higher incidences of suspension and expulsion, which ultimately can lead to higher dropout and incarceration rates. Thus, I review the discourse around middle school suspension to try to understand the current state of Black young men in middle and high school and their subsequent life outcomes.

Race, Identity, and Academic Achievement

The race and gender gaps in Black students' academic performance begin during middle school (Davis & Jordan, 1994; Ferguson, 2001; Polite & Davis, 1999). Researchers attribute these gaps to a range of individual, familial, environmental, cultural, and structural factors (Fordham & Ogbu, 1986; Mickelson & Greene, 2006; Noguera, 2003; Ogbu, 2003). Establishing a clear sense of individuality based on one's own personality and life circumstances is a significant development task in adolescence (Plummer, 1995). The middle school years represent a difficult time for most adolescents as they try to navigate the often contradictory processes of social acceptance and what it means to be an achiever in the school context. This task can be particularly challenging for a Black male adolescent, because the socially acceptable identity that he may want to embody is often culturally incongruent with what is useful for doing well in school. Thus, many Black male adolescents develop gendered racial identities that are oppositional (Fordham, 1996; Ogbu, 2003) to maintaining high academic performance in school, leading to their academic demise and behavioral misconduct. The healthy development of a Black male identity can be challenging at this stage of life because identity development is complicated by societally imposed constructions of who these students should be as *Blacks* and as *young men*. Their racial and gender identities are inextricably linked, through a history of oppression in a White male supremacist society, with negative societal stereotypes that have been socioculturally constructed.

Research on Black male achievement indicates that these students are particularly at risk for experiencing racial discrimination and for suffering grave academic and social consequences that result from experiences with individual and institutional racism while in school (Cunningham, 1999; Neblett, Chavous, Nguyen, & Sellers, 2009). The race-gendered nature of Black boys' identity is often culturally incompatible with the process of schooling (Ferguson, 2001; Howard, 2014; Noguera, 2008). For many Black male adolescents, their development through puberty (e.g., deepening of the voice and change in physical stature), coupled with gendered racial stereotyping as aggressive and violent, can result in teachers, peers, and society perceiving them as threatening and nonintellectual relative to other youth (Davis & Jordan, 1994). The "criminal archetypes" (Monroe, 2005) are socially acceptable to some peers but incongruent with behaviors akin to academic success. These racist societal stereotypes about adolescent Black males can result in these boys receiving more negative treatment from teachers and peers relative to other students (Swanson, Cunningham, & Spencer, 2003). The criminalization of Black boys at the societal level also forces them to develop a gendered racial identity that helps them to cope with racism, one of the stresses of being a young Black male in society. Majors and Billson (1992) suggest that Black boys learn to develop a "cool pose"—a distinctive style of dress, communication, walk, and presentation of self that counters the aggressive and violent stereotype.

Experiences with racial discrimination can cause Black youth to be more susceptible to stereotype threat (Steele, 1997) and academic disidentification and disengagement. Furthermore, Black adolescents' experiences with racism in the classroom are negatively associated with the value they place on doing well in school and academic performance (Chavous et al., 2008). Newer research suggests that Black adolescent boys and girls are developing ways to be "ethnic" as well as high academic performers. These students use academic achievement and school success as a way to counter experiences with racism; success represents various forms of resistance to racism (see Carter, 2008a; Carter Andrews, 2012; Fordham, 2008; Gayles, 2005; O'Connor, 1997; Sanders, 1997). While Black boys in middle school have been included in some of these samples, more research is needed on this specific population of students to better understand the various ways in which adolescent Black boys can construct racial, gender, and achievement identities that allow them to be achievers in the context of being Black (Oyserman, Gant, & Ager, 1995; Perry, Steele, & Hilliard, 2003). Race and racism play key roles in Black male adolescents' construction of identities—identities that can counter their third-class citizenship as criminals and reposition them as first-class citizens in middle school and beyond.

Black Boys in Special Education and Gifted Education

Several studies have documented the overrepresentation of Black students in special education classes and their underrepresentation in Advanced Placement and honors courses, as well as gifted education programs (Artiles, 2003; Donovan & Cross, 2002; Ford, 1996; Harry & Klingner, 2006; Howard, 2014; Noguera, 2003; Pollard, 1993). These deplorable patterns represent a new type of segregation of Black students, and Black boys specifically, from mainstream students. Furthermore, the processes by which Black students are identified for special education and subsequently locked into categorical tracks with little hope of getting out represent a form of structural racism. Researchers have called into question the accuracy of the professional judgments made in diagnosing educable mental retardation (EMR), learning disability (LD), and emotional disturbance (ED). Black students are overrepresented in the EMR and ED categories, and Black male students are more than twice as likely to be classified as EMR than White male students, despite research demonstrating that the percentage of students from all racial groups is approximately the same at each intelligence and emotional level (Harry & Klingner, 2006). In contrast to these data, White male students are more than twice as likely to be placed in gifted and talented programs than are Black male students (Howard, 2014; Schott Foundation for Public Education, 2010).

The segregation of Black male students is further exacerbated once they have received special education services. As Losen and Orfield (2002) state, "Both Latinos and African Americans are far less likely than whites to be educated in a fully inclusive general education classroom and far more likely to be educated in a substantially separate setting" (p. xxi). There is a consistent trend toward less inclusion for students of color at the national, state, and district levels. Further, when students of color do receive special education services, they are often inappropriate or inadequate. Black boys in middle schools who are on the fringe of academic failure are subject to poor-quality and misguided evaluations for special education, which contribute to their overrepresentation in special education and low-quality support services once placed (Harry & Klingner, 2006). Perhaps one of the most compelling compilations of research investigating racial discrimination in special education is Daniel Losen and Gary Orfield's (2002) edited text on racial inequity in special education. The volume includes studies that suggest a correlation between race and special education, with students of color overrepresented in special education. The research suggests that racial bias, stereotypes, and other race-linked factors significantly affect patterns of identification, placement, and quality of services for Black children. This collection of studies, along with others, points to special education as an institution within schools that serves to isolate adolescent Black boys and relegate them to a third-class citizenship through structural racism. While a growing body of research is examining the overrepresentation of Black students in special education, more studies that focus specifically on Black boys in middle school are needed to help us understand how special education can be used effectively to help Black boys persist academically through high school graduation.

Overrepresentation in School Suspensions

Racial disproportionality in exclusionary discipline points further to racism's permanence in schools and the relegation of Black boys to third-class citizenry. Research indicates that Black male students receive harsher punishments in school (e.g., suspensions and expulsions) than their White male counterparts for less severe offenses (e.g., defying school authorities, "bothering others," excessive noise; Howard, 2014; Losen & Skiba, 2010; Mendez & Knoff, 2003; Skiba, Michael, Nardo, & Peterson, 2002). More than twice as many Black male students as White male students receive out-of-school suspensions, and three times as many Black male students as White male students are expelled (Schott Foundation for Public Education, 2010). Because middle school is such a critical period for determining students' future academic success, understanding the long-term repercussions of suspension and expulsion for Black boys in middle school can help make sense of other phenomena like the school-to-prison pipeline and unemployment rates for Black men, for example.

Balfanz and his colleagues (2003) chronicled the educational trajectories of 400 youth incarcerated in ninth grade and found that adolescents most at risk of incarceration were identifiable by the time they reached middle school. Eighty percent of Balfanz's sample were Black, and 85% came from neighborhood schools. Mendez and Knoff (2003) examined out-of-school suspensions in a large, ethnically diverse school district by race, gender, school level, and infraction type and found that Black boys were overrepresented in suspensions across almost all infraction types. The disproportionate number of Black students being suspended was evident as early as elementary school, with Black boys more than three times as likely as White or Hispanic boys to experience a suspension. Overall, Black male middle school students had by far the highest number of suspensions per 100 students. In this study, 15 infractions made up approximately 90% of suspensions. By far the greatest number of suspensions (20%) were for disobedience and insubordination.

Disruptiveness (13% of all suspensions) and fighting (also 13% of all suspensions) were the next most frequent reasons for suspension. These findings are consistent with other research that concluded that Black boys are suspended at a higher rate than their White male counterparts for relatively minor misbehavior.

Losen and Skiba (2010) used 2006 data from the U.S. Department of Education Office for Civil Rights (OCR) to conduct an examination of school- and district-level out-of-school suspensions. Their report highlighted the use of suspension by middle schools in 18 of the nation's largest school districts to provide a clear picture of middle school disciplinary practices in large urban districts. Disaggregating the data by race and gender revealed great disparities in the use of out-of-school suspension. Slightly more than 28% of Black boys (28.3%) in middle school and 18% of Black girls in middle school were suspended. When comparing suspension rates by race and gender, there was an 18.3-percentage-point difference between White boys and Black boys, a 12.0-percentage-point difference between Black boys and Hispanic boys, and a 22.3-percentage-point difference between Black boys and Asian/Pacific Islander boys. In 11 of the 18 districts, more than 1 in 3 Black boys were suspended. Previous research has consistently found that racial/ethnic disproportionality in discipline persists even when controlling for poverty and other demographic factors (Skiba et al., 2002; Wallace, Goodkind, Wallace, & Bachman, 2009).

This discussion shows clearly that racial bias is prevalent in school disciplinary policies and procedures. Zero-tolerance policies in schools serve to exclude Black male adolescents and other students of color from the educational setting (Caton, 2012; Reyes, 2006). In fact, research on student behavior, race, and discipline has found no evidence that the overrepresentation of Black students in school suspension is due to higher rates of misbehavior (McFadden, Marsh, Price, & Hwang, 1992). In their research on racial and gender disparities in school punishments in urban settings, Skiba et al. (2002) found that White students were referred to the office significantly more frequently than Black students for offenses that were not as subjective in nature, such as smoking, vandalism, leaving without permission, and obscene language. Criminalizing Black boys this way—through school discipline procedures—speaks to the racist nature of school discipline and the need for educators to better understand how their views of middle school Black boys mediate their disciplinary actions in classrooms and school buildings (Monroe, 2005) and inevitably lead them to engage these boys in regular experiences with racial microaggressions in the learning environment (Allen, 2013; Solórzano, Ceja, & Yosso, 2000).

Restoring First-Class Citizenship to Black Male Adolescents

In this chapter I have raised three significant issues that contribute to the academic underperformance of many Black boys in middle schools and to their subsequent downward educational trajectory and their life outcomes. I remain hopeful that we can reposition Black male adolescents as first-class citizens in our public schools, particularly in urban environments where such students are most at risk of academically underperforming and falling through the cracks. I return to the major question asked at the beginning of this chapter about my nephew Tariq's academic and life trajectory: What are the necessary individual, institutional, and communal support structures that need to exist inside and beyond schools to help him maintain a positive racial identity, a positive gender identity, and a positive achievement self-concept as part of his overall self-perception? I offer two recommendations here that speak to the former question. One highlights how parents, educators, and community members can help Black boys develop identities as high achievers; the second focuses on helping educators deconstruct their negative stereotypes of Black boys so that teachers can better address these boys' academic and social needs. While much work is to be done at the policy level, I want to underscore the role of parents and teachers in helping Black boys construct healthy identities that can act as buffers against racism and other forces that put their academic and life success at risk.

Racial Socialization and Academic Achievement

A growing body of educational research indicates that positive racial socialization—the process by which parents and other adults teach children about the significance and meaning of race to their lives—can have a potentially important influence on academic achievement (Brown, Linver, Evans, & DeGennaro, 2009; Neblett, Philip, Cogburn, & Sellers, 2006; Neblett et al., 2009; O'Connor, 1997; Oyserman, Gant, & Ager, 1995; Perry, Steele, & Hilliard, 2003; Sanders, 1997; Spencer, Noll, Stoltzfus, & Harpalani, 2001; Ward, 2000). Over the past decade, my own research with Black middle and high school students in urban and suburban contexts reveals that when Black students feel connected to the Black community, understand racial discrimination as a potential barrier to their school and life success, and view themselves as achievers in the context of being Black, these factors prove significant to developing their critical race consciousness and shaping their achievement ideologies, academic engagement, and academic persistence in positive ways (see Carter, 2008a; 2008b; Carter Andrews, 2009). Helping adolescent Black boys develop self-concepts as achievers that also include positive racial self-concepts can serve as a buffer when they face racism in school. Similarly these Black boys' conceptions of their masculine selves can be reconstructed to include affirming ideas about race and achievement. The explicit and nonexplicit messages that Black parents convey to their sons about the significance of race and racism in their educational and life trajectories can serve to counteract experiences with racism, influence academic motivation, and lead to better academic performance (Cokley, 2003; Sellers, Chavous, & Cooke, 1998).

Parents of Black boys have to engage their sons in explicit conversations about racism as a potential barrier to their school and life success while conveying messages about racial group pride and personal self-worth (Neblett et al., 2009). These socialization practices should start in children's infancy so that a positive racial self-conception provides a solid foundation for overall identity in the middle school years and beyond. Doing so, along with developing and nurturing boys' self-efficacy[1] about their academic abilities, is a necessity. Self-efficacy is a key factor in resilience (Bandura, Barbaranelli, Caprara, & Pastorelli, 2001; Schwarzer & Warner, 2013), and given the social positioning of Black boys in this country, adolescent Black boys need to develop resilient, adaptive behaviors for succeeding in school. Parents, teachers, and other adults who are central in the lives of adolescent Black boys have to encourage self-efficacious beliefs in these young men so that they can reach full potential in their lives beyond middle and high school. Some ways to do this include helping these young men set reachable goals and identify many paths to the goals; helping them maintain motivation while pursuing their goals; and noticing, analyzing, and celebrating their successes. One approach is to encourage Black males to keep a success journal so that they can record their successes and list the skills, talents, and strategies used to achieve those successes. Adults can also nurture a growth mind-set (Dweck, 2007) in Black boys, helping them understand that intelligence is not fixed but is developed with hard work and effort. Process praise (praising youth for their efforts and the strategies they used to bring about success) can lead to greater mastery, persistence, and achievement. In his work with Black young men in schools, Whiting (2006) found that those boys with a "scholar identity" share common characteristics, such as high resilience, high self-confidence, and high self-control, and they reject negative stereotypes about Black boys that are imposed on them and instead deem themselves intelligent and talented. Positive racial socialization by parents, teachers, and other adults who play critical roles in the lives of adolescent Black boys can

---

[1] *Self-efficacy* is defined as an individual's belief in his or her own ability to complete a task and reach a goal (see the work of Albert Bandura for extensive research on the relationship between self-efficacy and academic achievement).

include the nurturing of all these characteristics. When engaging in this work with adolescent Black males, adults help these adolescents write their own counternarratives of Black male identity—narratives that reject the hegemonic discourse of Black maleness that is rooted in a history of racist policy and practice that has disproportionately affected Black males in school and society (Allen, 2013; Caton, 2012; Delgado & Stefancic, 2001).

Culturally Relevant Professional Development

While I focused in the previous section on how parents can positively racially socialize adolescent Black boys for academic success, teachers can help to promote critical race consciousness and self-efficacious beliefs about academic success as well. For teachers to engage in substantive identity development work with Black boys, they need opportunities to deconstruct stereotypes and biases that they bring to their interactions. Racial and gender stereotypes often undergird teachers' interactions with Black male students. Thus, many teachers, consciously or unconsciously, subscribe to the criminal archetype that has been constructed for Black young men and believe that these boys are less intelligent, even anti-intellectual, and present more disciplinary problems than girls or boys of other racial groups (Kunjufu, 2005; Monroe, 2005). Because school structure seldom provides opportunities for educators to observe each other's practices or engage in meaningful and courageous conversations about Black young men and their schooling experiences, many stereotypes and biases go unexamined, and the conscious or unconscious racism expressed toward Black boys persists. In-service professional development efforts have to provide opportunities for teachers to interrogate their beliefs about Black male students and consider pedagogies and instructional strategies that help them see adolescent Black boys as achievers.

Several years ago I conducted a two-year professional development series for pre-K to third-grade teachers in an urban school district who were part of a project directed at increasing the academic success of boys of color. While most of these teachers were White, there were teachers of color who brought diverse experiences to the conversations that helped to deconstruct negative societal stereotypes about Black boys. The teachers engaged in readings related to the construction of masculinity for boys of color, culturally relevant instructional strategies, and building home/school partnerships with families of color. The professional development seminars emphasized how issues of race, culture, and identity shape the schooling experiences of elementary-age boys of color. In these yearlong seminars, teachers were able to connect educational theories and empirical research with practice to establish innovative ways of meeting the academic needs of boys of color in their classrooms and strengthen their relationships with these students. Additionally, the teachers were able to interrogate their White privilege and have candid conversations—in what they considered to be a safe space—about race and its implications for the teaching and learning process. Teachers must engage in this type of professional development, I argue, to help adolescent Black boys reach their fullest potential. Such professional development courses produce teachers who have a heightened critical consciousness about how cultural nuances related to race and experiences with racism shape the identity development of adolescent Black boys, as well as their academic engagement and achievement. Having these types of teachers in middle school classrooms sets the stage for helping Black boys construct positive male identity narratives and for acquiring the first-class citizenship they deserve in public schools. With this heightened critical consciousness about race, power, and privilege, classroom teachers can employ culturally responsive disciplinary strategies in their classrooms and be more conscientious about the special education referral process.

Conclusion

I am hopeful that our public schools can provide the kind of educational experience that Tariq, and many boys like him, need to be successful beyond middle and high school. A holistic effort must take place on the part of families, schools, and communities to elevate Black boys to their rightful place as first-class citizens in this society. Although our public schools have failed many of them, the advancement of Blacks as a racial group since the time of slavery indicates that schooling has provided some measure of success for many Black boys. I do not want Tariq to grow up in a world where less than 50% of his same-race male peers graduate from high school. He should not have to accept that a Third America will continue for young men who look like him. Education is a civil right; thus, we have to work to make our public schools places where adolescent Black boys can experience their full humanity and realize their full potential.

References

Allen, Q. (2013). "They think minority means lesser than": Black middle-class sons and fathers resisting microaggressions in school. *Urban Education, 48*(2), 171–197.

Artiles, A. J. (2003). Special education's changing identity: Paradoxes and dilemmas in views of culture and space. *Harvard Educational Review, 73,* 164–202.

Balfanz, R., Spiridakis, K., Neild, R. C., & Legters, N. (2003). High-poverty secondary schools and the juvenile justice system: How neither helps the other and how that could change. *New Directions for Youth Development, 2003*(99), 71–89.

Bandura, A., Barbaranelli, C., Caprara, G. V., & Pastorelli, C. (2001). Self-efficacy beliefs as shapers of children's aspirations and career trajectories. *Child Development, 72*(1), 187–206.

Brown, T., Linver, M., Evans, M., & DeGennaro, D. (2009). African-American parents' racial and ethnic socialization and adolescent academic grades: Teasing out the role of gender. *Journal of Youth & Adolescence, 38,* 214–227.

Carter, D. J. (2008a). Achievement as resistance: The development of a critical race achievement ideology among Black achievers. *Harvard Educational Review, 78*(3), 466–497.

Carter, D. J. (2008b). Cultivating a critical race consciousness for African American school success. *Educational Foundations, 22*(1–2), 11–28.

Carter Andrews, D. J. (2009). The construction of Black high-achiever identities in a predominantly white high school. *Anthropology & Education Quarterly, 40*(3), 297–317.

Carter Andrews, D. J. (2012, January). East Lansing High School student school experience survey: A research component of the Achievement Gap Initiative (2008–2012). Prepared for Superintendent's Office, East Lansing Public Schools, East Lansing, MI.

Caton, M. T. (2012). Black male perspectives on their educational experiences in high school. *Urban Education, 47*(6), 1055–1085.

Chavous, T. M., Rivas-Drake, D., Smalls, C., Griffin, T., & Cogburn, C. (2008). Gender matters, too: The influences of school racial discrimination and racial identity on academic engagement outcomes among African American adolescents. *Developmental Psychology, 44*(3), 637–654.

Cokley, K. O. (2003). What do we know about the motivation of African American students? Challenging the "anti-intellectual" myth. *Harvard Educational Review, 73*(4), 524–558.

The College Board Advocacy & Policy Center. (2010, January). *The educational crisis facing young men of color: Reflections on four days of dialogue on the educational challenges of minority males.* Washington, DC: Author.

Cunningham, M. (1999). African-American adolescent males' perceptions of their community resources and constraints: A longitudinal analysis. *Journal of Community Psychology, 27,* 569–588.

Davis, J. E., & Jordan, W. J. (1994). The effects of school context, structure, and experiences on African American males in middle and high school. *Journal of Negro Education, 63,* 570–587.

Delgado, R., & Stefancic, J. (Eds.). (2001). *Critical race theory: An introduction.* New York: New York University Press.

Donovan, S., & Cross, C. (Eds.). (2002). *Minority students in special and gifted education.* Washington, DC: National Academy Press.

Dweck, C. S. (2007). *Mindset: The new psychology of success.* Ballantine Books.

Ferguson, A. A. (2001). *Bad boys: Public schools in the making of Black masculinity.* Ann Arbor: University of Michigan Press.

Ford, D. Y. (1996). *Reversing underachievement among gifted Black students: Promising practices and programs.* New York: Teachers College Press.

Fordham, S. (1996). *Blacked out: Dilemmas of race, identity, and success at Capital High.* Chicago: University of Chicago Press.

Fordham, S. (2008). Beyond Capital High: On dual citizenship and the strange career of "acting white." *Anthropology & Education Quarterly, 39*(3), 227–246.

Fordham, S., & Ogbu, J. U. (1986). Black students' school success: Coping with the burden of "acting white." *Urban Review, 18*(3), 176–206.

Gayles, J. (2005). Playing the game and paying the price: Academic resilience among three high-achieving African American males. *Anthropology & Education Quarterly, 36*(3), 250–264.

Harry, B., & Klingner, J. K. (2006). *Why are so many minority students in special education? Understanding race and disability in schools.* New York: Teachers College Press.

Howard, T. C. (2014). *Black male(d): Peril and promise in the education of African American males.* New York: Teachers College Press.

Kunjufu, J. (2005). *Keeping Black boys out of special education.* Chicago: African American Images.

Losen, D. J., & Orfield, G. (Eds.). (2002). *Racial inequity in special education.* Cambridge, MA: Harvard Education Press.

Losen, D. J., & Skiba, R. J. (2010). *Suspended education: Urban middle schools in crisis.* Los Angeles: Civil Rights Project, University of California, Los Angeles.

Majors, R., & Billson, J. M. (1992). *Cool pose: The dilemmas of Black manhood in America.* New York: Maxwell Macmillan.

McFadden, A. C., Marsh, G. E., Price, B. J., & Hwang, Y. (1992). A study of race and gender bias in the punishment of school children. *Education and Treatment of Children, 15*, 140–146.

Mendez, L. M., Raffaele, & Knoff, H. M. (2003). Who gets suspended from school and why: A demographic analysis of schools and disciplinary infractions in a large school district. *Education and Treatment of Children, 26*(1), 30–51.

Mickelson, R. A., & Greene, A. D. (2006). Connecting pieces of the puzzle: Gender differences in Black middle school students' achievement. *Journal of Negro Education, 75*, 34–48.

Monroe, C. R. (2005). Why are "bad boys" always Black? Causes of disproportionality in school discipline and recommendations for change. *Clearing House, 79*(1), 45–50.

Neblett, E. W., Chavous, T. M., Nguyen, H. X., & Sellers, R. M. (2009). "Say it loud—I'm Black and I'm proud": Parents' messages about race, racial discrimination, and academic achievement in African American boys. *Journal of Negro Education, 78*(3), 246–259.

Neblett, E. W., Jr., Philip, C. L., Cogburn, C. D., & Sellers, R. M. (2006). African American adolescents' discrimination experiences and academic achievement:

Racial socialization as a cultural compensatory and protective factor. *Journal of Black Psychology, 32,* 199–218.

Noguera, P. A. (2003). The trouble with Black boys: The role and influence of environmental and cultural factors on the academic performance of African American males. *Urban Education, 38*(4), 431–459.

Noguera, P. A. (2008). *The trouble with Black boys . . . and other reflections on race, equity, and the future of public education.* San Francisco: Jossey-Bass.

O'Connor, C. (1997). Dispositions toward (collective) struggle and educational resilience in the inner city: A case analysis of six African-American high school students. *American Educational Research Journal, 34*(4), 593–629.

Ogbu, J. U. (2003). *Black students in an affluent suburb: A study of academic disengagement.* New York: Lawrence Erlbaum.

Oyserman, D., Gant, L., & Ager, J. (1995). A socially contextualized model of African American identity: Possible selves and school persistence. *Journal of Personality and Social Psychology, 69,* 1216–1232.

Perry, T., Steele, C., & Hilliard, A. G. (Eds.). (2003). *Young, gifted, and Black: Promoting high achievement among African-American students.* Boston: Beacon Press.

Plummer, D. L. (1995). Patterns of racial identity development of African American adolescent males and females. *Journal of Black Psychology, 21*(2), 168–180.

Polite, V. C., & Davis, J. E. (Eds.). (1999). *African American males in school and society: Practices and policies for effective education.* New York: Teachers College Press.

Pollard, D. S. (1993). Gender, achievement, and African American students' perceptions of their school experience. *Educational Psychologist, 28*(4), 294–303.

Reyes, A. H. (2006). *Discipline, achievement, and race: Is zero tolerance the answer?* Lanham, MD: Rowman & Littlefield.

Sanders, M. (1997). Overcoming obstacles: Academic achievement as a response to racism and discrimination. *Journal of Negro Education, 66*(1), 83–93.

Schott Foundation for Public Education. (2010). *Yes we can: The Schott 50-state report on public education and Black males, 2010.* Cambridge, MA. Retrieved April 18, 2011 from http://www.schottfoundation.org

Schott Foundation for Public Education. (2012). *The urgency of now: The Schott 50-state report on public education and Black males, 2012.* Cambridge, MA. Retrieved from http://www.schottfoundation.org

Schwarzer, R., & Warner, L. M. (2013). Perceived self-efficacy and its relationship to resilience (pp. 139–150). In S. Prince-Embury & D. H. Saklofske (Eds.), *Resilience in children, adolescents, and adults.* New York: Springer.

Sellers, R. M., Chavous, T. M., & Cooke, D. Y. (1998). Racial ideology and racial centrality as predictors of African American college students' academic performance. *Journal of Black Psychology, 24*(1), 8–27.

Skiba, R. J., Michael, R. S., Nardo, A. C., & Peterson, R. L. (2002). The color of discipline: Sources of racial and gender disproportionality in school punishment. *Urban Review, 34,* 317–342.

Solórzano, D., Ceja, M., & Yosso, T. (2000). Critical race theory, racial microaggressions, and campus racial climate: The experiences of African American college students. *Journal of Negro Education, 69*(1–2), 60–73.

Spencer, M. B., Noll, E., Stoltzfus, J., & Harpalani, V. (2001). Identity and school adjustment: Revisiting the "acting white" assumption. *Educational Psychologist, 36*(1), 21–30.

Steele, C. M. (1997). A threat in the air: How stereotypes shape intellectual identity and performance. *American Psychologist, 52*(6), 613–629.

Swanson, D. P., Cunningham, M., & Spencer, M. B. (2003). Black males' structural conditions, achievement patterns, normative needs, and "opportunities." *Urban Education, 38*(5), 608–633.

Wallace, J. M., Jr., Goodkind, S., Wallace, C. M., & Bachman, J. G. (2009). Racial, ethnic, and gender differences in school discipline among U.S. high school students: 1991–2005. *Negro Educational Review, 59*, 47–62.

Ward, J. V. (2000). *The skin we're in: Teaching our children to be emotionally strong, socially smart, spiritually connected.* New York: Free Press.

Whiting, G. W. (2006). From at risk to at promise: Developing scholar identities among Black males. *Journal of Secondary Gifted Education, 17*(4), 222–229.

4

BLACK MALE HIGH SCHOOL STUDENTS

(Un)Accepted Failure in U.S. Schools

Terry K. Flennaugh

When I met Phillip, I could not help but feel that his story offered a powerful example of how society has accepted failure as the fate for young Black male students. At the time, I worked for a university-sponsored college readiness program that had recently begun to work with several of South Los Angeles's predominantly Black high schools to increase the number of students who applied and were admitted to competitive universities in California. I had spent several weeks working at the college center, talking with students about university admission requirements, before Phillip walked in to inquire about going to a prominent university in the area. I had seen Phillip, a senior at one of the high schools, pop in and out of the college center a few times since the beginning of the academic year, but we never spoke for any significant amount of time.

When we did finally speak at length, Phillip was clearly excited about the prospect of going to this specific university. He brought a copy of his high school transcript to our meeting; Phillip ranked in the top 10% of his class. Having had the opportunity to see the senior class rankings for his high school earlier in the year, I knew that young Black men were hardly present in the top quarter of the class. Needless to say, I was impressed by Phillip's academic record. Aware of the students' schooling experiences at this particular high school, I was encouraged to see a Black male student who, in the face of staggering structural challenges, found a way to excel in nearly all of his classes and position himself to go to college. However, after looking over Phillip's transcript further, I realized that he had taken only one foreign language course. I asked Phillip if he had taken any classes at a community college or elsewhere, hoping to hear that he satisfied his foreign language requirement outside of his high school. He said he had not taken any additional classes. For those not familiar with California's A-G requirements,[1] this status meant that Phillip was not eligible for admission to either the California State University or University of California systems.

I was immediately overwhelmed with frustration and questions as to how a student such as Phillip, who was in the top 10% of his class, could be assigned a course load that failed to satisfy the basic requirements for admission into any of California's publicly funded four-year universities. I was aware of the counseling challenges that existed in many of the urban schools with which my program was working, but it had not dawned on me that students who were otherwise headed down the path to college could be denied this opportunity (and others) because of neglect on the part of counselors and other school staff. Instead of talking with Phillip about applying to his dream university, I had to talk to him about enrolling in night school or community college to satisfy his foreign language requirement.

It was tough to see the shock on Phillip's face when he said that no one had told him that he needed more courses to be eligible for California's four-year universities. While we were able to develop a plan of action for Phillip for the next several months, I could not help but feel that Phillip's confidence and excitement for college had taken a major hit because of our conversation. I have always thought of Phillip and his experience as a catalyst for my work with young Black men.

Phillip's story, if nothing else, serves as a salient reminder that young Black men face persistent challenges in today's high schools, no matter what their academic profile looks like. I cannot say with certainty that Phillip, as a Black male student, was the victim of a broader conspiracy to fail young Black men, although scholars such as Kunjufu (2004) have articulated compelling arguments to support this theory. However, I believe wholeheartedly that school staff had accepted failure for Phillip before he even had a chance to demonstrate all of which he was capable. For far too long, the prevailing narrative that surrounds Black men in today's high schools has been dominated by the expectation for failure. As Howard (2008) argues, too

---

[1] The A-G Requirements (http://www.ucop.edu/agguide/a-g-requirements/) are a set of subject requirements that California high school students must satisfy in order to be eligible for admission to the California State and University of California systems.

many educators have accepted widespread failure as "business as usual" for young Black men. To be clear, a growing body of scholarship seeks to provide alternative narratives for academic failure and success for Black men in high school (Duncan, 2002; Ferguson, 2001; Harper et al., 2014; Kirkland, 2013; Nasir et al., 2013; Nasir, McLaughlin, & Jones, 2009; Terry, 2010); however, the challenges for Black male students such as Phillip remain.

Some may find it tempting to dismiss Phillip's story because it fundamentally conflicts with what we want to believe about the promise of American education. Many of us have yet to accept the reality of this pervasive framework that governs how we view young Black men, but it is imperative to shed light on these young men's experiences in high school so that we can move away from the complacency and apathy that dominate the broader discussion about young Black men in U.S. society. As the data show, a crisis exists for young Black men in high school. However, we must also acknowledge the powerful stories of Black male success in high school to demonstrate that young Black men are finding ways to succeed in the face of staggering challenges. In this chapter I lay out the current state of Black male academic performance, using graduation rates, subject-area proficiency, and college preparation in America's high schools. Further, I highlight promising efforts by educators across the country—educators who have rejected the business-as-usual approaches to young Black men in high school to stem troubling trends in the schooling of this population. Finally, I offer guidelines for evaluating emerging scholarship and programmatic interventions for Black male high school students.

Black Male Student Performance in High School

Over the past several decades, increasing attention has been paid to the dismal high school graduation rates of young Black men. Many social scientists and educational researchers have emphasized the institutional conditions that adversely affect the educational achievement of Black male students in secondary education (Howard, 2008, 2014; Jordan & Cooper, 2001; Noguera, 2003), while other scholars have pointed the finger at these students and their communities as the reasons for poor educational outcomes during high school (Bereiter & Engelmann, 1966; Fordham & Ogbu, 1986; Gibson & Ogbu, 1991; Ogbu & Simons, 1998). At the end of the day, the fact remains that Black male students who attain a high school diploma are being left behind at disturbing rates. Take Phillip, for example. Though his story is both heart wrenching and compelling, it is not unique in California. In 1960, the state adopted A Master Plan for Higher Education in California, which codified the California higher education structure. Though largely silent on issues of diversity, the broad intent of the Master Plan[2] was to configure an interrelated set of institutions that would provide access to higher education for *all* Californians. However, the California Department of Education (CDE) reports that only 22.9% of California's 13,520 Black male high school graduates completed courses that made them eligible for admission to either the California State University or University of California systems in 2012.[3] Coupled with the fact that only 31% of Black male ninth graders in 2008 graduated in 2012 means that just 7.1% of California's freshmen cohort of Black male students in 2008 acquired the courses necessary to enroll in any one of the state's publicly funded four-year universities. While the story of Black male academic performance in California is disturbing, young Black men in high school face similar situations across the country; this warrants further consideration, especially given the consequences of not having a high school degree in today's economy.

Now, perhaps more than any other time in U.S. history, education has serious implications for the social, political, and economic future of America's youth. Students such as Phillip will be three times more likely to vote if they complete college as opposed to their peers who fail to graduate from high school. Additionally, students who drop out of high school earn 28% less over a lifetime than do high school graduates (Baum, Ma, & Payea, 2013). Sadly, in its 2012 national report *The Urgency of Now: The Schott 50 State Report on Black Males and Public Education*, the Schott Foundation revealed that during the 2009–2010 academic year, 52% of young Black men did not receive diplomas with their classmates after four years of high school. In fact, the foundation reported that Black men who failed to graduate from high school were heavily concentrated in America's cities, such as New York, Cleveland, Detroit, and Rochester, where nonpeer-group completion rates were as high as 91%. The report identified Maine, Arizona, and Vermont as the only states to have Black male graduation rates above 82% (Schott Foundation for Public Education, 2012). These three states actually have the unique distinction of being the only states where Black male graduation rates exceeded those of their White male peers. However, the number of Blacks living in these three states constitutes only 0.1% of the entire Black population in the United States. On the other hand, the report identified New York, Florida, South Carolina, Georgia, and Louisiana as states that have Black male peer-group graduation rates between 37% and 49% (Schott Foundation for Public Education, 2012), where, collectively, Blacks make up 32.3% of the entire Black

---

[2] See Master Plan for Higher Education in California (http://www.ucop.edu/acadinit/mastplan/mp.htm).

[3] Data retrieved from California Department of Education (http://dq.cde.ca.gov/dataquest/).

population in the United States. But graduation rates are only one way to paint the picture of Black male performance in high school today.

Data from the National Assessment of Educational Progress (NAEP) 2009 *Nation's Report Card* describe a bleak situation for young Black men in high school. Overall, only 0.8% of all 12th-grade Black students were at or above proficient in algebra in 2008 (U.S. Department of Education, 2009). Further, when additional data are disaggregated to examine the percentage of students at or above proficient in reading by the eighth grade, we see that only 9% of young Black men were at or above proficient, as opposed to 22% of their White male counterparts (U.S. Department of Education, 2009). The only states in which the percent of Black male eighth graders reading at or above proficient exceeded 14% were Kentucky and New Jersey, although they came in at only 15%. Young Black men made up 9% of all students enrolled in public schools, yet they made up 24% of the out-of-school suspension population and 25% of those expelled; they were twice as likely to be classified as mentally retarded than their White male peers, and made up only 3% of those enrolled in AP science and mathematics (Schott Foundation for Public Education, 2008). Unfortunately, the struggle for high school–age Black men does not end there. According to the U.S. Bureau of Labor Statistics, high school–age (16–19 years old) Black men suffered unemployment rates as high as 55.5% in 2009, contributing to the 27.4% of Blacks living beneath the poverty line in the United States. Additionally, the Bureau of Justice Statistics reports that, in 2005, Black males represented more than 40% of the prison population in the United States, not including those on parole. The degree to which young Black men leave schoolyards and end up occupying prison yards has given rise to the school-to-prison pipeline, which has become the focus of an increasing amount of research (Alexander, 2012; Ferguson, 2001; NAACP, 2005; Wald & Losen, 2003). Consequentially, Black men who have little hope of obtaining educational, economic, and political opportunities have higher rates of homicide and shorter life expectancies than any other group (U.S. Department of Health and Human Services, 2013). While these facts may lead some people to make assumptions about this population of students and their ability to prosper in society, we must take a moment to critically reflect on the power that this particular narrative has on Black male adolescents and decide how helpful it is to create an alternative story of success for young Black men in high school.

The Danger of a Single Story

In her 2009 address to the Technology, Entertainment, Design (TED) Global Conference in Oxford, Nigerian novelist Chimamanda Ngozi Adichie described what she calls the danger of a single story. She explained that as a child she believed in a single story that existed about her family's houseboy, Fide. Her mother would send yams, rice, and old clothes to Fide's family. When Adichie sometimes failed to finish her meals, her mother would say, "Finish your food! Don't you know people like Fide's family have nothing?" Adichie felt enormous pity for Fide's family until the day she saw a beautiful handcrafted basket that Fide's brother had made. It had not dawned on her until that moment that anyone in Fide's family was capable of making any-thing. As an African living in the United States, she realized that single stories are anything but complete stories about groups of people. She warned that the real danger of the single story is that it robs people of their dignity. Pre-sumably, we all have our own single stories about various segments of society. Educators, researchers, and youth workers who focus on high school–age Black men can acknowledge that a single story of chronic underperformance and dismal chances for academic excellence exists for this population of stu-dents. This single story inhibits many of us from thinking about anything other than failure for young Black men in today's schools. Nonetheless, scholars such as Harper et al. (2014) and Noguera (2008) remind us that, despite the well-publicized shortcomings of young Black men in high school, it is important to recognize that Black men have found ways to achieve in today's school settings and that environmental and cultural factors play sig-nificant roles in the academic success of young Black men. Noguera's (2008) call for a paradigm shift that does *not* begin with what young Black men lack is important because it encourages those in education to accept the premise that the structures of many American institutions have failed to adequately address the needs of Black male students.

Scholars such as Ford (1996), Harper et al. (2014), Howard (2008, 2014), Kirkland (2013), Noguera (2008), and Whiting (2006) have been tremendously helpful in pushing against existing theoretical frameworks that examine Black male academic success in high school. Equally important to this push are the efforts of teachers, administrators, and community mem-bers across the United States. Their efforts, particularly with Black men in high school, are important to acknowledge, given that deficit-oriented frameworks about Black male academic success remain prevalent in public discourse.

Oakland Unified School District

In 2010 the Oakland Unified School District (OUSD) launched a bold ini-tiative to address the academic performance of young Black men with the creation of the Office of African American Male Achievement. The office's 2011 Task Force Summary Report indicated that Black babies born in West

Oakland are 7 times more likely to be born into poverty and 5.6 times more likely to drop out of school, and can expect to die almost 15 years earlier than a White child born in Oakland Hills (OUSD, 2011). In response to these figures, OUSD developed a six-year initiative to focus on seven areas aimed at improving educational and social outcomes for young Black men in Oakland: the achievement gap, graduation, literacy, suspension, attendance, incarceration, and middle school holding power (OUSD, 2011). The creation of this OUSD office in a post–Proposition 209 context[4] is significant, because it demonstrates the initiative and commitment at the school district level to confront the challenges that undermine young Black males' success in schools. As the district prepared to develop systemwide changes, the report listed a wide range of promising practices that support African American male achievement. These practices included engaging parents in educational forums that empower them to act as advocates for their children individually, as a group, and at the legislative level; eliciting perspectives of students, teachers, and parents; setting high expectations; providing engaging and culturally relevant coursework; promoting student-controlled classroom discourse; identifying alternatives to out-of-school suspension; and establishing pilot single-sex spaces based on research supporting the idea that such spaces improve the academic outcomes for young Black men (OUSD, 2011). When asked if this initiative would be different than previous efforts to address Black male academic performance in Oakland, Christopher Chatmon, executive director of the Office for African American Male Achievement, responded, "Well, it has to be different. . . . I think we as a people have become desensitized to the travesties, to the inequities that our children have faced for generations. So failure is no longer an option."[5]

Eagle Academy for Young Men

The first Eagle Academy for Young Men opened in the Bronx in 2004. At the time, it was the first single-sex public school for boys in New York City in approximately 30 years. Today, the Eagle Academy Foundation has expanded to five school sites across New York and New Jersey and stands out as another model approach to encourage Black male academic success. In the 2010–2011 school year, the Eagle Academy for Young Men in the Bronx enrolled an all-male student body that was 66% Black and 32% Latino, with 71% of all students eligible for free or reduced-price lunch (New York State

---

[4] In 1996, Proposition 209 was passed in California; it prohibited public institutions from using racial preferences in admissions and discriminating against individuals on the basis of protected attributes such as race or ethnicity.

[5] OUSD interview with Chris Chatmon (see http://www.youtube.com/watch?v=f0gYuOr_u3k).

Department of Education, 2011). Despite its similarities to other New York City urban schools, where overall graduation rates for Black males was 28% (Schott Foundation for Public Education, 2012), the Eagle Academy reports that its 2010 graduation rate was 70%, with 65% of graduates planning to enter college. Core elements of the Eagle Academy's mission include parent engagement, academic rigor, college preparation, extended day and Saturday programs, rituals to establish expectations among the entire school community, summer bridge programs for new students, and mentoring. When talking about the mission, President and CEO David Banks stated, "To fail here is not an option" (as quoted in Richardson, 2004). Eagle Academy was one of 40 schools in the New York City Black and Latino Male High School Achievement Study (see Harper et al., 2014). The following story about the Academy's principal is extracted from *Succeeding in the City*, a report from the Harper et al. study:

> Jonathan Foy, the principal, insisted that one of our team members use his office for interviews. He spent the entire day engaging with students and others around the school, which participants said was not at all unusual. At one point, Principal Foy apologized for having to interrupt one of our interviews; he needed to quickly enter his office to retrieve a book and folder. This former U.S. history and government teacher was on his way to tutor students in that subject, something he does multiple times each week. One participant's mom dropped by Eagle Academy that day. The principal took time to introduce our research team members to her. We later inquired about the multicolored sheets of paper taped to a whiteboard in his office; each had a student's name and some notes. Mr. Foy explained it was part of his method of checking in with students who were in jeopardy of not graduating on time. That an urban school leader has time to tutor and track the academic progress of individual students as well as introduce parents to researchers is remarkable. . . . Principal Foy told us he is usually at Eagle Academy until 7:00 most evenings. (2014, p. 21)

Urban Prep Academies in Chicago

Not long ago, a small charter school in Chicago captured the attention of many people in the education community who are concerned with the academic performance of young Black men in high school. Urban Prep Academies announced in 2013 that, for the fourth year in a row, 100% of its graduating class from its Englewood campus were accepted into college. Urban Prep Academies operates the country's first charter schools designed to meet the needs of young Black men. With a student population nearly 100% Black, 85% of whom are classified as low income (Urban Prep Academies,

2011), Urban Prep prides itself on being a system that educates young Black men from the city's most disadvantaged communities. While much more remains to be understood about Urban Prep's retention of students through their senior year, what *is* clear is the impact of additional instruction hours afforded by an extended school schedule and the core values that guide its mission: accountability, exceptionality, faith, integrity, relentlessness, resilience, selflessness, and solidarity (Urban Prep Academies, 2009).

New Approaches and Alternative Paradigms

These examples are not meant as an unequivocal stamp of approval for only these initiatives. In fact, efforts at Detroit's Paul Robeson/Malcolm X Academy, Long Beach Unified School District's Male Academies, or other locations across the United States could have easily been given as examples of places where education leaders are confronting Black male academic performance in their institutions. The reality is that a tremendous gap remains in the literature on Black male achievement in these types of learning contexts. Nonetheless, each example demonstrates educators' and community members' various efforts to redirect the educational and societal trajectory for many of our Black male high school students. Undoubtedly, now is an exciting time for those interested in Black male achievement, as this topic is receiving increasing attention from education researchers, and more and more school- and district-level initiatives to help young Black men are being created across the country. However, the work of Howard, Flennaugh, and Terry (2012) is important to consider as we begin to evaluate the scholarship and initiatives focused on young Black men in high school. In their article, Howard et al. (2012) propose five principles to help guide our thinking in research and practice with young Black men. I discuss four of the five principles here. These principles are not comprehensive but offer cautions, concerns, and considerations (Howard & Flennaugh, 2010) that may be useful in re-creating the narrative that surrounds Black men in high school.

The first principle calls for education researchers, practitioners, and youth workers to abandon theoretical approaches to Black men that are deficit oriented. Howard et al. (2012) argue that research on young Black men has historically focused on what these students and their communities lack intellectually, socially, and culturally. Howard et al. state,

> Researchers interested in students of color, in large part, have pathologized these populations by continuously studying those who are not doing well, or questioning their innate intelligence, or lack thereof (Bereiter & Engelmann, 1966; Terman, 1916). In many ways, contemporary researchers

have adopted similar stances, even as they attempt to disrupt discriminatory school practices. (p. 94)

The impact of the American eugenics movement and white supremacy on theoretical and methodological approaches to research on communities of color is often overlooked (Selden, 1999). With this in mind, Howard et al. (2012) suggest that the education community has often failed to acknowledge that young Black men do excel in the face of staggering structural challenges. Along with the work of scholars such as Harper et al. (2014) and Noguera (2008), Howard and his colleagues (2012) assert that work dealing with young Black men in today's schools should "highlight the prominence of the accomplishments, examine the practices and school culture, and then raise questions about the replicability of these outcomes given what has been learned" (p. 95). Using this specific approach to research initiatives such as that in the Oakland Unified School District would allow us to focus on the successful strategies being employed by district, school, and community leaders while allowing us to interrogate whether such efforts will lead to sustained improvement for young Black men across the district. The story of failure among young Black men in high school is one that we have heard repeatedly. Now is the time to identify those spaces and practices that challenge this single story and to critically evaluate the degree to which strength-based approaches can be transferred across varying educational contexts.

The second principle asks individuals to avoid perpetuating a false dichotomy focused on either the individual or the institution. Black adolescents who fail to successfully navigate secondary education are often among those students who attended severely underresourced schools. Scholars such as Kozol (1991) have documented at length the deplorable conditions that many of our students are still forced to endure in today's schools. Be it long-term substitutes, unsafe school environments, or the scarcity of education materials, schools continue to struggle with providing low-income children of color with the same caliber of education that is afforded students in more affluent communities. Nonetheless, Howard et al. (2012) warn that an exclusive focus on this point neglects the role that families play in their children's education or the role of individual agency on school failure and success:

> Work that focuses on failures of educational institutions is important; however, as educational researchers, we cannot turn a blind eye to disturbing data that reveals the high amount of television consumed by Black children, or the disconnect between educational aspirations and hours spent studying by Black students. (p. 95)

However, Howard and colleagues ask researchers to "avoid demonizing institutions or vilifying individuals and their communities" (2012, p. 96), and to consider all elements that influence Black male success in and outside the classroom.

In their third principle, Howard and colleagues call on us to acknowledge the complex identities and notions of self that young Black men have (Howard et al., 2012). Noting that the field of education has struggled for well over a century to sufficiently address the substantial challenges Black men face in constructing identities that function in schools, Howard and his colleagues highlight the work of Du Bois (1903), Harper and Nichols (2008), Harper and Harris (2010), Nasir et al. (2009), and Williams (2009) as examples of scholarship that rejects one-dimensional models of identity for Black men in today's schools. The early work of Du Bois (1903) and his concept of double-consciousness remain extremely important for educational researchers, practitioners, and youth workers because they serve as a foundation for multidimensional models of identity that contend with historic and contemporary discrimination in the United States. This foundation allows us to acknowledge that the ways Black men come to develop notions of self are not the same as the processes that members of the dominant group undergo during their high school years. Further, the work of Harper and Nichols (2008) and Harper and Harris (2010) pushes us to acknowledge that notions of masculinity and gender are not uniform among Black men. While the complexities of identity can be easily overlooked in research on Black men in high school, efforts to acknowledge these complexities are clear in the work being done at Eagle Academies in New York.

In their fourth principle, Howard et al. (2012) call for the voices of Black male students to be central in research and practice. Howard and colleagues point to the work of Duncan (2002), Giroux (1988), Howard (2008), Nieto (2004), and Waxman and Huang (1997) as examples of research that honors the narratives of students in educational settings. With specific references to counter-storytelling among young Black men (Howard, 2008) and narrative theory (Hoshmand, 2005), Howard et al. (2012) suggest that "the incorporation of narratives voiced by marginalized persons can also help to dismantle the dominant discourses surrounding race, class, and gender groups" (p. 97). They add, "Hearing people's own stories is a powerful way of getting oftentimes reluctant teachers, researchers, or policy makers in training to understand that the theories they are learning about have a material effect on individuals" (Howard et al., 2012, p. 98). Capturing the narrative of a student such as Phillip not only enables one to recognize the context of academic and college counseling for high-performing young Black men in urban schools, it also affords Phillip the opportunity and the agency to name the pain that he endured as a result of pervasive theories of failure and success for young Black men. His voice, in addition to other counter-stories, can represent a different truth and different experiences that challenge hegemony (Terry, 2010). Scholars and practitioners who work with young Black men in schools must strive to honor the voices of these students in all their efforts.

Conclusion

The story of school failure among young Black men in high school is one with which we all are familiar. Unfortunately, too few of us have attempted to disrupt this narrative, resulting in the types of educational injustices that students such as Phillip, or those who do not make it to their high school graduation, have suffered. However, it is important to acknowledge the work individuals and groups across the country are doing—in Oakland, New York, and Chicago. In these places and others like them, young Black men are not simply prescribed a single story of chronic failure. Through these efforts, new, more complete stories of Black male success and failure in high school are created. These efforts are quite promising. Nonetheless, we must continue to critically evaluate the ways in which theories of success are both constructed in research and implemented in practice for young Black men in high school. We simply cannot afford to continue business as usual for these students.

References

Alexander, M. (2012). *The new Jim Crow: Mass incarceration in the age of colorblindness.* New York: New Press.

Baum, S., Ma, J., & Payea, K. (2013). *Education pays 2013: The benefits of higher education for individuals and society.* New York: The College Board.

Bereiter, C., & Engelmann, S. (1966). *Teaching disadvantaged children in the preschool.* Englewood Cliffs, NJ: Prentice Hall.

Bureau of Justice Statistics. (2009, November 25). Retrieved from www.ojp.usdoj.gov/bjs

Du Bois, W. E. B. (1903). *The souls of Black folk.* New York: Penguin Group.

Duncan, G. A. (2002). Beyond love: A critical race theory ethnography of the schooling of adolescent Black males. *Equity & Excellence, 35*(2), 131–143.

Ferguson, A. A. (2001). *Bad boys: Public schools in the making of Black masculinity.* Ann Arbor: University of Michigan Press.

Ford, D. Y. (1996). *Reversing underachievement among gifted Black students: Promising practices and programs.* New York: Teachers College Press.

Fordham, S., & Ogbu, J. (1986). Black students school success: Coping with the "burden of acting white." *Urban Review, 18*, 176–206.

Gibson, M., & Ogbu, J. (1991). *Minority status and schooling: A comparative study of immigrant and involuntary minorities.* New York: Garland Publishing.

Giroux, H. (1988). *Schooling and the struggle for public life.* Minneapolis: University of Minnesota Press.

Harper, S. R., & Associates. (2014). *Succeeding in the city: A report from the New York City Black and Latino Male High School Achievement Study.* Philadelphia: University of Pennsylvania, Center for the Study of Race and Equity in Education.

Harper, S. R., & Harris, F. (Eds.). (2010). *College men and masculinities: Theory, research, and implications for practice.* San Francisco: Jossey-Bass.

Harper, S. R., & Nichols, A. H. (2008). Are they not all the same? Racial heterogeneity among Black male undergraduates. *Journal of College Student Development, 49*(3), 199–214.

Hoshmand, L. T. (2005). Culture, psychotherapy, and counseling: *Critical and integrative perspectives.* Thousand Oaks, CA: SAGE.

Howard, T. C. (2008). Who really cares? The disenfranchisement of African American males in preK–12 schools: A critical race theory perspective. *Teachers College Record, 110*(5), 954–985.

Howard, T. C. (2014). *Black male(d): Peril and promise in the education of African American males.* New York: Teachers College Press.

Howard, T. C., & Flennaugh, T. (2010). Research concerns, cautions, and considerations on Black males in a "postracial" society. *Race, Ethnicity & Education, 14*(1), 105–120.

Howard, T. C., Flennaugh, T. K., & Terry, C. L. (2012). Black males, social imagery, and the disruption of pathological identities: Implications for research and teaching. *Educational Foundations, 26* (1–2), 85–102.

Jordan, W., & Cooper, R. (2001). *Racial and cultural issues related to comprehensive school reform: The case of African American males.* Washington, DC: Office of Educational Research and Improvement.

Kirkland, D. (2013). *A search past silence: The literacy of young Black men.* New York: Teachers College Press.

Kozol, J. (1991). *Savage inequalities: Children in American schools.* New York: HarperCollins.

Kunjufu, J. (2004). *Countering the conspiracy to destroy Black boys.* Chicago: African American Images.

NAACP. (2005). Dismantling the school-to-prison pipeline. Retrieved from http://www.naacpldf.org/files/publications/Dismantling_the_School_to_Prison_Pipeline.pdf

Nasir, N., McLaughlin, M., & Jones, A. (2009). What does it mean to be African American? Constructions of race and academic identity in an urban public high school. *American Educational Research Journal, 46*(1), 73–114.

Nasir, N., Ross, K., McKinney de Royston, M., Givens, J., & Bryant, J. (2013). Dirt on my record: Rethinking disciplinary practices in an all-Black, all-male alternative class. *Harvard Educational Review, 83*(3), 489–512.

New York State Department of Education. (2011). *The New York state report card: Comprehensive information report 2010–11*. New York: Author. Retrieved from http://schools.nyc.gov/SchoolPortals/09/X231/AboutUs/Statistics/default.htm

Nieto, S. (2004). *Affirming diversity: The sociopolitical context of multicultural education*. Boston: Pearson.

Noguera, P. A. (2003). The trouble with Black boys: The role and influence of environmental and cultural factors on the academic performance of African American males. *Urban Education, 38*(4), 431–459.

Noguera, P. A. (2008). *The trouble with Black boys . . . and other reflections on race, equity, and the future of public education*. San Francisco: Jossey-Bass.

Oakland Unified School District. (2011). *African-American Male Achievement task force summary report*. Oakland, CA: Office of African American Male Achievement, Oakland Unified School District.

Ogbu, J., & Simons, H. (1998). Voluntary and involuntary minorities: A cultural-ecological theory of school performance with some implications for education. *Anthropology and Education Quarterly, 29*(2), 155–188.

Richardson, L. (2004, September 23). For principal, new boys' school is a call to action. *New York Times*, Retrieved from http://www.nytimes.com/2004/09/23/nyregion/23profile.html?_r=0

Schott Foundation for Public Education. (2008). *Given half a chance: The Schott 50-state report on public education and black males*. Cambridge, MA: Author.

Schott Foundation for Public Education. (2012). *The urgency of now: The Schott 50-state report on Black males and public education*. Cambridge, MA: Author.

Selden, S. (1999). *Inheriting shame: The story of eugenics and racism in America*. New York: Teachers College Press.

Terman, L. (1916). *The measurement of intelligence*. Boston: Houghton Mifflin Company.

Terry, C. L. (2010). Prisons, pipelines, and the president: Developing critical math literacy through participatory action research. *Journal of African American Males in Education, 1*(2), 73–104.

Urban Prep Academies. (2009). *Urban Prep Academies 2009 annual report*. Chicago: Author.

Urban Prep Academies. (2011). *Background information and preliminary FY11 data findings*. Chicago: Author.

U.S. Department of Education. (2009). *The nation's report card: Achievement gaps: How black and white students perform on NAEP*. Washington, DC: Institute of Education Sciences, U.S. Department of Education.

U.S. Department of Health and Human Services. (2013). *NCHS data brief: How did cause of death contribute to racial differences in life expectancy in the United States in 2010?* Washington, DC: Centers for Disease Control, U.S. Department of Health and Human Services.

Wald, J., & Losen, D. J. (2003). Editors' notes. In J. Wald & D. J. Losen (Eds.), *New directions for youth development: Deconstructing the school-to-prison pipeline* (pp. 1–2). San Francisco: Jossey-Bass.

Waxman, H. C., & Huang, S. (1997). Classroom instruction and learning environment differences between effective and ineffective urban elementary schools for African American students. *Urban Education, 32*(4), 7–44.

Whiting, G. (2006). Promoting scholar identity among African American males: Recommendations for educators. *Gifted Education Press Quarterly, 29*(3), 46–50.

Williams, R. F. (2009). Black-white biracial students in American schools: A review of the literature. *Review of Educational Research, 79*(2), 776–804.

5

BLACK MALE COLLEGIANS IN COMMUNITY COLLEGES

Factors Affecting Their Persistence and Academic Success

J. Luke Wood, Edward Bush, Terence Hicks, and Hassiem A. Kambui

In 1900, Joliet High School in Illinois began offering a selection of college-level classes. By 1901, the high school was providing a more comprehensive collegiate curriculum, and by 1902 it was officially sanctioned by the school's board of trustees. The board also approved offering these courses tuition free. This institution, later named Joliet Junior College, is credited as the oldest public two-year college in the nation (American Association of Community Colleges [AACC], 2009; Griffith & Blackstone, 1945; Joliet Junior College, 2012; Monroe, 1977). Its founding ushered in a new era, marking the establishment of a unique institution—the American community college. Today, there are more than 1,200 community colleges; as a whole, these institutions feature low-cost educational opportunities, open-access admissions, comprehensive educational programming, and a mission-driven dedication to meeting the needs (e.g., economic, social, cultural) of the local communities that they serve (Cohen & Brawer, 2003; Nevarez & Wood, 2010; Vaughan, 2006).

Despite these hallmarks and the institution's lofty vision of actualizing "broader postsecondary education for the people" (Tillery & Deegan, 1985, p. 5), these institutions have not rightly served all students. These students include, in particular, young Black men who—seeing community colleges as a venue for upward economic, social, and political mobility—are significantly less likely than other collegians to persist or complete their studies (Bush, 2004). Unfortunately, Joliet's one-year retention and three-year completion rates serve as examples of this perpetual pattern. Only 40.4% of young Black men who enter Joliet in the fall semester will still be enrolled the following year—the lowest retention rate among all male students; for instance, retention rates for other male racial/ethnic groups are as follows: Asian Americans, 53.8%; Latinos, 62.1%; and Whites, 62.5% (Joliet Junior College, 2005a). Another measure of community college student outcomes is completion rate (a statistic depicting the percentage of students who graduate, transfer, or are still enrolled three years after their initial enrollment). Again, young Black men at Joliet perform markedly lower than their counterparts from other racial groups, with a completion rate of 35.4%. In contrast, completion rates are 74.4%, 56.3%, and 60.5% for Asian American, Latino, and White men (Joliet Junior College, 2005b).

These differential outcomes are indicative of national trends for young Black men in community colleges. For instance, national data indicate that Black male completion rates are 41.1%, the lowest among all male groups; completion rates for other men are as follows: Asian Americans, 69.6%; Latinos, 50.3%; and Whites, 54.8% (U.S. Department of Education, 2009). These rates, among other measures of success, validate the ubiquitous discourse among researchers and practitioners on the disparate success of young Black men in community college. Rather than focusing on the multiple areas in which young Black men underperform in contrast to their counterparts (e.g., enrollment, persistence, graduation, transfer), we focus our discussion on why this occurs. We highlight certain background characteristics of young Black men to provide insight into the general attributes of this population. Then we discuss the most salient factors that affect Black male success. These factors are gathered from the literature on young Black men in community college. In conclusion, we offer recommendations that can be used to enhance academic outcomes for young Black men in community college. We begin, however, by sharing some of our concerns.

Four Initial Concerns

As educators we have dedicated our careers, through our research and practice, to improving young Black men's experience in community college. As such, we are especially concerned about current academic outcomes for these men. Our concern is rooted in four notions. First, young Black men overwhelmingly select community college as their primary point of entry into postsecondary education. For example, in 2008, 44.2% of young Black men were enrolled in public two-year institutions while the remainder attended public four-year (26.0%); private, not-for-profit four-year (10.9%); private for-profit (12.0%); and other (6.9%) colleges and universities. Given the large proportion of young Black men who attend community college, that these institutions are not facilitating their success is troubling; this situation has significant ramifications for social stratification, economic inequities, and workplace disparities, among other issues. In many ways, young Black men have been sold a false bill of goods: the promise of a better life through educational opportunities. Sadly, a limited number of Black men will realize that promise.

Second, the outcomes young Black men in community college experience are preventable. Institutions committed to curbing the disastrous success rates of these students can do so with guidance and dedication. While students must be held accountable, colleges bear the lion's share of the responsibility for student success. In the past, the community college operated on a philosophy that students have the *right to fail*, meaning that the schools provided students with access to postsecondary education without employing "all reasonable means" to advance student success. Instead, community colleges must foster a *right-to-succeed* philosophy, creating an environment supportive of students' efforts bolstered by policies, structures, training, and an affirming climate (Wood, 2012a). Bush (2004) and Bush and Bush (2004) have compared the notion that institutions are responsible for student outcomes to the Gospel of Matthew, Chapter 7, in which Jesus provides instruction to his followers about how they may discern false prophets from true prophets. Jesus stated, "By their fruit you will recognize them. Do people pick grapes from thornbushes, or figs from thistles? Likewise, every good tree bears good fruit, but a bad tree bears bad fruit" (Matt. 7:16–17). In this light, the tree represents the institution, and the fruit, the students. As such, good student outcomes (good fruit) are indicative of efficacious institutions (good trees), while poor student outcomes (bad fruit) come from ineffective institutions (bad trees). This metaphor helps us understand the importance of reframing the discourse from a cultural-deficit perspective, which blames young Black men, their families, and their communities for their underachievement, to one in which the burden of student outcomes is placed on colleges themselves.

Third, Black men are commonly portrayed in the media as gangsters, rapists, womanizers, drug dealers, and thugs. These immoral caricatures of Black men present a false and dehumanizing narrative (Wood & Hilton, forthcoming). In the community college context, the implications of these perceptions are often unconscious. Faculty, staff, and peers may hold stigmatized views of Black men that unknowingly communicate that they are not welcome or do not belong on a college campus. Interestingly, recent research on young Black men in community college presents a counternarrative. For example, Wood and Harris (2012) examined differences in personal goals between Black men and other men in community college and found that Black men were more likely (than one or more of their peer groups) to want to be community leaders, help others, and have meaning and purpose in their lives. Further, research from Wood, Hilton, and Hicks (in press) indicates that Black men are motivated to succeed in college by the desire to create better futures for themselves and their families, their aspirations to serve as role models to others and make their families proud, and their desire to disprove negative perceptions of Black men. Taking these factors into account, Black men (like other men in college) clearly have noble goals, dreams, and civic desires. Because they do, we remain concerned about their dehumanizing portrayals, which invite conscious and unconscious disregard for their well-being.

Fourth, well-intentioned efforts to support the success of Black men in community college are often plagued by assumptions of applicability. Many college officials assume that research and strategies used for teaching Black men in four-year colleges will be useful in a two-year context. While this assumption is in some respects accurate, extant research illustrates that, in many ways, Black men in two- and four-year colleges are two distinct populations with differing factors affecting their success (Wood, 2011a). Two research studies (Flowers, 2006; Wood, 2011b) illustrate why this assumption of applicability should be approached with caution. Flowers (2006) conducted a study in which he compared academic and social integration experiences of Black men in two- and four-year colleges. He found that Black men in two-year colleges have significantly lower levels of academic integration (e.g., attending study groups, talking with faculty, meeting with advisers) and social integration (e.g., participating in clubs, attending fine arts performances, participating in sports, going places with friends) than their counterparts from other racial groups. While we are not concerned with differences in social integration, which have been found to be negative predictors of Black male success in two-year institutions (a point we return to later; Bush & Bush, 2010; Wood, 2012d), differences in academic integration are troubling. Further, Wood (2011b) illustrated that Black men have important differences in backgrounds. Two-year collegians are significantly more likely to be older, have dependents, be independent, be married, and have delayed their enrollment into higher education. Further, men in two-year colleges were less likely to have higher degree expectations, have attended private schools, or have enrolled in collegiate preparation courses in critical areas (e.g., mathematics, science, foreign language). Bearing these differences in mind, we present an analysis of themes from the literature on Black men in community college.

Salient Factors Affecting Black Male Success

In this section we highlight recurrent themes from the literature, using a meta-synthesis approach to identify the most salient themes. Literature meta-synthesis is a research procedure whereby research is collected, annotated, and synthesized to find emergent themes (Turner, Gonzalez, & Wood, 2008). This procedure (sometimes referred to as *integrative review*) is akin to other research synthesis procedures such as meta-analysis (for quantitative studies) and meta-ethnography (for qualitative studies). In short, meta-synthesis is used to synthesize works from qualitative and quantitative works, by treating a significant variable as equivalent to an emergent theme. Using numerous databases (e.g., ERIC, Google Scholar, JSTOR, EBSCOhost, Project MUSE), we identified published and unpublished documents about Black men in the community college. We limited the included works to peer-reviewed journal articles, book chapters, dissertations, editor-reviewed works, and refereed conference presentations. From this process, we identified more than 100 total studies conducted since 1971. Only a small portion of these works (about 15 in all) were published,[1] with only half of these being peer-reviewed. We then generated extensive annotations for each work collected, focusing our efforts in the following areas:

- Topic of interest
- Problem that prompted the study
- Theoretical framework(s) employed
- Methodology
- Study findings
- Recommendations for policy
- Recommendations for practice

We coded our annotations for each article in these areas; then we extracted emergent themes from study findings.

What follows is a presentation of the most recurrent themes, relevant to academic, social, psychological, and environmental factors affecting Black male success in community college. While we recognize the importance of

---

[1] The vast majority of the identified documents were doctoral dissertations. In general, these documents are unpublished works.

background factors (e.g., high school grade point average and educational goals) in facilitating student success, our focus is on explicating the factors directly relevant to the collegiate experience. First we discuss the importance of a positive campus climate—a factor that directly or indirectly affects all the domains we examined.

Institutional Climate

A positive campus climate has been found to be associated with better outcomes for Black male students (Beckles, 2008; Ihekwaba, 2001; Roberts, 2009). On the other hand, unwelcoming, hostile, and alienating campus climates lead to negative student outcomes for young Black men in community college (Harrison, 1999; Wilkins, 2005). For example, Riley (2007) found evidence of a negative campus climate at the institution she studied, noting that campus police repeatedly harassed Black students there. Bush and Bush (2010) found that a positive institutional climate was a strong predictor of Black men's probability of transferring to a four-year college and academic achievement. Similarly, Wood (2010) found that a positive campus climate served as a driver for student success. In his study, participants spoke about their relationships with campus staff (e.g., advisers, tutors, janitors, librarians), noting that these staff checked in on the students' academic progress and encouraged achievement. Many participants in this study noted, on the other hand, that faculty purposely avoided them on campus to evade conversation. In a more hostile vein, Bush's (2004) findings from focus groups with Black men illustrated these men's perceptions that they were singled out for disruptive or "off-task" behaviors when other students were displaying the same behaviors. In particular, Black men noted that faculty members would "hover" over them to enact disciplinary measures but walk past them when their hands were raised for help. Campus personnel, whose actions, behaviors, or dispositions create an unwelcoming climate for young Black men, must be held responsible for their actions.

Academic Factors

Successful academic patterns, habits, and dispositions are positive contributors to Black male success in community college. First and foremost, students must attend class. Absenteeism has been shown to detract from student success (Mason, 1994, 1998). Simply put, when students do not attend class, they miss valuable information that prevents them from performing well in the course. Habitual absenteeism detracts from peer and faculty relationship-building, which are critical components needed for student achievement. Students in Wood's (2010) study identified numerous factors that contributed to their absenteeism, such as: "(a) dislike for a particular class; (b) disinterest in school, in general; (c) transportation issues; (d) lack of motivation or 'will' to attend classes due to external relationship factors; (e) family issues (e.g., death in the family); and (f) antipathy toward a particular student in class or a perception that an instructor is overly strict" (p. 265). Regardless of the cause, the effects of absenteeism are the same: lost time receiving materials and information that are critical to passing and (more important) excelling in class.

Scholars have also identified full-time attendance as a critical determinant of student success. For example, Freeman (2003), Freeman and Huggans (2009) Hampton (2002) and Hagedorn, Maxwell, and Hampton (2001–2002) have noted that young Black men who attend community college on a part-time basis are significantly less likely to persist. Though the findings are slightly short of being statistically significant, Wood (2012b) reported that young Black men who attended college full-time as opposed to less than full-time had greater odds, by 78.8%, of persisting. In essence, when students attend college full-time, they have more opportunities to engage with faculty, access campus resources, and focus on their studies. Using data from the Educational Longitudinal Study, Wood (n.d.a) noted that the three primary reasons why young Black men enroll part-time in community college are work (74%), financial reasons (42%), and family responsibilities (30%).[2] These factors pull students' time and attention away from their academic pursuits, limiting their ability to focus on their studies.

Research also highlights the importance of faculty-student interactions on student success. Bush and Bush (2010) noted that young Black men are significantly less likely than their peers to meet with faculty. Wood (2012b) found that Black male students who talked with their faculty members were 283% more likely to persist than those who did not. However, as Wood and Turner (2010) noted, the burden of this interaction does not rest solely on the student. Faculty members are also responsible for facilitating positive interactions. In particular, Wood and Turner concluded that it is important for faculty members to make contact first and invest in time with young Black men, rather than taking an "approach me first" or "prove yourself first" attitude. This issue is important, Wood (2014) notes, since young Black men may be apprehensive to engage faculty, given previous negative experiences in school leading to fear of being perceived as academically inadequate. Wood (2012a) and Wood and Turner (2010) provide direction on how faculty members should establish relationships with young Black men in community college; collectively, these researchers offer the following steps:

---

[2] Students could indicate more than one category.

- Initiate first contact with students.
- Illustrate an authentically friendly and caring disposition.
- Be proactive in monitoring students' academic progress.
- Be attentive to and solicit students' concerns.
- Be encouraging and affirming to students.

The authors of this chapter add,

- Be cognizant of racial microaggressions (subtle, often unconscious racial indignations) and stereotypes.

While these steps may seem simplistic, too often they are not taken.

Another recurrent theme in the literature on young Black men in community college is the importance of studying. Simply put, the more hours students spend studying, and the more they hone their study skills, the more likely they are to persist (Mason, 1994, 1998). Some scholars have suggested that group studying is more effective in facilitating positive outcomes for young Black men than individual studying (Freeman, 2003; Riley, 2007). Researchers note that group studying allows young Black men to practice collectivity, relying on one another for support and seeing one another's success and failure as their own. Wood's (2010) interviews with young Black men indicated several strategies that maximized the benefits of studying: "(a) studying right after class so that the material is still fresh, (b) studying every day, (c) studying for classes several days in advance to the next session, (d) making the library their hangout, and (e) avoiding distractions to studying" (p. 225). The suggestion to make the library their "hangout" has particular importance for student success. As Wood (2012b) noted, young Black men who study in the campus library had greater odds (by 97.7%) of persistence than those who did not.

Using academic support services has also been shown to be important for student success. In particular, numerous scholars (e.g., Beckles, 2008; Freeman, 2003; Glenn, 2003–2004; Ihekwaba, 2001; Mason, 1994, 1998; Riley, 2007 Scaggs, 2004; Travis, 1994) have highlighted that greater levels of participation in tutoring or academic advising resulted in greater success rates for Black men. For example, using a persistence model that included background characteristics and social and academic variables, Wood (2012b) found that young Black men who used academic advising services had significantly greater odds (by 69.1%) of persisting in college. These support services provide students with an opportunity to get assistance in identifying the most appropriate course schedule for their academic goals and to receive academic support for their coursework. Given research from Stevens (2006), which noted that young Black men were reluctant to seek out academic support from faculty, having accessible tutoring services available is paramount.

Social Variables

Foundational research on students in higher education has suggested the importance of students' social integration and involvement in college settings for their academic success (Astin, 1977; Tinto, 1975, 1988, 1993). Essentially, the literature on integration and involvement surmises that the more students are submerged into the social milieu on campus, the more likely they are to succeed. In general, social participation in campus life has been measured by involvement in clubs or organizations, development of campus friendships, going places with friends from college, participation in intramural or varsity sports, and attendance at fine arts activities. Counter to this point, Bean and Metzner (1985) suggested that students who are nontraditional (e.g., older, first-generation, commuters, part-timers, low-income, and students of color) are more affected by environmental factors (addressed later in this section) than by social immersion. Primarily, a lower focus on social participation is attributed to external factors (e.g., family commitments, work) that prevent students' full incorporation in the college social environment.

Research conducted on young Black men in community college has been divergent on the importance of social participation. For example, Poole (2006) suggested that on-campus friendships serve as a facilitator of institutional commitment and, as a result, student success. In contrast, Faison (1993) identified a negative correlation between peer-group dependence and two psychological outcomes positively correlated with student success: students' autonomy and internal locus of control. As a result, Faison concluded "that lower-achieving inner-city black male [community] college students are more likely to harbor feelings of powerlessness vis-à-vis the political system and to exhibit a peer group" dependence (p. 143). Similarly, Bush (2004) suggested that interaction with peers served as a barrier to Black male success. Bush and Bush (2010) extended this, suggesting that peer interactions are "symptomatic" of young Black men's disconnection from college. They presented focus-group findings that indicated that young Black men viewed their peers, particularly those who were also Black men, as "having a negative impact on their ability to succeed academically. Peer interaction with African American men is perceived as something that African American male students had to overcome to be successful as opposed to a tool for success" (p. 55). In general, Black men noted that their peers were disinterested in college and mostly spent time "hanging out" or discussing topics unrelated to college. Wood (2010) and Wood, Hilton, and Harrell (2011) helped to further delineate the nuanced effects of peer interactions. Through interviews with 28 young Black men, Wood (2010) found that campus friendships that placed excessive emphasis on nonacademic factors (e.g., relaxing, partying, athletics, sexual pursuits) distracted from college, while those friendships built around academic matters (e.g., academic encouragement, studying, discussing topics from class, tutoring) served as critical facilitators of student achievement. Thus, it is not simply important to have friendships, but to have the "right" friendships.

The literature has also been split on the importance of athletics. In an institution-level analysis, Scaggs (2004) suggested that institutions with high athletic involvement (varsity and nonvarsity) benefit from high Black persistence and graduation rates. Stevens (2006) suggested that athletic participation eased the college adjustment process, which was believed to facilitate student persistence. In contrast, Riley (2007) found athletic commitments to be a negative factor for student success. These students' athletic aspirations detracted from their focus on education and were reified by "unrealistic family members, a manipulative media empire, [and] enterprising coaches" (p. 167). Wood (2012b) distinguished the effects of intramural and varsity sports on Black male success. He found that Black men who participated in intramural sports had greater odds (by 94.3%) of persisting, while varsity athletes had lower odds (by 35.7%) of persisting. These findings seem to complement Riley's (2007) findings of the deleterious effects of varsity participation. While participation in intramural sports is shown to have a positive effect on Black male success, the utility of this finding is limited as not all community colleges feature such programs.

Finally, findings on participation in extracurricular activities have also been incongruous. Wood (2012b) found that Black men who participated in extracurricular activities had significantly lower odds of persisting, by 68.2%. This contrasts with Wood's (2010) findings, which illustrated that participation in clubs or organizations and campus events served to support student academic success. Wood found in his 2010 study that participation in these activities motivated Black men to come to campus, placed them in contact with academically focused students, provided them an opportunity to learn about campus resources, facilitated regular contact with faculty and counselors, and exposed students to speakers who provided advice. To further examine this dichotomy, Wood (2012d) conducted a logistic regression analysis using Beginning Postsecondary Students (BPS) Longitudinal Study data. Wood investigated the effect of select social integration variables on first-year persistence (controlling for age, full-time status, and hours worked per week). The findings, which were nonsignificant, indicated that participation in fine arts activities led to slightly lower odds of persistence (by 11.4%), while participation in school clubs led to greater odds of persistence (by 16.7%). Further delineation among different types of extracurricular activities (e.g., student government, clubs or organizations, attending fine arts activities) is needed. However, we believe that extracurricular activities that foster academic excellence will likely lead to greater student success, while those activities that are primarily social in nature may serve to detract from student success. With this in mind, practitioners should be cautious about encouraging participation in *all* kinds of activities, instead using their experiential knowledge to direct Black men toward activities that will facilitate their success in college.

Psychological Variables

Historically, psychological variables have been important considerations in the student success puzzle (Bean & Metzner, 1985; Mason, 1994). Contemporarily, Wood (2011c) stated that some of "the most predominant factors affecting the success of Black men are psychological in nature, resulting directly from barriers, negative messages, and stressors in and out of the college . . . impact[ing] students' motivation, focus on academic endeavors, and academic confidence" (p. 24).

Several scholars have explored the effect of self-efficacy on Black male success in community college (e.g., Bates, 2007; Ihekwaba, 2001; Wilkins, 2005; Wood, 2010). *Self-efficacy* refers generally to students' self-confidence. In an academic context, it refers to confidence in one's own academic abilities. Bates (2007), in an examination of anxiety about mathematics, found a significant positive relationship between self-efficacy and students' academic preparedness. Students with greater levels of preparedness had higher self-efficacy. More interestingly, he found that as students' self-efficacy increased, their anxiety about mathematics decreased. Ihekwaba (2001) also discussed the importance of self-efficacy. Using focus groups, Ihekwaba found that Black men and women both perceived that confidence in their ability to perform academically was a critical facilitator of persistence. In a converse approach, Wood (2010) noted that students perceived a lack of confidence in their academic abilities as a hindrance to their achievement and persistence in community college. Further advancing the notion of self-efficacy, Wilkins's (2005) interviews with young Black men showed that self-efficacy aided students in achieving their educational goals. In this study, Black male participants saw themselves as exceptionally intelligent, distinguishing themselves from their peers as rarities. Specifically, Wilkins noted that high self-efficacy allowed participants to embrace academic challenges, especially when faculty doubted their abilities. Their confidence in their ability to perform academically allowed these challenges to serves as motivators—in essence, opportunities to prove themselves.

Utility refers to students' perceptions of the worthiness of their collegiate endeavors. Mason (1994, 1998), in a quantitative study of persistence among young Black men in an urban community college, found utility to have a strong positive relationship with persistence. In essence, he concluded that having a greater belief in the usefulness of one's education, program, degree, or coursework led the student to enhanced outcomes. Wood (2010) noted that young Black men who had low utility believed that their success (personal and professional) was best obtained outside of the classroom setting. In contrast, those Black men with high degrees of utility often view education as the "door to opportunity." Still, Wood (2012c) noted that some young Black men may experience a utility conflict, whereby their "perceptions of the benefits of school conflict with their experiences, perceptions, and immediate needs (e.g., food, housing)" (p. 24). He noted that while Black men may deem education to have a high value, actualizing that ideal, based on their prior educational experiences and negative media messages, may seem more likely to happen through other means (e.g., employment, military, illicit activities).

Several authors have discussed the psychological effects of racism, often in the language of stereotype threat. In classroom settings, stereotype threat occurs when negative stereotypes about groups are evident. When students are in situations that can reinforce negative perceptions (e.g., standardized tests, classroom discussions), students experience anxiety that can have dismal effects on their academic performance (Steele, 1997, 1999). As a result of being educated in stereotype-laden classroom environments, young Black men may exhibit disidentification, which is psychological disengagement from academic matters and pursuits as a protective mechanism against racism and stereotypes (Aronson, Blanton, & Cooper, 1995; Aronson, Fried, & Good, 2001; Osbourne, 1995). In essence, students begin to "'dis'-identify" as academic beings. Many scholars have discussed academic disengagement that occurs as a result of stereotypes and negative perceptions of Black men (Bush, 2004; Bush & Bush, 2010; Foster, 2008; Stevens, 2006; Wood, 2011d). For example, Stevens (2006) conducted in-depth interviews with Black male students and focus groups with faculty members at a community college. Stevens found that Black men did not speak during class, a circumstance that Black male students attributed to their being fearful of reflecting negatively on their race. This behavior created tension with faculty members, who viewed reluctance to participate as a lack of commitment to academics. Stevens suggested that these students' actions were evidence of disidentification. Wood (2011d), too, found that young Black men were apprehensive about fully engaging as active agents in their academic pursuits. In his study, Black men refused to make contact with teachers, engage in small group discussions or activities, attend faculty office hours, or provide answers to classroom discussions. Most disturbing, participants in his study noted that they desired to fully engage, but they were apprehensive due to fear of being perceived as "stupid" or "dumb." Overwhelmingly, scholars (Bush, 2004; Foster, 2008; Stevens, 2006; Wood, 2011d) have noted that disidentification is an institutional problem, resulting from faculty members who unknowingly (although sometimes knowingly) affirm stereotypes and perceptions of Black men as unintelligent, noncognitive beings.

Environmental Factors

Unlike four-year collegians, community college students tend to be at greater risk of succumbing to environmental variables, which include factors that occur outside of the institution (i.e., in students' homes, communities, and work settings) that can have negative effects on students' experiences and outcomes inside college. Not all environmental factors are negative, but these factors tend to have a negative influence. In large part, the reason is important background differences between students in these two types of schools, as evidenced by Wood (2011b), who used national data from the BPS study to illustrate these key background differences between young Black men in two- and four-year institutions. For example, Black men in two-year colleges are significantly more likely to be older and to have delayed their enrollment into postsecondary education. More importantly, young Black men have greater odds than other students of having dependents (by 555%), being married (by 284%), and being independent (by 464%). When Wood controlled for age and income differences, he still found Black men to have greater odds of being independent (by 202%) and having dependents (by 246%). With this in mind, Black men in community college are more likely than their four-year counterparts to be affected by environmental factors that pull them away from their academic pursuits.

Wood (2012b) also illustrated the integral role of environmental variables on persistence. In a model of persistence, he found that four environmental variables, without the effect of other variables (e.g., background, social, academic), accounted for 54.1% of the variance in persistence. Take, for example, family responsibilities; Wood found that students who were supporting others had lower odds (by 74.4%) of persisting, which is in line with extant research illustrating that family responsibilities are integral to student success (Beckles, 2008; Freeman, 2003; Ihekwaba, 2001; Mason, 1994, 1998). According to Wood (n.d.b), 39.2% of Black men who leave college report doing so due to family responsibilities. Wood (2012e) noted that this trend of leaving for family obligations tends to be greater for Black men in comparison to other men during their first year of college, but less likely after several years of enrollment. Thus, family obligations are initial factors that weed out many Black men before their collegiate careers are fully under way. However, this is not to say that family responsibilities have only a negative effect on student success. In contrast, Wood (2010) noted that family members serve as an important source of inspiration, emotional encouragement, and monetary support. Scholars such as Ihekwaba (2001) and Stevens (2006) provide details about how family members encourage and establish high expectations for students that push them to succeed. Overwhelmingly, this support comes from strong mothers and familial matriarchs (e.g., aunts, grandmothers).

Student finances and costs associated with attending college are recurrent themes in the literature (see Hampton, 2002; Jordan, 2008; Offutt, 1971). Mason (1994, 1998) examined the relationship between finances and Black male persistence. He found a strong, direct, negative relationship between income and persistence, meaning that as family income decreased, student persistence decreased. Similarly, findings from Wood (2010) illustrated that financial instability negatively affected students' academic success. Through interviews, student participants noted that their lack of financial stability served as a distraction from their education. A number of students expressed that their financial problems placed them in difficult circumstances, forcing them to choose between having their basic needs met—such as gas, housing, and even food—or concentrating on school. Similarly, Hampton (2002) asserted that colleges that address Black men's financial barriers help to refocus students' attention on college (as opposed to more elemental needs). Jordan (2008) noted that the cost of books was a major challenge that Black men face in community college. In some cases, students with limited funds may be unable to purchase a course's reading materials, which can negatively affect their success. On the other hand, Mason (1994, 1998) found that as college costs increased, there was a strongly positive increase in student persistence. This notion may seem counterintuitive at first; however, we believe that community colleges with higher costs serve as a deterrent for enrollment, eliminating those students who are on the margins of commitment to their educational goals. In essence, access to postsecondary education is likely stripped from students who are ambivalent about their academic pursuits.

A related theme to student finances is the effect that employment has on Black male success. When students lack the finances needed to focus on school, they often work to support themselves. This circumstance has led to discussions about students' ability to balance college and work. Wood (2011c) stated,

> One environmental challenge that has become increasingly evident in recent years is the work-college balance, the balancing act that takes

place between being a student and an employee. My research on Black males has illustrated that current economic conditions may have made balancing college and work more difficult as fewer available jobs can lead to unemployment, underemployment or fewer employment options. (p. 24)

Research on the effect of work on college has been conflicting. Some research illustrates that work has a positive effect on college. For example, Shannon (2006) noted that having a job was a positive facilitator of student success. Still, some scholars, such as Mason (1994, 1998), have found no relationship between employment commitments and student persistence. In contrast, Wood (2012c) found that work served as a barrier to students' academic success. He highlighted the intensified difficulties in balancing work and school commitments when transitioning into new work environments. Further, he noted that Black men had difficulty finding employment opportunities to begin with (a problem that intensified with the economic downturn). As a result, these men were forced to work long hours, usually at night, performing physically demanding jobs (e.g., moving boxes, stocking shelves), which made them too tired to fully engage in their studies. Other researchers have presented more nuanced views.

Shannon (2006) noted that work tended to serve as a barrier to school success for Black men who were parents. Shannon found that these men needed to work more hours per week (35 on average) than their nonparent counterparts and had to work overtime to support themselves and their families. These men did not use campus support services as often as their peers, and they enrolled in more credit hours than men who were not parents but were less likely to complete those hours. In contrast, Black men who did not have children worked fewer hours per week, were more likely to complete coursework, and made somewhat greater use of campus support services. Wood (2012b) also presented a more nuanced view of work, noting that more hours worked per week was initially strongly predictive of persistence, a trend that had less stability after 21 to 30 hours worked per week. Research from Wood, Hilton, and Lewis (2011) is also instructive on the effect of work on student achievement. Using data from the National Postsecondary Student Aid Study, they examined students' perspectives on the effect of work on their academic achievement. Students noted a positive effect when their employment helped them to understand their coursework, provided them greater work experience in their desired field, and did not limit the number of courses they took. Further findings indicated that students who paid their own educational expenses were significantly more likely to believe that work had a negative effect on their academic success.

Advancing Black Male Student Success in Community College

Campus Climate

A number of recommendations can be employed to enhance the success of Black men in community college. In terms of the campus climate, we noted that positive campus climates, particularly those affirming diversity, can facilitate Black male success. All campus personnel should place high importance on positive interactions with Black men. To facilitate this process, campus administrators and human resource personnel should meet one-on-one with new and prospective employees to ensure that they are willing to commit to this process. Furthermore, to ensure that campus personnel are capable of fostering a supportive campus climate conducive to the needs of a diverse cadre of students, all prospective hires should be required to complete a cultural sensitivity inventory. Milton Bennett's (1993) developmental model of intercultural sensitivity is a well-respected inventory. This inventory rates individuals on a continuum from ethnocentrism to ethnorelativism, including three stages associated with each concept. Possessing a minimum qualification of ethnorelativism should be required of faculty members. In addition to one-on-one meetings, campus personnel should also require new hires to participate in intensive formal training on campus climate expectations and guidelines. Further, faculty members who create nonsupportive environments for Black men must be identified. Colleges should monitor average GPAs and course completion rates for Black and other minority men by faculty member within each respective discipline to better identify faculty members who serve as detractors from Black male success. This process should be part of the faculty performance evaluation process.

Academic Factors

We advocate implementing early warning systems that identify concerning behaviors (e.g., absenteeism, late withdrawals, poor performance) and require students to meet with counselors who can mandate that students meet with campus support services. Positive faculty-student interactions are imperative to student success. However, numerous barriers to positive interactions exist, chief among them microaggressions (i.e., common, everyday racial slights). To address such behavior, all campus faculty should be trained to understand what microaggression is, the underlying assumptions communicated to students, and how they affect student success. In particular, we suggest that trainers use Sue and colleagues' (2007) typology of microaggressions as a framework to educate faculty on subtle, often unconscious racial indignations toward Black and other minority men. Further, faculty must be made aware of common stereotypes specific to Black men (e.g., gangsters, players, hustlers; see Oliver, 2006) and be engaged in a reflective process in which they interrogate their own perceptions of Black men.

Societal Factors

In this chapter we addressed the nuanced effect of social variables on Black men. We noted that these variables tend to have a small negative effect on Black male persistence and success. With this in mind, we suggest that retention-based services deemphasize social programming and instead focus on academic-related activities. Primarily, we discourage campus officials from urging students to get involved on campus for the sake of involvement. Instead, these officials must be strategic, directing students toward social integration activities that have a documented track record of leading to positive outcomes for Black men. Furthermore, students must be encouraged to establish friendships that are academically oriented. This should be a regular topic of conversation emanating from all campus personnel—faculty, staff, and administrators.

Psychological Factors

We recommend that colleges require students to take a short inventory regarding the psychological constructs of utility, self-efficacy, and disidentification prior to enrolling in their courses. Students illustrating low scores on utility, self-efficacy, or identification can be more closely monitored throughout their academic career. These students can also be referred to career counselors. This process serves as a way to identify career fields that may increase students' perception of degree utility. Further, faculty members must be authentically affirming and supportive in the classroom. Low self-efficacy and high disidentification often stem from negative classroom climates and poor interactions with faculty. This notion again emphasizes the importance of racial microaggression training for community college faculty.

Environmental Factors

As we also noted, some of the most challenging barriers facing Black men are environmental. These factors (e.g., supporting dependents, working, and finances) have a direct effect on student success. Institutional personnel must be attentive to the challenges facing their students. Each semester, academic counselors should inquire about environmental factors when meeting with students, and this information should be used to help students determine an appropriate course schedule and course load. Moreover, faculty must establish personal relationships with students, so that the faculty become attuned to changes in disposition, academic habits, and behavior that may be indicative of external factors. Once aware of such problems, faculty must be proactive, talk with students about their challenges, and refer them to counselors who can connect them with support services.

The fact that students work while attending college is a trend that is unlikely to change. Thus, selecting the right job is as important as having one. Students transitioning into new jobs should be encouraged to take lighter loads in school to provide them the time needed to adjust to their new professional positions. Students should also be encouraged to find employment that is relevant to their degree goals or academic pursuits.

In all, the recommendations presented merely highlight some of the many actions that community colleges can take to support the success of enrolled Black men. The key to understanding which strategies are most impactful requires campus personnel to disaggregate data by race and ethnicity, gender, and other characteristics, and engage in reflective conversations (rooted in extant research) that guide organizational decision making. Community colleges have the capacity to make the most strident changes for Black male postsecondary success—capacity that should not be wasted.

References

American Association of Community Colleges (AACC). (2009). Historical information. Washington, DC: Author. Retrieved from http://www.aacc.nche.edu/AboutCC/history/Pages/default.aspx

Aronson, J., Blanton, H., & Cooper, J. (1995). From dissonance to disidentification: Selectivity in the self-affirmation process. *Journal of Personality and Social Psychology, 58*, 1062–1072.

Aronson, J., Fried, C. B., & Good, C. (2001). Reducing the effects of stereotype threat on African American college students by shaping theories of intelligence. *Journal of Experimental Social Psychology, 38*, 113–125.

Astin, A. W. (1977). *What matters in college? Four critical years.* San Francisco: Jossey-Bass.

Bates, V. M. (2007). *The impact of preparedness, self-efficacy, and math anxiety on the success of African American males in developmental mathematics at a community college* (Doctoral dissertation). Retrieved from ProQuest Dissertations and Theses database. (UMI No. 3258440)

Bean, J. P., & Metzner, B. S. (1985). A conceptual model of nontraditional undergraduate student attrition. *Review of Educational Research, 55*(4), 485–540.

Beckles, W. A. (2008). *Redefining the dream: African American male voices on academic success* (Doctoral dissertation). Retrieved from ProQuest Dissertations and Theses database. (UMI No. 3314150)

Bennett, M. J. (1993). Towards ethnorelativism: A development model of intercultural sensitivity. In R. M. Paige (Ed.), *Education for the intercultural experience* (pp. 21–71). Yarmouth, ME: Intercultural.

Bush, E. C. (2004). *Dying on the vine: A look at African American student achievement in California community colleges* (Doctoral dissertation). Retrieved from ProQuest Dissertations and Theses database. (UMI No. 3115606)

Bush, E. C., & Bush, L. (2004). Beware of false promises. *Community College Journal, 74*(5), 36–39.

Bush, E. C., & Bush, L. (2010). Calling out the elephant: An examination of African American male achievement in community colleges. *Journal of African American Males in Education, 1*(1), 40–62.

Cohen, A. M., & Brawer, F. B. (2003). *The American community college* (4th ed.). San Francisco: Jossey-Bass.

Faison, A. C. (1993). *The effect of autonomy and locus-of-control on the academic achievement of Black male community college students* (Doctoral dissertation). Retrieved from ProQuest Dissertations and Theses database. (UMI No. 9315460)

Flowers, L. A. (2006). Effects of attending a 2-year institution on African American males' academic and social integration in the first year of college. *Teachers College Record, 108*(2), 267–286.

Foster, D. W. (2008). *Student engagement experiences of African American males at a California community college* (Doctoral dissertation). Retrieved from ProQuest Dissertations and Theses database. (UMI No. 3331201)

Freeman, T. L. (2003). *Theoretical model for studying year-to-year persistence of two-year college students by ethnicity using the beginning Postsecondary Students Longitudinal Study 1996–98* (Doctoral dissertation). Retrieved from ProQuest Dissertations and Theses database. (UMI No. 3094695)

Freeman, T. L., & Huggans, M. A. (2009). Persistence of African-American male community college students in engineering. In H. T. Frierson, W. Pearson Jr., & J. H. Wyche (Eds.), *Black American males in higher education: Diminishing proportions* (pp. 229–252). Bingley, UK: Emerald Group.

Glenn, F. S. (2003–2004). The retention of Black male students in Texas public community colleges. *Journal of College Student Retention, 5*(2), 115–133.

Griffith, C. R., & Blackstone, H. (1945). *The junior college in Illinois*. Chicago: University of Illinois.

Hagedorn, L. S., Maxwell, W., & Hampton, P. (2001–2002). Correlates of retention for African-American males in the community college. *Journal of College Student Retention, 3*(3), 243–263.

Hampton, P. (2002). *Academic success for African-American male community college students* (Doctoral dissertation). Retrieved from ProQuest Dissertations and Theses database. (UMI No. 3073786)

Harrison, C. K. (1999). *Perceptions of African American male student-athletes in higher education* (Doctoral dissertation). Retrieved from ProQuest Dissertations and Theses database. (UMI No. 9987606)

Ihekwaba, R. H. (2001). *A comparative analysis of African American male and female students' perceptions of factors related to their persistence at a Texas community college.* (Unpublished doctoral dissertation). University of Texas, Austin.

Joliet Junior College. (2005a). *Retention of Joliet Junior College and Illinois community college students.* Joliet, IL: JCC Office of Institutional Research and Effectiveness.

Joliet Junior College. (2005b). *Completion rates by ethnicity at Joliet Junior College and Illinois community college.* Joliet, IL: JCC Office of Institutional Research and Effectiveness.

Joliet Junior College. (2012). *College information.* Retrieved from http://www.jjc.edu/about/college-info/Pages/history.aspx

Jordan, P. G. (2008). *African American male students' success in an urban community college: A case study* (Doctoral dissertation). Retrieved from ProQuest Dissertations and Theses database. (UMI No. 3311541)

Mason, H. P. (1994). *The relationships of academic, background, and environmental variables in the persistence of adult African American male students in an urban community college* (Doctoral dissertation). Retrieved from ProQuest Dissertations and Theses database. (UMI No. 9430242)

Mason, H. P. (1998). A persistence model for African American male urban community college students. *Community College Journal of Research and Practice, 22*(8), 751–760.

Monroe, C. R. (1977). *Profile of the community college.* San Francisco: Jossey-Bass.

Nevarez, C., & Wood, J. L. (2010). *Community college leadership and administration: Theory, practice, and change.* New York: Peter Lang.

Offutt, B. R. (1971). *A comparison of self-perceived needs among Black and non-Black males attending an inner-city community college and those attending a suburban community college* (Doctoral dissertation). Retrieved from ProQuest Dissertations and Theses database. (UMI No. 7216485)

Oliver, W. (2006). "The streets": An alternative Black male socialization institution. *Journal of Black Studies, 36*(6), 918–937.

Osbourne, J. W. (1995). Academics, self-esteem, and race: A look at the underlying assumptions of the disidentification hypothesis. *Personality and Social Psychology Bulletin, 21*, 449–455.

Poole, J. S. (2006). *Predictors of persistent Black male students' commitment to rural Mississippi two-year public institutions* (Doctoral dissertation). Retrieved from ProQuest Dissertations and Theses database. (UMI No. 3211245)

Riley, N. M. (2007). *A steady drop will wear a hole in the rock: Feminism, the John Henry myth, and the Black male experience in higher education: A persistence case study* (Doctoral dissertation). Retrieved from ProQuest Dissertations and Theses database. (UMI No. 3291817)

Roberts, A. A. (2009). *Institutional factors supporting the enrollment and persistence of African-American males in Virginia community colleges* (Doctoral dissertation). Retrieved from ProQuest Dissertations and Theses database. (UMI No. 3354265)

Scaggs, S. L. (2004). *The retention of Black male students at Mississippi public community and junior colleges: Identifying best practices in rural Mississippi community col-*

leges (Doctoral dissertation). Retrieved from ProQuest Dissertations and Theses database. (UMI No. 3120822)

Shannon, V. (2006). *A case study: Higher education and parenting—African American female and male persistence and the community college experience* (Doctoral dissertation). Retrieved from ProQuest Dissertations and Theses database. (UMI No. 3205348)

Steele, C. M. (1997). A threat in the air: How stereotypes shape intellectual identity and performance. *American Psychologist, 52,* 613–629.

Steele, C. M. (1999). Thin ice: Stereotype threat and Black college students. *The Atlantic.* Retrieved from http://www.theatlantic.com/doc/199908/student-stereotype

Stevens, C. D. (2006). *Skating the zones: African-American male students at a predominantly white community college* (Doctoral dissertation). Retrieved from ProQuest Dissertations and Theses database. (UMI No. 3247770)

Sue, D. W., Capodilupo, C. M., Torino, G. C., Bucceri, J. M., Holder, A. M. B., Nadal, K. L., & Esquilin, M. (2007). Racial microaggressions in everyday life: Implications for clinical practice. *American Psychologist, 62*(4), 271–286.

Tillery, D., & Deegan, W. L. (1985). *Renewing the American community college.* San Francisco: Jossey-Bass.

Tinto, V. (1975). Dropouts from higher education: A theoretical synthesis of recent research. *Review of Educational Research, 45*(1), 89–125.

Tinto, V. (1988). Stages of student departure: Reflections on the longitudinal character of student leaving. *Journal of Higher Education, 59*(4), 438–455.

Tinto, V. (1993). *Leaving college: Rethinking the causes and cures of student attrition.* Chicago: University of Chicago Press.

Travis, R. L. (1994). *Noncognitive predictors of academic success for nontraditional students at a large, southeastern, urban community college* (Doctoral dissertation). Retrieved from ProQuest Dissertations and Theses database. (UMI No. 9420383)

Turner, C. S. V., Gonzalez, J. C., & Wood, J. L. (2008). Faculty of color in academe: What 20 years of literature tells us. *Journal of Diversity in Higher Education, 1*(3), 139–168.

U.S. Department of Education. (2009). Community college student 3-year retention and attainment 2006 by race/ethnicity (with multiple) and gender, for first institution type 2003–04 (Public 2-year). 2004/2009 Beginning Postsecondary Students Longitudinal Study, second follow-up. Washington, DC: National Center for Education Statistics.

Vaughan, G. B. (2006). *The community college story* (3rd ed.). Washington, DC: Community College Press.

Wilkins, R. D. (2005). *Swimming upstream: A study of Black males and the academic pipeline* (Doctoral dissertation). Retrieved from ProQuest Dissertations and Theses database. (UMI No. 3244696)

Wood, J. L. (n.d.a). *Factors influencing part-time enrollment.* Retrieved from http://jlukewood.com/black-male-statistics-report/

Wood, J. L. (n.d.b). *Black males in the community college—Dashboard statistical report.* Retrieved from http://jlukewood.com/black-male-statistics-report/

Wood, J. L. (2010). *African American males in the community college: Towards a model of academic success* (Doctoral dissertation). Retrieved from ProQuest Dissertations and Theses database. (UMI No. 3410569)

Wood, J. L. (2011a, August 5). Developing successful Black male initiatives. *Community College Times.* Retrieved from http://www.communitycollegetimes.com/Pages/Opinions/Developing-successful-black-male-programs-and-initiatives.aspx

Wood, J. L. (2011b). *The same . . . but different: Examining background characteristics among Black males in public two-year colleges.* Paper presented at the Council on Ethnic Participation Pre-Conference, Association for the Study of Higher Education, Charlotte, NC.

Wood, J. L. (2011c, October 13). Falling through the cracks: An early warning system can help Black males on the community college campus. *Diverse Issues in Higher Education, 28*(18), 24.

Wood, J. L. (2011d). Black males in the community college: Self-agency, stereotypes and the classroom. Paper at the Council on Ethnic Participation Pre-Conference, Association for the Study of Higher Education, Charlotte, NC.

Wood, J. L. (2012a). From the *right to fail* to the *right to succeed*: Faculty interactions with Black males in community colleges. *About Campus, 17*(2), 30–32.

Wood, J. L. (2012b, April). *Persistence factors for Black males in the community college: An examination of background, academic, social, and environmental variables.* Paper presented at the American Association of Community Colleges, Orlando, FL.

Wood, J. L. (2012c). *Black males' perceptions of the work-college balance: The impact of employment on academic success.* Paper presented at the Council for the Study of Community Colleges, with Marissa Vasquez, Orlando, FL.

Wood, J. L. (2012d). Black males in the community college: Using two national datasets to examine academic and social integration. *Journal of Black Masculinity, 2*(2), 56–88.

Wood, J. L. (2012e). Leaving the two-year college: Predictors of Black male collegian departure. *Journal of Black Studies, 43*(3), 303–326.

Wood, J. L. (2014). Apprehension to engagement in the classroom: Perceptions of Black males in the community college. *International Journal of Qualitative Studies in Education, 27*(6), 785–803.

Wood, J. L., & Harris, F. (2012). Apprehension to engagement in the classroom: Perceptions of Black males in the community college. Paper presented at the annual meeting of the African American Male Education Network and Development (A²Mend) conference, Los Angeles, CA.

Wood, J. L., & Hilton, A. A. (Forthcoming). Moral choices: Towards a conceptual model of Black male moral development (BMMD). In C. M. Ellis & J. Carlson (Eds.), *Resiliency, achievement, and manhood: Promoting the healthy development of African American men.* New York: Routledge.

Wood, J. L., Hilton, A. A., & Harrell, I. (2011). *African American males in the community college: Peer relationships and academic success.* Paper presented at the Council for the Study of Community Colleges, Denver, CO.

Wood, J. L., Hilton, A. A., & Hicks, T. (In press). Motivational factors for academic success: Perspectives of African American males in the community college. *International Journal of Africana Studies.*

Wood, J. L., Hilton, A. A., & Lewis, C. (2011). Black male collegians in public two-year colleges: Student perspectives on the effect of employment on academic success. *National Association of Student Affairs Professionals Journal, 14*(1), 97–110.

Wood, J. L., & Turner, C. S. V. (2010). Black males and the community college: Student perspectives on faculty and academic success. *Community College Journal of Research & Practice, 35*(1), 135–151.

6

UNDERSTANDING THE UNIQUE NEEDS AND EXPERIENCES OF BLACK MALE SUBGROUPS AT FOUR-YEAR COLLEGES AND UNIVERSITIES

Mauriell H. Amechi, Jonathan Berhanu, Jonathan M. Cox, Keon M. McGuire, Demetri L. Morgan, Collin D. Williams Jr., and Michael Steven Williams

Black undergraduate men's experiences and outcomes at four-year colleges and universities have garnered considerable attention from journalists, educators, and foundations over the past two decades (Harper, 2014; Harper & Harris, 2012; Palmer, Wood, Dancy, & Strayhorn, 2014; Shah & Sato, 2014). Stagnant enrollments, persistent patterns of disengagement, and low college completion rates are among a handful of issues that compelled many campuses to launch mentoring programs, host one- to two-day Black male summits, start local and multicampus men-of-color initiatives, and employ a range of other efforts to improve student success. Despite the popularization of programs focused on Black male collegians and their problems, Harper (2014) observed that most efforts enacted between 1997 and 2012 did little to actually improve the status of these students in U.S. higher education. Among the numerous explanations he offers for this is the monolithic mistreatment of Black men. "'Which Black men?' is not a question that seems to have been carefully contemplated in the design and implementation of many Black male initiatives and campus activities" (Harper, 2014, p. 129). He suggested that well-intentioned educators and others failed to recognize and effectively address the within-group diversity that exists among Black undergraduate men.

Harper and Nichols (2008) posed the following question in their multi-institution study of Black male collegians: Are they not all the same? Their results revealed considerable diversity among Black male participants as well as subgroup-specific challenges and experiences. The misperception of homogeneity sustains a one-sided narrative that fails to adequately capture what Harper, Wardell, and McGuire (2011) termed *complex individuality*. Furthermore, it overlooks the diverse identities that Black men develop, perform, and negotiate within particular subgroups (McGuire, Berhanu, Davis, & Harper, 2014). For this reason, a better understanding of within-group diversity is necessary.

There are two other critical reasons to examine the unique experiences of Black male subgroups in four-year campus contexts. First, Harper and Nichols (2008) contend that overlooking different subpopulations of Black male undergraduates misses important interactions and forms of peer engagement that take place within groups. Second, the proclivity for treating all Black undergraduate men as the same often leads to one-size-fits-all programmatic interventions on campuses, such as Black Male Summits that are not relevant to some subpopulations at best and at worst are hostile and alienating to others (Harper, 2014; Harper & Nichols, 2008).

In our effort to advance a more sophisticated understanding of Black male collegians, we divide this chapter into six sections, each focusing on a distinct subpopulation:

1. Black gay and bisexual men
2. Black men in historically Black fraternities
3. Black male student-athletes
4. Black undergraduate men at historically Black colleges and universities
5. Black underprepared, disengaged low performers
6. Black male college achievers and student leaders

Offered in each section are group-specific insights from education research and practice. Note that the subpopulations written about in this chapter do not fully capture the within-group diversity that exists among Black male collegians. Others about whom little has been published include immigrants and first-generation Black American men, Black men with disabilities, Black male returning adult learners, Black men at for-profit institutions and in online degree programs, transgender Black men, and Black male veterans, to name a few. Although we have chosen to focus on six particular subgroups, we believe that more research and strategic intentional institutional responses are needed to better understand Black male students and help them *all* succeed at four-year colleges and universities.

Black Gay and Bisexual Men in College

While many scholars and educators have increasingly focused on the educational experiences of Black men in postsecondary settings, significantly fewer have explored one subgroup of this population: nonheterosexual Black male students (Patton, 2011; Strayhorn, Blakewood, & DeVita, 2008; Strayhorn & Mullins, 2012). Although in other disciplines, such as psychology and sociology, studies exist that examine the life worlds of gay, bisexual, or queer (GBQ) Black male students, higher education scholars have only recently begun to substantively engage this topic (Goode-Cross & Good, 2009; Harris 2003; Patton, 2011, 2014; Washington & Wall, 2010). In fact, prior to recent efforts to raise awareness concerning GBQ Black men's unique educational experiences, one may have erroneously surmised that all Black men attending four-year public colleges and universities were heterosexual and all GBQ men were White.

A participant in Washington and Wall's (2010) study may have articulated it best when he referred to the tenuous positioning of GBQ Black men within an "invisible middle." As such, the research discussed here represents a critical scholarly intervention in the field of higher education and allows educators to develop a more comprehensive, yet complex, "profile" of the twenty-first-century Black male student attending four-year colleges and universities. Prior to reviewing literature that explicitly concerns college students, this section briefly engages a few studies that address the macro sociohistorical context within which postsecondary institutions exist. In addition, we briefly discuss one model (Wilson, 2008) of identity and identity formation to frame our discussion of these concepts among GBQ Black college men.

As several scholars (Brown, 2005; Lewis, 2003; Patton, 2014; Wilson, 2008) have noted, conservative attitudes toward both sexual and gender norms are prevalent within the Black community. While we cautiously employ the phrasing "Black community"—a reductionist phrase often (over) used to assert essentialized claims about an extremely diverse group of people—we attempt to capture how GBQ Black men experience and engage with Black family members, peers, church parishioners, and other Black persons they encounter throughout their lives. Such sexually conservative ideological positions construct spaces where GBQ Black men are the natural targets of social, political, spiritual, psychoemotional, and physical penalties. To productively negotiate these environments, Black nonheterosexual men "wear the mask," prohibiting them from resolving tensions that exist between their raced identities and sexual orientation (Brown, 2005).

As identity formation does not occur in a social vacuum, GBQ Black men are forced to manage ever evolving internal processes with cues, messages, and symbols from their environments (Wilson, 2008). Wilson's dynamic-ecological model of identity formation effectively captures this developmental process and emphasizes three central tenets:

1. Ecological factors affect ethnic, sexual, and masculine (ESM) identity formation and conflict.
2. ESM identity formation and conflict occur through dynamic, interrelated, and overlapping processes in which identities shape each other.
3. ESM identity formation and conflict occur through dynamic processes in which individuals shape their social contexts, and thereby shape their identities.

The dynamic-ecological model is particularly useful in accounting for how internal, individual development is informed by and influences one's social networks, community norms and values, and macrocontextual factors. In addition, Wilson does not reduce sexual orientation to sexual attraction. Rather, the model is employed to consider gender as distinct from, yet informed by, ethnicity and sexual orientation.

Scholars who explore the experiences of GBQ Black men in postsecondary settings have discovered similar findings—namely, that the institutional environment in college selection (Strayhorn, Blakewood, & DeVita, 2008); identity development (Goode-Cross & Good, 2009; Patton, 2011); and the general "politics" of identity (Patton, 2011, 2014; Strayhorn & Mullins, 2012; Washington & Wall, 2010) is important. Concerning the last, Washington and Wall (2010) found that GBQ Black male students are often faced with the dilemma of choosing a primary identity. For example, they are expected to decide if they are Black or gay first. However, being gay, bisexual, or queer already positions these young men outside of the (narrow) stereotypical conceptions of Blackness, which are commonly associated with religious conservatism on issues related to sexual orientation. Often, GBQ Black men have to take significant risks to establish support networks and must use caution in determining to whom they can reveal their whole selves (Goode-Cross & Good, 2008; Patton, 2011). As such, many GBQ Black men are selective about the people to whom they disclose their sexual orientation.

Moreover, GBQ Black men have to live with the negative perception that most nonheterosexual Black men are on the "down low"—meaning, they are not explicitly public about their sexual preferences. This homophobic suspicion surrounding GBQ Black male students creates a particularly hostile campus environment. One consequence of this institutional and interpersonal homophobia is the loneliness that GBQ Black men experience (Patton, 2011, 2014).

Another consistent finding in the research has been that, with limited or no access to role models, GBQ Black men may struggle to locate spaces on campus that fully engage their raced and gendered identity as well as their sexual orientation (Harris, 2003; Washington & Wall, 2010). Programmatic offices (e.g., cultural and LGBTQ centers) often fail to fully support GBQ Black men who occupy this invisible middle. Although for some GBQ Black men, their raced and gendered identities are most salient in their lives (Goode-Cross & Good, 2009), this is not true for all men. The experiences of GBQ Black men tend to vary depending on the type of institution. At predominantly White institutions (PWIs), GBQ Black men face not only homophobia but also acts of overt and covert racism (Harris, 2003). As PWIs have significantly fewer Black students when compared to minority-serving institutions, GBQ Black men may seek a safe space among their same-race peers. Again, however, these communities may promote gender and sexual conservatism, creating a space that does not welcome GBQ Black men.

Conversely, historically Black colleges and universities (HBCUs), although commonly associated with more welcoming and supportive environments for Black students when compared to PWIs, have espoused values and embraced traditions that marginalize GBQ Black male students (Patton, 2011, 2014). In addition to experiencing the similar identity formation processes as their counterparts at PWIs, these students have to negotiate the challenges of not fitting into the (heterosexist) ideal of Black maleness on campus. Students in Patton's (2011) study, who all attended an HBCU, articulated the necessity to be "selectively out" as well as resisting the gender-performative stereotypes about GBQ Black men—specifically that they were flamboyant, feminine, and loud.

Several implications have emerged from the research, including, but not limited to, the need for programmatic efforts that address the whole identity of GBQ Black male students; a redefining of what it means to "come out," considering the racial implications for Black male students; the need for psychoemotional support to manage induced feelings of depression, marginalization, and loneliness; and the need for educators to examine institutional practices and traditions to see how they may promote homophobia (Harris, 2003; Patton, 2011, 2014; Strayhorn et al., 2008; Strayhorn & Mullins, 2012;

Washington & Wall, 2010). In addition, while differences exist between the campus climates at HBCUs and PWIs, rather than comparing the intensity of homophobic hostility in Black communities versus non-Black communities, a more productive analytical approach would examine how race informs homophobia (*raced homophobia*). For example, future studies could consider how whiteness intersects with homophobia to create hostile spaces for GBQ Black men.

Members of Historically Black Fraternities

Since the 1989 hazing-induced death of a Morehouse College student pledging a Black Greek-letter organization (BGLO), historically Black fraternities have faced significant scrutiny (Harper & Harris, 2006; Jones, 2000; Kimbrough, 2003). From mainstream media to scholarly studies, discourse on Black fraternities has been dominated by violent, ritualistic pledging (Harper, 2008a). Still, select research has strategically circumvented this issue to discover what else can be learned about Black male undergraduates who choose to participate in Black Greek life. Beyond violence, undergraduate chapters of Black fraternities can serve as spaces that inculcate homophobia, misogyny, and paternalism in the minds of their members, as well as indirectly promote divisive, exclusionary behavior and, at times, academic mediocrity (DeSantis & Coleman, 2008; Harper & Harris, 2006; Kimbrough, 1995, 2003). Simultaneously, Black fraternities address and cater to specific needs of Black male undergraduates and larger Black communities, leading to myriad positive outcomes (McClure, 2006a). BGLOs can provide valuable supports, where students are afforded cultural connections and a sense of belonging that fosters increased participation in campus activities; easier transitions to college environments; and ultimately increased levels of classroom participation, campus satisfaction, and postcollege success (Harper, 2008a; Harper & Harris, 2006; Kimbrough, 1995; McClure, 2006a, 2006b). Here, we explore the positive and negative outcomes for Black undergraduate men who pledge a Black fraternity.

Several scholars (Harper & Harris, 2006; Jones, 2000; Kimbrough, 2003) suggest that elements of hazing have always been a part of the Black fraternity-sanctioned pledge process; however, it was not until a series of deaths and injuries in the late 1980s and early 1990s that the five national organizations—Alpha Phi Alpha, Kappa Alpha Psi, Omega Psi Phi, Phi Beta Sigma, and Iota Phi Theta—along with the four historically Black national sororities, banned pledging altogether. The new "membership intake process" (MIP), birthed in 1990, was not highly regarded by current, alumni, or aspiring brothers of these organizations, and the majority of their voices went unheard during this critical transition. For many, the MIP was enacted too quickly; failed to accurately define *hazing*; did not allow enough time for the proper learning of history, sufficient bonding, and the formation of life-long connections; and promoted disunity within organizations, as the transition created a rift between pre- and post-1990 initiates (Kimbrough, 1997). Due to this unrest among members, the once systematic acts of pledging and hazing became quasi-universal aspects of a secretive, unmonitored, and considerably more precarious "underground" process of induction (Harper & Harris, 2006; Jones, 2000; Kimbrough, 2003). Members of Black fraternities began to judge each other on how much they endured during their underground process, fueling inter- and intraorganizational tension. Moreover, those who did not pledge were frequently referred to as going "paper" or "skating," and were, for the most part, not considered "real" brothers; they were overtly ostracized by members of the other organizations as well as their own. Unfortunately, this preoccupation with brutality and survival is not the only manifestation of hypermasculinity within Black fraternities.

In their study of attitudes about homophobia in Black fraternities, DeSantis and Coleman (2008) not only concluded that "anti-homosexual bias is deeply engrained in the rules, laws, and collective psyche of these organizations" (p. 308), but they also uncovered that Black fraternity members strongly associated manhood and masculinity with being physically strong and dominating, being hypersexual and promiscuous, and maintaining a persona that was not overly academic. Furthermore, the various justifications for why homosexuality had no place in Black fraternities—religion; the laws of nature and reproduction; deviance from accepted social norms; and inhibition of vital fraternal functions like pledging, bonding, and relationship building—share a thematic undercurrent of members protecting their chapters and larger organizations from internal division and external scrutiny. These discriminatory practices perhaps speak to persistent anti-homosexual sentiments in larger Black American communities, ones that undergraduate Black Greeks demonstrate little interest in confronting and reluctance to stop perpetuating.

Other behaviors that warrant concern and further substantive research are the splintering of the Black community through "Greek-only" events, the choice of some fraternity brothers to interact only with one another, and the exclusionary selection processes by which members are chosen; the meager academic performance of Black fraternity members relative to members of mainstream Greek organizations and campuses at large; and the stifling of their members' individuality (DeSantis & Coleman, 2008; Harper & Harris, 2006). Despite these issues, the positive effects from participating in Black fraternities indicate a need for their further examination.

Kimbrough (1995) assessed the impact of BGLO participation on members' leadership skills, level of activity on campus, and general engagement. He found that students regarded leadership as a prominent aspect of their campus experience and that BGLOs, early and often, afforded their members opportunities for leadership development. White-dominated student groups had few opportunities for Black women and men to gain access to leadership positions, and culturally relevant groups such as the gospel choir, for example, were limited in scope. The breadth of BGLO activities helped to develop a range of leadership skills, from campus programming to community service planning and social event marketing (Kimbrough, 1995). Similarly, McClure (2006b) employed a social constructionist framework that "focuses on the meaning-making process engaged in by individuals and the ways in which social processes shape and are shaped by our perceptions" (p. 1042) to determine how participation in Black fraternities impacted members' understandings of themselves and their experiences. As a result of their fraternity membership, the men in her study experienced additional positive connections to one another, the campus, and Black history (McClure, 2006b). This social network support system also provided connections that resulted in positive professional outcomes after college.

In another study, McClure (2006a) juxtaposed two models of masculinity, hegemonic and Afrocentric, and illustrated the ways that Black fraternities' organizational structure provides a context where Black men can develop an *amalgamation identity*, in which they combine positive aspects of each contrasting model of identity formation. Through interviews with undergraduate members, McClure discovered that Black fraternities nurture a fluid identity model in which Black men can both subscribe to the mainstream hegemonic ideals of success, achievement, and self-sufficiency and to the Afrocentric ideals of cooperation and connectedness with one another and larger Black communities (McClure, 2006a).

The literature circulating about BGLOs and campus engagement regularly leaves the classroom unexamined. Harper (2008a) focused specifically on these environments to evaluate how BGLOs were carrying out their academic missions. In his study of 131 members from 7 of the 9 BGLOs at a large midwestern PWI, he observed a positive correlation between fraternity and sorority membership and classroom participation, as long as White teachers and students did not put specific pressure on members to represent their entire race. In his active participation model, Harper identified three themes that led to positive outcomes in PWI classroom environments: underrepresentation, voluntary race representation, and collective responsibility. By participating more in class, Black Greeks were able to contribute a missing perspective on their own self-negotiated terms, positively represent their organizations by demonstrating their grasp of the material to teachers and other students, and earn better grades, improving their chapter's collective academic standing.

In an earlier study, Harper and Harris (2006) examined the role of Black fraternities in the holistic Black male undergraduate experience. The positive outcomes of fraternity membership are broken down into four subgroups: racial identity development, leadership development, development of practical competence, and cognitive development. Black fraternities emphasize a social and cultural awareness and collectivism that allow Black men who participate to embrace a strong and positive sense of their racial selves. While BGLOs seek out persons with leadership potential, participation in Black Greek life provides those with such potential opportunities to exercise and enhance their leadership. Fraternity membership and activity have also been associated with the construction of transferable skills that supplement and put into practice classroom experiences—time management, collaborative work in diverse environments, enhanced communicative ability, efficient multitasking and delegating, and improved persuasion and negotiation techniques (Harper & Harris, 2006). Finally, participation in Greek life may help the typically disengaged Black male undergraduate to become more engaged in school and, hence, to learn more.

Black Male Student-Athletes

The body of literature on Black male student-athletes in postsecondary education is growing. Between 2007 and 2010, Black men were 2.8% of full-time, degree-seeking undergraduate students, but 57.1% of the football teams and 64.3% of the basketball teams at Division I institutions, the National Collegiate Athletic Association (NCAA)'s most competitive and profitable competition level (Harper, Williams, & Blackman, 2013). Some researchers have explored the effects of intercollegiate sports participation on academic achievement, career outcomes, and the exploitation these students face (Beamon, 2010; Beamon & Bell, 2006; Benson, 2000; Harper, Williams, & Blackman, 2013; Overly, 2005), while others have written about various concerns related to engagement and the larger sociopolitical implications of Black overrepresentation in college sports (Comeaux & Harrison, 2007; Donnor, 2005). Even though this research has been primarily focused on student-athletes at four-year institutions (specifically NCAA Division I schools) and revenue-generating sports (football and men's basketball), it offers valuable insights into the experiences and challenges facing this subset of Black male collegians across institutions and NCAA divisions.

That stakeholders often fail to create educationally supportive environments for student-athletes has been well documented, but especially disturbing are the negative effects of athletics-driven socialization on Black players (Beamon, 2010; Beamon & Bell, 2006; Benson, 2000; Comeaux & Harrison, 2007; Donnor, 2005; Harper, Williams, & Blackman, 2013; Howard, 2014; Overly, 2005). The problems start at home. Beamon and Bell (2006) found that, as early as childhood, parents of Black athletes were more likely than their White counterparts to emphasize athletics over academics. Further, as the parental emphasis on athletics increased, the collegiate academic performance of the students decreased, and their expectation of a career in professional sports increased. "Though many aspire to play professional sports after college, the National Football League (NFL) and the National Basketball Association (NBA) will draft fewer than 2% of student-athletes each year" (Harper, Williams, & Blackman, 2013, p. 2).

Benson's (2000) qualitative study of Black men on a Division I football team revealed that many of them were socialized to prioritize athletic achievement over academic achievement in high school. This ethos persisted, and was perhaps reinforced, when they enrolled in college. Coaches, administrators, advisers, faculty members, and many Black student-athletes themselves are part of an interlocking system responsible for rampant academic underachievement as evidenced by low grade point averages and low graduation rates (Beamon, 2010; Benson, 2000; Comeaux & Harrison, 2007; Harper, Williams, & Blackman, 2013; Overly, 2005). According to former players, coaches only expressed concern with education if it threatened to impact their eligibility to play the sport (Beamon, 2010; Benson, 2000). Without respect for their interests or career goals, a number of Black student-athletes reported being counseled into certain majors that were perceived as less demanding by coaches and academic advisers. In some extreme cases, players were robbed of their agency altogether, with their majors and course load predetermined by academic officials without their consultation (Beamon, 2010; Benson, 2000; Overly, 2005).

Time constraints due to their athletic endeavors not only precluded some Black student-athletes from pursuing desired majors but also hampered their engagement in the larger campus community (Beamon, 2010; Benson, 2000; Comeaux and Harrison, 2007). In fact, Comeaux and Harrison (2007) found that engagement with faculty, in particular, had positive effects on academic achievement for Black and White male student-athletes alike, but professors were more likely to engage with White student-athletes. The NCAA bears responsibility as well, with policies that allow athletes to be admitted with questionable academic credentials (Overly, 2005). As a result, many Black student-athletes arrive on campus ill prepared to compete academically and with few realistic options to remedy this deficit (Beamon, 2010; Beamon & Bell, 2006; Comeaux & Harrison, 2007; Donnor, 2005; Overly, 2005). These issues help explain the following inequities that Harper, Williams, and Blackman found in graduation rates at NCCA Division I universities:

> Across four cohorts, 50.2% of Black male student-athletes graduated within six years, compared to 66.9% of student-athletes overall, 72.8% of undergraduate students overall, and 55.5% of Black undergraduate men overall.
> 96.1% of these NCAA Division I colleges and universities graduated Black male student-athletes at rates lower than student-athletes overall.
> 97.4% of institutions graduated Black male student-athletes at rates lower than undergraduate students overall. On no campus were rates exactly comparable for these two comparison groups. (2013, p. 1)

Beamon (2010) found that Black male student-athletes often left colleges and universities feeling exploited. To many, the education they received as compensation paled in comparison to the millions in profits and prestige the universities enjoyed for their athletic toil. In their eyes, they were more aptly termed *athlete-students* than student-athletes. This overemphasis on athletic achievement at the expense of educational attainment and career development for Black male student-athletes has far-reaching social and political implications (Benson, 2000; Donnor, 2005; Harper, Williams, & Blackman, 2013; Overly, 2005). Benson (2000) has noted that researchers, when studying the underachievement of Black athletes, have either employed a deficit perspective highlighting their deficiency compared to other groups or connected poor academic performance to "problems within society at large, suggesting that these students' underachievement may be caused in part by the way schools are structured to maintain prevailing social and economic order" (p. 225).

The challenges facing Black male student-athletes are multifaceted, and the responsibility for dealing with them extends to various stakeholders and the students themselves. Parents need to promote academic-centered values when socializing children who are potential athletes (Beamon & Bell, 2006; Harper, Williams, & Blackman, 2013). Coaches and academic advisers need to stress the importance of academic achievement and align students with majors that can lead to careers outside of sports (Beamon, 2010; Benson, 2000; Donnor, 2005; Harper, Williams, & Blackman, 2013; Overly, 2005). College and university faculty need to intentionally expand opportunities for engagement with these Black male student-athletes (Comeaux & Harrison, 2007; Harper, Williams, & Blackman, 2013). Black student-athletes must also take personal responsibility for educational achievement, striving to align their academic life and campus engagement with their future goals (Beamon, 2010). Unless a collective effort takes place on behalf of all these stakeholders to develop Black male student-athletes, low graduation rates, unsatisfactory academic progress, and narrowly circumscribed career opportunities beyond graduation will persist.

Black Undergraduate Men at HBCUs

A wealth of scholarly work exists about HBCUs and the benefits they provide for Black students. Currently, HBCUs are responsible for producing almost 20% of all undergraduate degrees and one fifth of all first professional degrees awarded to this population, despite these schools representing only 3% of all institutions of higher education (Lundy-Wagner & Gasman, 2011; Palmer & Gasman, 2008). Studies consistently indicate more positive outcomes attained for Black students at HBCUs over their same-race peers at PWIs because of the nurturing, family-like environments; supportive faculty and administration; and greater number of more culturally desirable engagement outlets, despite schools having fewer resources (Harper, Carini, Bridges, & Hayek, 2004; Palmer & Gasman, 2008).

Scholars of HBCUs have discovered that despite clear benefits for HBCU attendees, there is still a need for improvement (Kimbrough & Harper, 2006). Overall enrollment has declined, and gender disparities (while existing across the board at colleges and universities) are most pronounced at HBCUs, with women far outnumbering men (Kimbrough & Harper, 2006; Lundy-Wagner & Gasman, 2011; Palmer & Gasman, 2008). The graduation rates are also sinking. As reported by the National Center for Education Statistics in 2003, 14 of just over 100 HBCUs graduated their students at a rate above 50%; only 7 of these institutions graduated more than 50% of their Black men, an even bleaker proposition (Harper et al., 2004; Kimbrough & Harper, 2006).

Studies have also revealed experiential concerns that students deal with once enrolled, particularly related to the conservatism of many of these institutions. In their study, Harper and Gasman (2008) suggest that HBCUs often impose conservative views on attendees, including limitations on free speech, self-expression, and sexuality. This conservatism is often so entrenched in the school's culture that many students are afraid or disinclined to oppose it, to the point that some may not persist due to what they perceive to be an oppressive climate. Additionally, when discussing their experiences at HBCUs, many students often told stories of disorganization at the institutional level, particularly with financial aid processes, and of having to deal with negativity from some staff members (Kimbrough & Harper, 2006). Despite these negatives, students still commonly report positive beliefs about HBCUs. They tell of accessible and caring professors who regularly go beyond teaching to serve as mentors; the benefits of being surrounded by other Black peers motivated to succeed (Palmer & Gasman, 2008); learning how to appreciate the variety of subcultures within their race (Kimbrough & Harper, 2006); and feeling more connected to their institution (Harper et al., 2004). Clearly, despite perceived and real troubles, many students regard their experiences at HBCUs as positive.

Scholars more recently have recognized a gap in the literature: it had not adequately addressed differences in the experiences of male and female students at HBCUs (Palmer & Gasman, 2008). As a result, research that explores HBCUs using a gendered lens emerged, but more often than not these works have focused largely on women and not men. As Lundy-Wagner and Gasman (2011) suggested in their literature review, "Critical analysis of historical data from the mid-19th to early 21st century indicates that African American males have indeed been neglected in analyses of student enrollment, experiences, and degree completion at HBCUs" (p. 947). Within the past decade, however, many scholars have begun to disaggregate the experiences of Black students by gender, shedding more light on male-female differences, and in particular, Black men, at these institutions. As previously stated, male students at HBCUs are attending and graduating at much lower rates than their female counterparts (Harper et al., 2004; Kimbrough & Harper, 2006). An undeniable reason for this difference is that Black men are much less engaged in their collegiate experiences, both in and outside the classroom. As Kimbrough and Harper (2006) found, male students at HBCUs dedicated considerably less time to educational pursuits such as studying, homework, and writing, and were less often involved in organizations or leadership positions, as compared to their female peers. Several possible reasons for this disengagement are offered in their study, many of which relate to how Black men make meaning of what is considered "cool" or successful in terms of their racial identity. Because of popular culture, many men at HBCUs find themselves stuck between pervasive social stereotypes and defining their success through completion of their degree programs. As a result, many Black male students choose athletic involvement or the pursuit of romantic relationships with women over organizational affiliation or becoming a campus leader (Kimbrough & Harper, 2006).

Studies of 11 men who entered an HBCU classified as "academically underprepared" yet persisted to graduation offer more insights into the experiences of Black men at HBCUs (Palmer, Davis, & Maramba, 2010; Palmer

& Gasman, 2008; Palmer & Strayhorn, 2008). Participants indicated many barriers to academic success, including their family and home life, pride that inhibited them from seeking assistance, a lack of financial means (Palmer, Davis, & Maramba, 2010), and the inherent social nature of the university, which caused some students to lose focus (Palmer & Strayhorn, 2008). These studies also suggested that the presence of certain elements led to an increase in persistence and engagement for Black men at HBCUs. These elements included noncognitive variables, such as initiative, resolve, and effort (Palmer & Strayhorn, 2008); faculty who showed support for academic as well as personal success; access to role models and mentors, particularly those who had commonalities with the students, such as background and ethnicity; and supportive relationships with similarly motivated, same-race peers (Palmer et al., 2010; Palmer & Gasman, 2008). Interestingly, all but two of the men in the study were either members of organizations or leaders on campus; they noted, however, that a majority of their male counterparts were disengaged in out-of-class activities (Palmer et al., 2010).

In general, Black men at HBCUs are enrolling and graduating at lower rates and are less engaged than their female counterparts, more disproportionately than any other population in higher education (Kimbrough & Harper, 2006; Lundy-Wagner & Gasman, 2011; Palmer & Gasman, 2008). Participants in Kimbrough and Harper's (2006) study identified several possible reasons for these statistics: a lack of maturity, manifesting itself in less focus on academic pursuits and more attention given to romantic relationships, fraternity membership, and other social endeavors; the belief that men were not subject to the same expectations to go to college as women; the perception that their female counterparts were more academically prepared, received better support both in and outside class, and were given preferential treatment by professors; and men had too much pride, preventing them from taking full advantage of resources on campus. According to Lundy-Wagner and Gasman (2011), other possible reasons that Black male students at HBCUs are disengaged, underrepresented, and do not persist through to degree attainment are "systematic racism, poor primary and secondary school preparation, and lagging achievement" (p. 938). While providing meaningful insights into the HBCU experience for Black men, their data are potentially limited in applicability to the population of male HBCU students as a whole, due to the specificity and size of the research groups (Lundy-Wagner & Gasman, 2011). This and related research should not be discounted, however, or seen as less valid; rather, it should serve as a springboard for more research, utilizing a greater number and a wider variety of students and institutions. Only then will we truly have a full picture of the experiences of Black men at HBCUs and how we can continue to improve available support for them.

Underprepared, Disengaged Low Performers

In recent decades, scholars investigating the unique experiences of Black college students have highlighted the alarming disparities that prevent these students' progression through and success in higher education (Bonner & Bailey, 2006; Bush & Bush, 2010; Cuyjet, 1997, 2006; Harper, 2009). In particular, a myriad of studies shed light on the precarious predicament of Black men in college and throughout the educational pipeline. For example, higher education scholars and administrative stakeholders have characterized a significant portion of Black male college students as an "endangered species," given their severely high attrition rates (Cuyjet, 1997, p. 6). The declining educational attainment of Black men has resulted in poor employment rates and low social status for this group.

As evidenced by data from the American Council on Education (Palmer & Young, 2009), college participation rates have gradually risen among all racial/ethnic groups, yet Black men lag significantly behind their female counterparts in terms of their college enrollment, retention, and degree attainment (Bonner & Bailey, 2006; Cuyjet, 1997, 2006; Harper, 2009; Palmer, Davis, & Hilton, 2009). When numbers are closely examined across racial/ethnic groups, the gender gap among men in general and Black men in particular becomes even more pronounced.

Despite the proliferation of college access and the development of academic support programs that target at-risk student populations, Black male underrepresentation and attrition remain endemic across many higher education institutions, including minority-serving institutions (Cuyjet, 1997; Palmer et al., 2009; Palmer & Young, 2009). Among the Black men who do successfully matriculate into college, a disproportionately high number are underprepared for college-level work. As evidenced by Cuyjet's (1997) extensive review of the literature, academic deficiencies among Black male collegians have been linked to a number of conditions: poor K–12 schooling opportunities, financial hardships that hinder college access, lowered expectations among significant adults and peers about academic achievement, limited access to suitable mentors and role models, and assorted barriers related to racism. Unfortunately, these young men often enter higher education with "developmental disadvantages" that contribute to their dismal academic performance (Cuyjet, 1997, p. 7).

Further, based on 6,765 Black student respondents to the College Student Experiences Questionnaire, Cuyjet (1997) found that Black men spent considerably less time studying and taking class-related notes, were less likely to engage in collaborative academic experiences, and designated less time for writing and revising papers compared to their female counterparts. Cuyjet also found that Black men were less likely to participate in campus events and student organizations. Similar trends were noted within Harper's (2009) study on Black male student disengagement. For example, whereas Black women capitalized on leadership roles and other purposeful engagement opportunities, Black men devoted much of their time to working out in campus fitness centers, playing basketball, and pursuing romantic relationships with women.

These trends corroborate findings from Harper, Carini, Bridges, and Hayek's (2004) study based on the National Survey of Student Engagement. Using a sample of 1,167 Black undergraduates at 12 HBCUs, the researchers found that while men reported greater interactions with faculty, they still lagged significantly behind their female counterparts in time spent on studying, reading, and writing, and working diligently to meet professors' expectations. Unquestionably, the general perception, even among Black male student leaders in Kimbrough and Harper's (2006) qualitative study, is that Black men are grossly disengaged.

Black male student leaders in Kimbrough and Harper (2006) and Harper (2009) believed that Black men also regarded sports, athleticism, and physical activity as "cooler" and socially acceptable. Black male student leaders also believed that Black men generally encounter difficulty working together. The continuing shortage of Black male role models and mentors offers further explanation as to why some Black men undervalue campus involvement (see also Cuyjet, 1997).

Palmer et al. (2009) and Palmer and Young (2009) have addressed factors that promote academic success among underprepared Black men at HBCUs. Palmer et al.'s (2009) study explored the experiences of 11 Black male juniors and seniors who entered a public HBCU through its remedial program and persisted to graduation. Among the key findings from their study was that participants encountered financial barriers to paying for college. While this finding was not unusual given the institutional context, what was striking was that most Black men in the study described how pride interfered with their willingness to seek out campus support services. Furthermore, external issues in the homes and communities of Black male students often posed a constant threat to their success in college. In sum, these findings underscore significant impediments to Black male student achievement and engagement.

While most participants in Palmer and Young's (2009) study perceived campus involvement and faculty interactions as conducive to their academic success and personal development, Black men frequently expressed dissatisfaction about their social exclusion on campus as a result of institutional negligence. As Bush and Bush (2010) posit, "The role of the institution must be taken into consideration by colleges that are attempting to improve student achievement" (p. 57), as opposed to solely addressing individual behaviors.

As research consistently shows, perceptions of institutional support play a critical role in explaining academic attrition and disengagement among students in general and Black male students in particular (Bonner & Bailey, 2006; Bush & Bush, 2010; Palmer, Davis, & Maramba, 2010). For instance, even once minority male students become academically integrated and savvy to the college setting, particularly at PWIs, they confront daily negative perceptions about their intellectual abilities, discrimination, racial stereotypes, and a hostile campus environment generally (Bonner & Bailey, 2006; Bush & Bush, 2010; Cuyjet, 1997).

Furthermore, Black male collegians often struggle to develop effective coping strategies to fit in and succeed at PWIs, which engenders what some scholars call a "cool pose," or a "ritualized form of masculinity" that empowers Black men and gives them a sense of control (Bonner & Bailey, 2006, p. 34). Despite the considerable attention already devoted to exploring Black men in the educational pipeline (Bonner & Bailey, 2006; Bush & Bush, 2010; Cuyjet, 1997; Harper, 2009; Palmer, Davis, & Maramba, 2010), institutions must continue to allocate resources to investigating outcome disparities and social inequities. Ultimately, to reverse these growing gender gaps, institutions must first recognize the value of engaging, retaining, and graduating all Black male students, from underprepared and disengaged low performers to student-athletes, achievers, and student leaders.

Black Male College Achievers and Student Leaders

The dearth of literature regarding Black male achievers and leaders in college has garnered attention from scholars (Bonner, 2010; Fries-Britt, 1997; Harper, 2008b, 2009, 2012; Harper & Quaye, 2007; Harper et al., 2011; Martin & Harris, 2006; Warde, 2008). Their premise is to alter the discourse on Black male collegians and develop a counter-narrative whose realities are unlike those (mis)represented in higher education literature, media portrayals, and society as a whole. These scholars intend to remount the argument and illuminate a segment of Black male achievers who persist toward degree attainment and do so with high records of academic achievement and co-curricular engagement.

In her seminal piece "Identifying and Supporting Gifted African American Men," Fries-Britt (1997) painstakingly (re)defines *gifted and talented* to include contemporary meanings and understandings. Using Howard Gardner's theory of multiple intelligences, Renzulli's "three ring" concept of giftedness, and the federal government's definition of *giftedness*, Fries-Britt settles on a combination of interpersonal skills, academic prowess, high levels of engagement and creativity, and unusual leadership capabilities as elements of her definition (Fries-Britt, 1997, p. 66). Applying Fries-Britt's definition, Black male achievers can be categorized as gifted leaders, in that they exemplify the traits and characteristics that Gardner, Renzulli, and the federal government have put forth. Additionally, we can frame the experiences of Black male achievers using Bonner's (2010) six influential factors essential to their development: relationships with faculty, peer relationships, family influence and support, college selection, self-perception, and institutional environment.

The "gifted and talented" designation, however, if erroneous, can do more harm than good. Labeling Black male achievers as such often comes with the assumption that they do not require academic support or resources, and that they are well-adjusted socially and academically to their college environments, particularly when compared to their Black male counterparts who exhibit low levels of academic achievement and high levels of disengagement (Bonner, 2010; Fries-Britt, 1997). On the contrary, their experiences are far more congruent with their less well adjusted Black male counterparts than they are contradictory.

Bonner (2010) substantiates the claims put forth by other scholars that Black male collegians attending PWIs find their environments to be cold, uninviting, and inhospitable. Their classroom experiences range from marginalization to being viewed by their peers as the authority on all racial matters pertaining to Blacks in America (Bonner, 2010). Moreover, Black male college students frequently refer to the unequal treatment from professors in comparison to their White peers. Many would argue that forming these types of relationships is essential to successfully navigating academia. Bonner also draws attention to the "proving process" that Black men in college undergo to be viewed by their professors as legitimate and capable academically. Similarly, Harper's (2009) and Harper et al.'s (2011) counter-narrative of Black men in college revealed that Black male achievers were met with the task of having to separate themselves from negative depictions and portrayals of Black men. The Black men in these studies were intentional in disrupting the ubiquitous perception of Black men as hypersexual, hypermasculine, criminals, underachievers, irresponsible fathers, and "products" of dysfunctional families (Harper, 2008b, 2009, 2012; Harper et al., 2011).

The defining factor that sets Black male achievers apart from their counterparts is their ability to overcome the challenges discussed previously and simultaneously to maintain high records of academic success and cocurricular engagement. Harper and Quaye (2007), Harper (2012), and Martin and Harris (2006) reveal the obligation that Black male achievers feel to racially uplift the Black community on and off campus. In an attempt to debunk Black myths and stereotypes, Black male achievers joined and led Black affinity groups on campus (e.g., Black student unions or Black fraternities) to address issues that directly affected the Black community, creating venues to help younger Black students self-actualize academically (e.g., study hall and study groups). Likewise, some Black male achievers aspired for high-ranking positions within majority organizations (e.g., student government associations) to ensure financial support for Black organizations and their initiatives (Harper & Quaye, 2007).

For Black male achievers, improved educational outcomes and moving the Black community forward were only parts of the advantages of leadership. As active members of the campus community, their leadership positions and high academic standing granted them access to top-level university administrators (e.g., deans, provosts, vice presidents, presidents)—relationships that their peers did not have. Harper (2008b) illuminated the relationships that Black male achievers fostered with their university president and other senior-level administrators. Fostering these relationships led to invitations to join exclusive and highly coveted committees, scholarships and other academic opportunities, university awards, and letters of recommendation. A number of students mentioned having direct access to the president and other senior administrators. As one student stated, "The president actually has my cell phone number and calls me whenever he needs something or there is someone important on campus he wants me to meet" (Harper, 2008b, p. 1039). As a result, these Black male achievers acquired the social capital needed to advance within academia.

Conclusion

Our purpose in this chapter was to complicate what is known about Black undergraduate men and to move beyond the popular approach of treating them all the same. We hope to have made clear that different groups of Black male students have population-specific needs and challenges. The six groups discussed in this chapter offer only a glimpse into who Black men at four-year institutions are. Without a nuanced understanding of differences within and across subpopulations, educators will continue to face challenges in fostering environments where all Black males succeed. Furthermore, future research must focus more on the institutional contexts in which diverse groups of Black men live, learn, and interact. To assume that the experiences of subpopulations are the same across all four-year institutions (HBCUs, predominantly White liberal arts colleges, Ivy League universities, religiously affiliated institutions, for-profit universities, urban commuter schools, etc.) is as erroneous as assuming that all Black male students are the same. Success for these students cannot be advanced in the absence of strategies that respond appropriately to within-group heterogeneity and institutional diversity.

References

Beamon, K. K. (2010). Used goods: Former African American college student-athletes' perceptions of exploitation by Division I universities. In S. R. Harper & F. Harris III (Eds.), *College men and masculinities: Theory, research, and implications for practice* (pp. 504–522). San Francisco: Jossey-Bass.

Beamon, K. K., & Bell, P. A. (2006). Academics versus athletics: An examination of the effects of background and socialization on African American male student athletes. *Social Science Journal, 43*(3), 393–403.

Benson, K. F. (2000). Constructing academic inadequacy: African American athletes' stories of schooling. *Journal of Higher Education, 71*(2), 223–246.

Bonner, F. A., II. (2010). *Academically gifted African American male college students.* Santa Barbara, CA: Praeger.

Bonner, F. A., II, & Bailey, K. W. (2006). Enhancing the academic climate for African American college men. In M. J. Cuyjet (Ed.), *African American men in college* (pp. 24–46). San Francisco: Jossey-Bass.

Brown, E., II. (2005). We wear the mask: African American contemporary gay male identities. *Journal of African American Studies, 9*(2), 29–38.

Bush, E. C., & Bush, V. L. (2010). Calling out the elephant: An examination of African American male achievement in community colleges. *Journal of African American Males in Education, 1*(1), 41–62.

Comeaux, E., & Harrison, C. K. (2007). Faculty and male student athletes: Racial differences in the environmental predictors of academic achievement. *Race, Ethnicity, and Education, 10*(2), 199–214.

Cuyjet, M. J. (1997). African American men on college campuses: Their needs and their perceptions. In M. J. Cuyjet (Ed.), *Helping African American men succeed in college. New Directions for Student Services* (no. 80, pp. 5–16). San Francisco: Jossey-Bass.

Cuyjet, M. J. (2006). African American college men: Twenty-first-century issues and concerns. In M. J. Cuyjet (Ed.), *African American men in college* (pp. 3–23). San Francisco: Jossey-Bass.

DeSantis, A. D., & Coleman, M. (2008). Not on my line: Attitudes about homosexuality in Black fraternities. In G. S. Parks (Ed.), *Black Greek-letter organizations in the 21st century: Our fight has just begun* (pp. 291–312). Lexington: University Press of Kentucky.

Donnor, J. K. (2005). Towards an interest-convergence in the education of African American football student-athletes in major college sports. *Race, Ethnicity and Education, 8*(1), 45–67.

Fries-Britt, S. L. (1997). Identifying and supporting gifted African American men. In M. J. Cuyjet (Ed.), *Helping African American men succeed in college. New Directions for Student Services* (no. 80, 65–78). San Francisco: Jossey-Bass.

Goode-Cross, D. T., & Good, G. E. (2008). African American men who have sex with men: Creating safe spaces through relationships. *Psychology of Men & Masculinity, 9*(4), 221–234.

Goode-Cross, D. T., & Good, G. E. (2009). Managing multiple-minority identities: African American men who have sex with men at predominately white universities. *Journal of Diversity in Higher Education, 2*(2), 103–112.

Harper, S. R. (2008a). The effects of sorority and fraternity membership on class participation and African American student engagement in predominantly white classroom environments. *College Student Affairs Journal, 27*(1), 94–115.

Harper, S. R. (2008b). Realizing the intended outcomes of *Brown*: High-achieving African American male undergraduates and social capital. *American Behavioral Scientist, 51*(7), 1030–1053.

Harper, S. R. (2009). Niggers no more: A critical race counternarrative on Black male student achievement at predominantly white colleges and universities. *International Journal of Qualitative Studies in Education, 22*(6), 697–712.

Harper, S. R. (2012). *Black male student success in higher education: A report from the National Black Male College Achievement Study*. Philadelphia: University of Pennsylvania, Center for the Study of Race and Equity in Education.

Harper, S. R. (2014). (Re)setting the agenda for college men of color: Lessons learned from a 15-year movement to improve Black male student success. In R. A. Williams (Ed.), *Men of color in higher education: New foundations for developing models for success* (pp. 116–143). Sterling, VA: Stylus.

Harper, S. R., Berhanu, J., Davis, C. H. F., III, & McGuire, K. M. (2015). Engaging college men of color. In S. J. Quaye & S. R. Harper (Eds.), *Student engagement in higher education: Theoretical perspectives and practical approaches for diverse populations* (2nd ed., pp. 55–74). New York: Routledge.

Harper, S. R., Carini, R. M., Bridges, B. K., & Hayek, J. C. (2004). Gender differences in student engagement among African American undergraduates at historically Black colleges and universities. *Journal of College Student Development, 45*(3), 271–284.

Harper, S. R., Davis, R. J., Jones, D. E., McGowan, B. L., Ingram, T. N., & Platt, C. S. (2011). Race and racism in the experiences of African American male resident assistants at predominantly white universities. *Journal of College Student Development, 52*(2), 180–200.

Harper, S. R., & Gasman, M. (2008). Consequences of conservatism: Black male students and the politics of historically Black colleges and universities. *Journal of Negro Education, 77*(4), 336–351.

Harper, S. R., & Harris, F., III (2006). The role of Black fraternities in the African American male undergraduate experience. In M. J. Cuyjet (Ed.), *African American men in college* (pp. 128–153). San Francisco: Jossey-Bass

Harper, S. R., & Harris, F., III (2012). *A role for policymakers in improving the status of Black male students in U.S. higher education*. Washington, DC: Institute for Higher Education Policy.

Harper, S. R., & Nichols, A. H. (2008). Are they not all the same? Racial heterogeneity among Black male undergraduates. *Journal of College Student Development, 49*(3), 199–214.

Harper, S. R., & Quaye, S. J. (2007). Student organizations as venues for Black identity expression and development among African American male student leaders. *Journal of College Student Development, 48*(2), 133–159.

Harper, S. R., Wardell, C. C., & McGuire, K. M. (2011). Man of multiple identities: Complex individuality and identity intersectionality among college men. In J. A. Laker & T. Davis (Eds.), *Masculinities in higher education: Theoretical and practical considerations* (pp. 81–96). New York: Routledge.

Harper, S. R., Williams, C. D., Jr., & Blackman, H. W. (2013). *Black male student-athletes and racial inequities in NCAA Division I college sports.* Philadelphia: University of Pennsylvania, Center for the Study of Race and Equity in Education.

Harris, W. G. (2003). African American homosexual males on predominantly white college and university campuses. *Journal of African American Studies, 7*(1), 47–56.

Howard, T. C. (2014). *Black male(d): Peril and promise in the education of African American males.* New York: Teachers College Press.

Jones, R. L. (2000). The historical significance of sacrificial ritual: Understanding violence in the modern Black fraternity pledge process. *Western Journal of Black Studies, 24*(2), 112–124.

Kimbrough, W. M. (1995). Self-assessment, participation, & value of leadership skills, activities, and experiences for Black students relative to their membership in historically Black fraternities and sororities. *Journal of Negro Education, 64*(1), 63–74.

Kimbrough, W. M. (1997). The membership intake movement of historically Black Greek-letter organizations. *NASPA Journal, 34*(3), 229–243.

Kimbrough, W. M. (2003). *Black Greek 101.* Madison, NJ: Fairleigh Dickinson University Press.

Kimbrough, W. M., & Harper, S. R. (2006). African American men at historically Black colleges and universities: Different environments, similar challenges. In M. J. Cuyjet (Ed.), *African American men in college* (pp. 189–209). San Francisco: Jossey-Bass.

Lewis, G. B. (2003). Black-white differences in attitudes toward homosexuality and gay rights. *Public Opinion Quarterly, 67*(1), 59–78.

Lundy-Wagner, V., & Gasman, M. (2011). When gender issues are not just about women: Reconsidering male students at historically Black colleges and universities. *Teachers College Record, 113*(5), 934–968.

Martin, B. E., & Harris, F., III. (2006). Examining productive conceptions of masculinities: Lessons learned from academically driven African American male student-athletes. *Journal of Men's Studies, 14*(3), 359–378.

McClure, S. M. (2006a). Improvising masculinity: African American fraternity membership in the construction of a Black masculinity. *Journal of African American Studies, 10*(1), 57–73.

McClure, S. M. (2006b). Voluntary association membership: Black Greek men on a predominantly white campus. *Journal of Higher Education, 77*(6), 1036–1057.

McGuire, K. M., Berhanu, J., Davis, C. H. F., III, & Harper, S. R. (2014). In search of progressive black masculinities: Critical self-reflections on gender identity development among Black undergraduate men. *Men & Masculinities, 17*(3), 253–277.

Overly, K. B. (2005). The exploitation of African-American men in college athletic programs. *Virginia Sports and Entertainment Law Journal, 5*(1), 31–62.

Palmer, R. T., Davis, R. J., & Hilton, A. A. (2009). Exploring challenges that threaten to impede the academic success of academically underprepared Black males at an HBCU. *Journal of College Student Development, 50*(4), 429–445.

Palmer, R. T., Davis, R. J., & Maramba, D. C. (2010). Role of an HBCU in supporting academic success for underprepared Black males. *Negro Educational Review, 61*(1–4), 85–106.

Palmer, R. T., & Gasman, M. (2008). "It takes a village to raise a child": Social capital and academic success at historically Black colleges and universities. *Journal of College Student Development, 49*(1), 52–70.

Palmer, R. T., & Strayhorn, T. L. (2008). Mastering one's own fate: Non-cognitive factors associated with the success of African American males at an HBCU. *NASAP Journal, 11*(1), 126–143.

Palmer, R. T., Wood, J. L., Dancy, T. E., & Strayhorn, T. L. (2014). *Black male collegians: Increasing access, retention, and persistence in higher education.* ASHE Higher Education Report (vol. 40, no. 3). San Francisco: Jossey-Bass.

Palmer, R. T., & Young, E. M. (2009). Determined to succeed: Salient factors that foster academic success for academically underprepared Black males at a Black college. *Journal of College Student Retention, 10*(4), 465–482.

Patton, L. D. (2011). Perspectives on identity, disclosure, and the campus environment among African American gay and bisexual men at one historically Black college. *Journal of College Student Development, 52*(1), 77–100.

Patton, L. D. (2014). Preserving respectability or blatant disrespect? A critical discourse analysis of the Morehouse Appropriate Attire Policy and implications for intersectional approaches to examining campus policies. *International Journal of Qualitative Studies in Education, 27*(6), 724–746.

Shah, S., & Sato, G. (2014). *Building a beloved community: Strengthening the field of Black male achievement.* New York: Foundation Center.

Strayhorn, T. L., Blakewood, A. M., & DeVita, J. M. (2008). Factors affecting the college choice of African American gay male undergraduates: Implications for retention. *NASAP Journal, 11*(1), 88–108.

Strayhorn, T. L., & Mullins, T. G. (2012). Investigating Black gay male undergraduates' experiences in campus residence halls. *Journal of College and University Student Housing, 39*(1), 141–160.

Warde, B. (2008). Staying the course: Narratives of African American males who have completed a baccalaureate degree. *Journal of African American Studies, 12*(1), 59–72.

Washington, J., & Wall, V. A. (2010). African American gay men: Another challenge for the academy. In S. R. Harper & F. Harris III (Eds.), *College men and masculinities: Theory, research, and implications for practice* (pp. 136–147). San Francisco: Jossey-Bass.

Wilson, P. A. (2008). A dynamic-ecological model of identity formation and conflict among bisexually behaving African-American men. *Archives of Sexual Behavior, 37*(5), 794–809.

7

BLACK MEN IN MASTER'S DEGREE PROGRAMS

Status, Distribution, and Achievement

Terrell L. Strayhorn

According to the Council of Graduate Schools' (CGS; 2009) annual report of graduate degrees (most recent data available), which is based on responses from 699 graduate schools in the United States that enroll approximately 1.8 million students in certificate, education specialist, master's, and doctoral degree programs, 71% of graduate students are White/non-Hispanic, while only 12% are Black/African American.[1] Furthermore, underrepresented minority first-time graduate students were less likely than Whites and Asian American and Pacific Islanders (AAPIs) to be enrolled in science, technology, engineering, and math (STEM) fields, such as biological/agricultural sciences, math, and computer science. Consider the following statistics that reflect the proportional representation in STEM by race: 28% AAPI, 15% White, 12% Latino, 12% American Indian/Alaskan Native (AI/ANs), and only 8% Black.

Disaggregating these data further revealed interesting trends in terms of race/ethnicity and sex.[2] For instance, CGS (2009) data indicated that 71% of Black full-time graduate students were women, one of the largest sex gaps among both sexes and all races. Furthermore, recent data from the National

---

[1] Statistic includes U.S. citizens and permanent residents only.

[2] In this chapter, the term *sex* refers to one's biological assignment at birth as male or female.

Science Board (2012) indicated that 62% of Black graduate students in science and engineering (S&E) were women. Indeed, Black men in S&E fields were unevenly distributed across major fields and disciplines; for instance, surprisingly, fewer than 10 Black men nationally were enrolled in graduate fields such as anatomy ($n = 7$), botany ($n = 7$), zoology ($n = 3$), earth/ocean science, astronomy, linguistics, and even mining or agricultural engineering.

The status and representation of Black men in graduate education is measured not only through enrollment statistics but can also be understood through attainment or degree completion information. Given this chapter's focus on Black men in master's degree programs, I found it useful to analyze the most recent data from the U.S. Department of Education's National Center for Education Statistics' (NCES) Integrated Postsecondary Education Data Systems (IPEDs) completions survey (2009). Data suggest several major trends: Blacks earn approximately 9% of master's degrees awarded annually; the majority of master's degrees awarded to Blacks are in non–S&E fields, with only 15% earned in S&E fields; and Black women compose the largest share of Black master's degree awardees. Of all master's degrees awarded, Black men earned fewer than 40 in agricultural science, sociology, and materials engineering; fewer than three in atmospheric sciences and linguistics; and, surprisingly, zero in ocean sciences, astronomy, anthropology, and several other fields.

Although national and survey data provide a useful glimpse at the status—that is, representation, distribution, and achievement or attainment—of Black men in graduate education generally and master's degree programs specifically, this information sheds little light on just why so few Black men enroll in and graduate from master's degree programs in the United States. To understand the underlying mechanism that gives rise to such statistics, additional information is needed about the experiences of Black men in master's degree programs specifically. In this chapter I address this gap in the literature.

Purpose

I seek here to expand on the statistics presented in the previous section by focusing on the status, distribution, and achievement of Black men in master's degree programs. I use national statistics reported by federal and higher education agencies, such as the CGS, NCES, and the National Science Foundation (NSF). In this chapter, I also break new ground by sharing findings from a multi-institutional survey of Black men in graduate degree programs. Given the specific focus, my survey analysis is based on a sample of 306 Black men in master's degree programs, making it one of the largest studies of this particular subpopulation to date. Last, I offer recommendations for educational policies and practices that hold promise for enhancing the success of Black men in master's degree programs. Before describing the study and its major findings and implications, let's consider the theoretical and conceptual underpinnings that frame graduate students' experiences.

Frameworks

I have pointed out elsewhere (Strayhorn, 2009) that although we know relatively little about the experiences of Black men in graduate school, we know far more—at least theoretically—about the demographic, institutional, and academic factors that appear to influence students' success in higher education generally (e.g., Tinto, 1993) and graduate education specifically (e.g., Strayhorn, 2005, 2010). Thus, in this chapter I employ a blended conceptual framework based on existing theories to establish relationships among the variables studied (e.g., test scores, campus type) and to guide the selection of variables that are included in the analyses that follow. As in previous work, I seek to bring together a set of interconnected theoretical propositions that provide useful constructs for talking about Black men in master's degree programs. Indeed, blended frameworks of this sort are useful, as they allow researchers to see in new and different ways what otherwise might seem overly complex, ordinary, or completely unrelated. Framing this examination of the status and achievement of Black men in master's degree programs are theories of graduate student persistence and socialization.

Graduate Student Persistence

In his second edition of *Leaving College: Rethinking the Causes and Cures of Student Attrition*, Vincent Tinto (1993) devotes 229 pages of the 244-page volume (excluding notes and references) to explicating the determinants of undergraduate student departure from institutions of higher education specifically and "the broader system of higher education" altogether (p. 8). Despite its near paradigmatic status (Braxton, 2000), Tinto's model of undergraduate student retention is not the only theoretical contribution of his book's second edition. Tucked in the back of the book—Appendix B to be exact—and spanning just 14 pages is his theory on doctoral/graduate student persistence, which is far less cited. Generally speaking, Tinto posits graduate student persistence as a function of three stages—transition/adjustment, attaining candidacy, and completing independent research requirements (e.g., dissertation, thesis) and makes the following points about his longitudinal model of graduate persistence:

1. Individual attributes and educational experiences prior to graduate school shape individual goals and commitments at entry. Graduate student persistence is a function of several external factors that operate independent of the institution (e.g., family, work). Participation patterns also are important.

2. Graduate student persistence is primarily shaped by local communities that frame department life; thus, primary reference groups are local student and faculty communities that exist in the units in which the degree is pursued. Consequently, graduate student persistence is likely to be more strongly related to the particular normative and structural character of the field of study than the university at large.

3. Graduate student persistence is framed by the particular types of student/faculty communities that exist in local units (e.g., colleges, schools, departments); thus, academic and social integration are more closely tied for graduate than undergraduate students.

4. Local graduate communities are nested within the broader university and "external professional communities that frame the field of study" (p. 233).

5. The availability, amount, and type of financial assistance are important, although it's less clear whether "they matter in the same way at different stages of the [degree] completion process" (p. 237).

The model's infrequent use in studies of graduate students does not necessarily reflect its utility for research. In other words, the model has several strengths, in my opinion, that make it appropriate for the current discussion. First, the model is based on prior research, including empirical examinations of graduate student persistence (or, conversely, retention; e.g., Girves & Wemmerus, 1988; Ott, Markewich, & Ochsner, 1984; Zwick, 1991). Second, the model is parsimonious and lends itself to meaningful operationalization of central constructs (e.g., commitment to graduate degree, social interactions with graduate peers). Parsimonious models help to alleviate the paradox of theory—that "workable models are too complex to research and researchable models are too simplified to be useful in practice" (Parker, 1977, p. 420). Last, Tinto's model has been applied in other studies of graduate student outcomes (e.g., Strayhorn, 2009, 2010); thus, some knowledge has accumulated over time about the applicability of his theoretical propositions to various groups of graduate students. Taken together, these criteria lend support to the utility of the model and its applicability to this discussion of Black men in master's degree programs.

With this information in mind, I decided to include several measures of students' individual attributes, prior educational experiences, participation patterns, and formal and informal academic or social interactions with peers and faculty, as well as relevant competencies and skills in the analysis of survey data from Black men in master's degree programs. While Tinto's (1993) longitudinal model of graduate student persistence was helpful in identifying variables to include in the statistical analysis, socialization theory provided constructs for talking about the underlying mechanism of Black male students' success (or lack thereof) in master's degree programs.

Socialization

Socialization has been defined in several ways. For instance, a growing body of research has employed socialization theory to understand the "process by which persons acquire the knowledge, skills, and dispositions that make them more or less effective members of their society" (Brim, 1966, p. 3). Jablin and Miller (1990) identified four stages[3] in the vocational socialization process that focus on the entry and exit of new members of a field or career: (1) vocational socialization (i.e., how one learns about a role or job function); (2) anticipatory socialization (i.e., how one develops expectations of the organization and roles within it); (3) encounter (i.e., entry into the organization, experiences that either affirm or challenge expectations); and (4) exit. Another prevailing definition posits socialization as a "learning process through which the individual acquires the knowledge, skills, the values and attitudes, and the habits and modes of thought of the society to which he belongs" (Bragg, 1976, p. 3). In the context of student socialization, this learning process is often defined by three phases: anticipatory socialization, encounter, and change or acquisition (Feldman, 1981).

Perhaps the most widely cited conceptualization of socialization is the one that Weidman, Twale, and Stein (2001) proposed. The authors simplify the socialization process into three phases: knowledge acquisition, investment, and involvement. *Knowledge acquisition* typically refers to acquiring cognitive and affective knowledge and skills, while *investment* refers to devoting something of personal value (e.g., time) to preparing for a graduate or professional role. Participating in any activity that prepares one for such a role is the essence of *involvement*. In several ways, Weidman et al.'s conceptualization reflects central aspects of Tinto's (1993) graduate student persistence model; for instance, Weidman et al.'s concept of knowledge acquisition is related to Tinto's notion of developing competence, which can be demonstrated by attaining candidacy.

---

[3] Some scholars discuss socialization in terms of *stages* (Thornton & Nardi, 1975), whereas others refer to *phases* (Wanous, Reichers, & Malik, 1984).

Weidman et al.'s (2001) theoretical orientation to socialization has been applied to a number of groups in higher education. Prior research has examined the socialization experiences of working-class students (Wegner, 1973), doctoral students (Austin & McDaniels, 2006), and faculty members (Tierney & Rhoads, 1993). Although ample evidence ties socialization to the success of students and faculty in general, the extent to which it applies to Black male graduate students is not fully substantiated. To my knowledge, however, only one scholarly work (Strayhorn, 2009) applies socialization theory to understanding the status and achievement of Black men in graduate school generally and master's degree programs specifically. I settled on this framework because it offered useful language for describing the processes by which Black men acquire the knowledge and skills needed to participate successfully in master's degree programs. This understanding was immeasurably useful when discussing the study's major findings and identifying specific areas that should be the object of institutional action for enhancing Black men's success in graduate education.

What We Know About Black Men in Graduate Education

Two lines of scholarship relate to my focus in this chapter: statistical reports on the representation and distribution of Black men in graduate education and a handful of empirical research studies on Black men in graduate school. Over time, a growing body of research has amassed on the nature and purpose of graduate education (Berelson, 1960; Bowen & Rudenstine, 1992; Burgess, 1997; Golde & Walker, 2006; LaPidus, 1997), as well as the structure and function of graduate degrees (e.g., Advisory Board for the Research Councils, 1993). For instance, LaPidus (1997) posited several major issues and themes that shape the nature of graduate education in the United States. Chief among them are money (i.e., cost of graduate education), politics (i.e., affirmative action, immigration, labor market), and technology (as a way of building capacity to meet the increasing demands for graduate training). Enrollment growth and the perceived overproduction of some graduate degrees (e.g., MBAs, JDs) also have generated widespread interest in the quality of graduate education (Conrad, Haworth, & Millar, 1993; Holdaway, 1997).

The vast majority of published reports on graduate education focus on the number of students enrolled in graduate degree programs across the country. Consider the following list of annual reports that document, at least in part, the representation and distribution of students across graduate degree fields: CGS's (2009) *Graduate Enrollment and Degrees*, the American Council on Education's (2007) *Minorities in Higher Education* annual report, the U.S. Department of Education's (2009) *Condition of Education*, and the

National Science Board's (2006) *Science and Engineering Indicators* report, to name a few. Several trends can be identified from these national reports. First, a master's education is an important part of the graduate enterprise, as a swelling number of scientific and technical jobs now require at least a master's degree (U.S. Department of Education, National Center for Education Statistics, 2009). Second, more than 90% of all students who earn graduate degrees complete a master's degree, a trend that has persisted for more than 30 years. Disaggregating these data by race/ethnicity and sex reveals another noticeable enrollment pattern that deserves explicit mention, given the focus of the present chapter—that Black women outnumber their same-race male counterparts in both enrollment in and completion of master's degrees, even in S&E fields.

Despite the increased attention given to graduate education generally and minority graduate student rates specifically, comparatively little scholarly attention has been given to master's education. This situation led Conrad and his colleagues (1993) to conclude that the master's degree was assigned "second-class and consolation prize status, mostly by individuals associated with colleges and universities" (p. 314). In fact, Clark's (1993) observation is still true when it comes to the higher education literature:

> The first degree level [i.e., bachelors] has historical primacy, predominates numerically and possesses a deep hold on traditional thought and practice. It comes first in budget determination, public attention and the concerns of governments. Graduate or advanced education is then prone to develop at the margin as an add-on of a few more years of unstructured work for a few students. (p. 356)

Indeed, more information is needed if graduate education is to do more than "develop at the margin" and if educators are expected to promote conditions that enable graduate student success, particularly the success of those who may be least likely to achieve it without additional support, such as Black men who face significant challenges in higher education.

Empirical Research on Black Men in Higher Education

A shift toward examining the academic and social experiences of Black or African American men in higher education has taken place fairly recently (e.g., Cuyjet, 2006), with most attention devoted to students at the undergraduate level. Despite steadily increasing attrition and time-to-degree (TTD) rates, the little attention given to Black men in graduate education is surprising. What is known focuses on demographic differences in students' decisions to enroll in graduate school (Perna, 2004), application decisions among students of color in higher education administration (Poock, 1999), the influence of financial aid on master's degree completion (Luan & Fenske, 1996; Strayhorn, 2010), and even master's students' perspective on diversity of their education (Talbot, 1996). Very few of these, however, focus on Black men explicitly, with one exception (Strayhorn, 2009).

In most cases, Black men are part of the analyses of "sex differences" as men or "race differences" as Black students, but rarely are a separate and distinct category with a few exceptions (e.g., Wood & Turner, 2011). However, in a previous study of Black male graduate students (Strayhorn, 2009), I found that educational aspirations, age, and salary were associated for Black men with enrollment in and completion of a graduate degree program. Additionally, Black men who had highly educated parents (i.e., parents with a graduate degree) were more likely than those with less educated parents to enroll in and complete graduate school themselves. A careful review of the literature on Black men in graduate education generally and master's degree programs specifically yields one major conclusion: much more information is needed to understand the status, distribution, and achievement of Black men in such settings, which is the objective of the study that framed this chapter.

The Study

Since I was interested in describing the status, distribution, and achievement of Black men in master's degree programs, I drew upon data from a larger, multiyear quantitative research project that examines the academic and social experiences of 635 Black men in graduate school, including master's, doctoral, and first-professional-degree programs. Although the larger study consists of responses from students at all levels of graduate education, this chapter is based on data from Black men enrolled in or recent graduates from (i.e., within three years of survey participation) master's degree programs only. For more information about the survey study, see Strayhorn (2011).

A total of 306 Black men provided information that formed the basis for this chapter. Generally speaking, 70% of sample participants were currently enrolled in graduate school, 30% were recent graduates; 79% were single, 19% were married, and 2% were widowed or divorced; 7.5% attended historically Black colleges and universities (HBCUs), 1.6% attended Hispanic-serving institutions (HSIs), and the vast majority (83%) attended predominantly White institutions (PWIs). Table 7.1 describes the sample in more detail.

TABLE 7.1
Demographics of Survey Respondents

Variable	%	M	SD
Marital status			
Single	79		
Married	19		
Widowed/divorced	2		
Campus composition			
Predominantly White	83		
Historically Black	8		
Hispanic-serving	2		
Other	7		
Participation pattern			
Full-time	55		
Part-time	16		
Recent graduate	30		
Age		28.49	6.93
Time to degree		2.47	1.12
Undergraduate GPA		3.12	0.39
Graduate GPA		3.32	0.98

Using a combination of descriptive and multivariate statistics, I analyzed the survey data to illuminate the status, distribution, and achievement of Black men in master's degree programs. In many ways, this represents one of the first large-scale survey studies of this sample. This analysis is of significance, as this population may be in need of additional support to achieve success in higher education. The next section highlights the study's major findings, followed by a discussion of these results in light of the previous literature.

Key Findings

Tinto's (1993) model noted the important role that individual attributes play in determining graduate student persistence; thus, I included several background and individual trait measures. The mean age (in years) of Black men in the master's-only sample was 28.49 (SD = 6.93), with ages ranging from 20 to 63 years. As previously mentioned, 79% of Black men in the sample were single, 19% were married, and 2% were widowed or divorced. On average, parents' level of education varied among survey respondents. For instance, 3.8% indicated that their mother's highest level of education was a doctoral degree, 10.4% master's, 20% bachelor's, and 66% associate's or less. On the other hand, the father's highest level of education ranged from 4.2% doctoral, 11% master's, 13.8% bachelor's, to 71% associate's or less.

Prior educational experiences are also important in terms of graduate student persistence. Consider the survey's results regarding Black men's performance as undergraduates and prior to entry into graduate school. For example, the mean undergraduate grade point average (GPA) among the sample was 3.12 (SD = 0.39). Undergraduate majors also varied: 25% STEM fields, 14% humanities, 27% other social sciences, 9% education, 15% business, and 11% "all others."

Fifty percent of the sample reported taking the Graduate Record Exam (GRE). Of these, two mean scores were calculated for each subscale: GRE Verbal (M = 424.3; SD = 175.5) and GRE Quantitative (M = 499.8; SD = 206.9). As a benchmark, compare these results against the national averages reported by the Educational Testing Service (ETS): 470 on the GRE Verbal and 610 on the GRE Quantitative. In terms of achievement, the mean graduate (i.e., master's) GPA among the sample was 3.32 (SD = 0.98). TTD ranged from one to eight years with a mean TTD of 2.47 years (SD = 1.12).

Recall that Tinto (1993) also pointed out the importance of participation patterns. Among the sample of Black men in master's degree programs, 54.6% were enrolled full-time while 16.3% were enrolled part-time; the balance of the sample did not indicate an enrollment status since they had recently graduated. Interestingly, 13.6% of the sample had *stopped out*, defined as being unenrolled for at least one semester not including summer terms unless they are required by one's program.

According to Tinto (1993), graduate student persistence is a function of external commitments (e.g., family) as well as individual commitments to one's institution/program and the goal of degree completion. Recall that most men in the sample (79%) were single, 19% were married, and 2% were widowed or divorced. Cross-tabulations revealed that participation patterns varied significantly by marital status. For instance, 30% of married students in the sample were enrolled part-time compared to only 13% of single students, which represents a significant difference in marital and time status— $\chi2$ (4) = 14.60, p < 0.01. Further, 24% of married students had stopped out at some point during their graduate education, compared to only 12% of single students—$\chi2$ (2) = 1.05, p < 0.01. Taken together, these findings may lend support to Tinto's conclusion that marital status affects participation patterns, including for Black men in master's degree programs.

One of the major concepts in Weidman et al.'s (2001) graduate student socialization model is *investment*, defined as to the degree of personal time and energy devoted to activities that facilitate one's involvement in communities to which one seeks membership. Time spent studying in graduate school may be an appropriate proxy for investment, as it reflects the degree of personal time and energy devoted to learning activities (Tinto, 1993), although it may be related to personal attributes and external commitments as well. Here is how Black men in the sample fared on time spent studying weekly in graduate school: 17% spent one to five hours, 29% spent six to 10 hours, 25% spent 11 to 15 hours, 16% spent 16 to 20 hours, and 11% spent 21 or more hours per week studying. Consider that 12% of single Black men in the sample devoted 21 or more hours per week to academic assignments, while only 6% of married Black men did so.

Socialization theory also describes the process through which individuals attain bona fide membership in a community, such as graduate school, by way of involvement with others who hold membership in or aspire to become members of a group or community (Weidman et al., 2001). To this end, I analyzed several items that assessed whether Black men in the sample had worked with faculty members on research while in graduate school, had published journal articles or chapters with graduate faculty, or had published with other graduate students. Although 40% of the sample reported "working with" faculty on research while in graduate school, only 5% had published with a faculty member(s), and a mere 3% had published with other graduate students. Given the importance of meaningful involvement in educationally purposeful activities, such as research and writing, to graduate students' success (Gardner & Barnes, 2007; LaPidus, 1997), I think that much more can be done to facilitate Black men's involvement in such activities while they pursue a master's degree.

Discussion of Findings

Recall that the purpose of this chapter was threefold: (1) to expand on the existing body of research by describing the status, distribution, and achievement of Black men in master's degree programs; (2) to report new findings from a multi-institutional survey of Black men in master's degree programs; and (3) to offer recommendations for educational policies and practices that hold promise for enhancing the success of Black men in master's degree programs. Herein I identify approximately 10 factors that relate to Black men's success in such programs, including: age, parents' level of education, marital status, participation patterns, time spent studying, and involvement in research activities, to name a few. Generally, my findings coincide with the assumptions of graduate student persistence and professional socialization theories (Tinto, 1993; Weidman et al., 2001). Using these findings as a guide, I offer the following recommendations for future policy and practice.

Recommendations for Policy

In light of the national statistics reported in this chapter's introduction, federal and state policies must play a continued role in increasing the participation rates of Black men in graduate school. Financial aid, precollege intervention (e.g., TRIO programs), and research and development (R&D) policies should be fashioned to reduce, if not eliminate, the academic and financial barriers that may restrict Black men from graduate school. For example, student aid policies can be redesigned to offer compensation packages to Black men that permit them to attend graduate school full-time versus part-time, or aid options that satisfy the needs of Black men with partners and other dependents.

A large number of Black male undergraduates aspire to earn graduate degrees, according to recent studies (Sax, 2008; Strayhorn, 2007), although we lose a significant number of them at critical junctures throughout the educational pipeline. To increase participation rates among this group at the graduate level, policies are needed that establish pipelines or pathways to and through graduate education. For instance, graduate departments might create programs that work with undergraduate departments or local school districts to provide early support and assistance to young Black men as they navigate through high school graduation, undergraduate courses, and the graduate school application process.

Interestingly, the mean GRE scores for Black men in the survey sample were lower, on average, than the national norms published by the ETS; in other words, Black men perform lower than their counterparts on the GRE, all sections considered. What does this mean for Black men when so many graduate departments place a premium on GRE scores during the admission decision-making process? The answer is that comparatively few Black men would qualify for admission to graduate school based on GRE scores alone, although they may have the requisite knowledge, skills, and dispositions to excel in graduate study. My opinion is that basing admissions decisions solely on GRE scores is poor wisdom, as a persuasive body of information has shown that graduate school success depends on myriad factors, such as learning motivation, financial support, self-efficacy, and time spent studying, to name a few (Gardner & Barnes, 2007; Strayhorn, 2010). Instead I advocate for a more holistic review process whereby graduate deans and faculty consider a host of factors that are associated with graduate student success, some of which were included in the current chapter: undergraduate preparation for graduate study, academic major, family and work commitments, motivation, and predisposition to scholarly activities and research, for example. Admissions policies, then, could be designed or revised to expand the criteria upon which decisions are made.

Recommendations for Practice

In this chapter I present new information from a multi-institutional survey of Black men in master's degree programs across the country. One key finding relates to the proportion of Black men who stop out at some point during their master's education, as well as the overrepresentation of married students among those who stop out. Results may reflect what happens when Black men in master's degree programs struggle to balance the demands of married life with the academic requirements of graduate school. To the extent that this is true, college student educators and graduate faculty might develop programs and outreach services to support such students. More information is needed to understand their specific needs, but they may likely benefit from childcare services, financial management workshops, conflict resolution strategies, study skills seminars, and even private audiences with Black men in similar situations who have successfully completed their degrees.

Investment of personal resources (e.g., time) in activities that prepare one for a graduate or professional role is important. Data from the survey suggest that time spent studying is important, although the amount of time devoted to such activities varied among the sample. Student affairs officers within graduate departments might consider these results when working with students. For instance, school officers might sponsor programs on study habits, note-taking strategies, and time management. Perhaps students need a place to study; graduate deans, department heads, and provosts might consider this point when designing physical spaces on campus. Institutions such as Virginia Tech and Washington State University recently have devoted considerable resources to building graduate student life centers that offer student housing, study rooms, computer labs, and even dining areas, which have proven to be effective in enhancing the graduate student communities on their campuses.

I close where I began: much more information is needed to understand the experiences of Black men in master's degree programs. Practitioners and scholars can respond to this recommendation by documenting their work with such students through reports, conference presentations, and publications ranging from theses to journal articles, chapters to book-length volumes. And as college educators implement the recommendations offered in this chapter, they should document their efforts and share the results of such initiatives with others through similar means. All of this effort will add to what we know about Black men in master's degree programs, which remains a noticeable gap in the current literature.

These recommendations hold promise for promoting and improving the status, distribution, and achievement of Black men in master's degree programs. When considering these and other strategies for influencing the factors that condition Black men's success in graduate school, I urge educators, administrators, and leaders to remember that institutional responses of this sort can be difficult to mount, but difficulty can be no excuse for retreat. Working together, we can enact policies and fashion effective educational practices that support the ability of Black men to master the curriculum, both formal and informal, that leads to earning a master's degree.

References

Advisory Board for the Research Councils. (1993). *Nature of the Ph.D.: A discussion document.* London: HMSO.

American Council on Education. (2007). *Minorities in higher education: Twenty-third annual status report.* Washington, DC: Author.

Austin, A. E., & McDaniels, M. (2006). Preparing the professoriate of the future: Graduate student socialization for faculty roles. In J. C. Smart (Ed.), *Higher education: Handbook for theory and research* (vol. 21, pp. 397–456). Netherlands: Springer.

Berelson, B. (1960). *Graduate education in the United States.* New York: McGraw-Hill.

Bowen, W. G., & Rudenstein, N. L. (1992). *In pursuit of the Ph.D.* Princeton, NJ: Princeton University Press.

Bragg, A. K. (1976). *The socialization process in higher education.* Washington, DC: American Association of Higher Education.

Braxton, J. M. (2000). Introduction: Reworking the student departure puzzle. In J. M. Braxton (Ed.), *Reworking the student departure puzzle* (pp. 1–8). Nashville: Vanderbilt University Press.

Brim, O. G. (1966). Socialization through the life cycle. In O. G. Brim & S. Wheeler (Eds.), *Socialization after childhood* (pp. 3–49). New York: John Wiley and Sons.

Burgess, R. G. (1997). The changing context of postgraduate education in the United Kingdom. In R. G. Burgess (Ed.), *Beyond the first degree: Graduate education, lifelong learning, and careers* (pp. 3–17). Buckingham, UK: Open University Press.

Clark, B. R. (Ed.). (1993). *The research foundations of graduate education.* Berkeley: University of California Press.

Conrad, C. F., Haworth, J. G., & Millar, S. B. (1993). *A silent success: Master's education in the United States.* Baltimore, MD: Johns Hopkins University Press.

Council of Graduate Schools (CGS). (2009). *Graduate enrollment and degrees: 1999 to 2009.* Washington, DC: Author.

Cuyjet, M. J. (2006). African American college men: Twenty-first-century issues and concerns. In M. J. Cuyjet & Associates (Eds.), *African American men in college* (pp. 3–23). San Francisco: Jossey-Bass.

Feldman, D. C. (1981). The multiple socialization of organization members. *Academy of Management Review, 6*(2), 309–318.

Gardner, S. K., & Barnes, B. J. (2007). Graduate student involvement: Socialization for the professional role. *Journal of College Student Development, 48*(4), 369–387.

Girves, J., & Wemmerus, V. (1988). Developing models of graduate student degree progress. *Journal of Higher Education, 59*(2), 163–189.

Golde, C. M., & Walker, G. E. (Eds.). (2006). *Envisioning the future of doctoral education: Preparing stewards of the discipline.* San Francisco: Jossey-Bass.

Holdaway, E. A. (1997). Quality issues in postgraduate education. In R. G. Burgess (Ed.), *Beyond the first degree: Graduate education, lifelong learning, and careers* (pp. 60–78). Buckingham, UK: Open University Press.

Jablin, F. M., & Miller, V. D. (1990). Interviews with applicant questioning behavior in employment interviews. *Management Communication Quarterly, 4*, 51–86.

LaPidus, J. B. (1997). Issues and themes in postgraduate education in the United States. In R. G. Burgess (Ed.), *Beyond the first degree: Graduate education, lifelong learning, and careers* (pp. 21–39). Buckingham, UK: Open University Press.

Luan, J., & Fenske, R. (1996). Financial aid, persistence, and degree completion in master's degree programs. *Journal of Student Financial Aid, 26*(1), 17–31.

National Science Board. (2006). *Science and engineering indicators, 2006* (2 vols.). Arlington, VA: National Science Foundation.

National Science Board. (2012). *Science and engineering indicators, 2012.* Arlington, VA: National Science Foundation.

Ott, M. D., Markewich, T. S., & Ochsner, N. L. (1984). Logit analysis of graduate student retention. *Research in Higher Education, 21*(4), 439–460.

Parker, C. A. (1977). On modeling reality. *Journal of College Student Personnel, 18*(5), 419–425.

Perna, L. W. (2004). Understanding the decision to enroll in graduate school: Sex and racial/ethnic group differences. *Journal of Higher Education, 75*(5), 487–527.

Poock, M. C. (1999). Students of color and doctoral programs: Factors influencing the application decision in higher education administration. *College and University, 74*(3), 2–7.

Sax, L. J. (2008). *Gender gap in college: Maximizing the developmental potential of women and men.* San Francisco: Jossey-Bass.

Strayhorn, T. L. (2005). More than money matters: An integrated model of graduate student persistence. *Dissertation Abstracts International, A66*(2), 519.

Strayhorn, T. L. (2007). Educational aspirations of Black millennials in college. *NASAP Journal, 10*(1), 20–34.

Strayhorn, T. L. (2009). African American male graduate students. In M. H. Howard-Hamilton, C. L. Morelon-Quainoo, S. D. Johnson, R. Winkle-Wagner, & L. Santiague (Eds.), *Standing on the outside looking in: Underrepresented students' experiences in advanced degree programs* (pp. 124–146). Sterling, VA: Stylus.

Strayhorn, T. L. (2010). Money matters: The influence of financial factors on gradu-ate student persistence. *Journal of Student Financial Aid, 40*(3), 4–25.

Strayhorn, T. L. (2011, April). *Quantifying the socialization process for Black male doctoral students and its influence on sense of belonging.* Paper presented at the annual meeting of the American Educational Research Association (AERA), New Orleans, LA.

Talbot, D. M. (1996). Master's students' perspectives on their graduate education regarding issues of diversity. *NASPA Journal, 33*, 163–178.

Thornton, R., & Nardi, R. M. (1975). The dynamics of role acquisition. *American Journal of Sociology, 80*, 870–885.

Tierney, W. G., & Rhoads, R. A. (1993). Postmodernism and critical theory in higher education: Implications for research and practice. In J. C. Smart (Ed.), *Higher education: Handbook of theory and research* (pp. 308–343). New York: Aga-thon.

Tinto, V. (1993). *Leaving college: Rethinking the causes and cures of student attrition* (2nd ed.). Chicago: University of Chicago Press.

U.S. Department of Education, National Center for Education Statistics. (2009, June). *The condition of education, 2009* (NCES Report No. 2009-081). Washing-ton, DC: U.S. Government Printing Office.

Wanous, J. P., Reichers, A. E., & Malik, S. D. (1984). Organizational socialization and group development: Toward an integrative perspective. *Academy of Manage-ment Review, 4*, 670–683.

Wegner, E. L. (1973). The effects of upward mobility: A study of working-status college students. *Sociology of Education, 46*(3), 263–279.

Weidman, J. C., Twale, D. J., & Stein, E. L. (2001). Socialization of graduate and professional students in higher education: A perilous passage? *ASHE-ERIC Higher Education Report 28*, 25–54.

Wood, J. L., & Turner, C. S. V. (2011). Black males and the community college: Student perspectives on faculty and academic success. *Community College Journal of Research & Practice, 35*, 1–17.

Zwick, R. (1991). *Factors contributing to persistence in graduate school.* Paper pre-sented at the annual meeting of the American Educational Research Association, Chicago.

8

IMPROVING ATTAINMENT, EXPERIENCES, AND CAREER OUTCOMES AMONG BLACK MALE STUDENTS IN DOCTORAL DEGREE PROGRAMS

Shaun R. Harper and Robert T. Palmer

Vanderbilt University was Ian's top choice for doctoral study, but he was denied admission. Despite numerous indicators of academic accomplishment (including 3.5 and 3.9 cumulative grade point averages in his bachelor's and master's degree programs, respectively) and strong advocacy from faculty in the program to which he applied, the dean at Vanderbilt's Peabody College of Education deemed Ian's Graduate Record Exam (GRE) scores too low for admission. Ian took the GRE four times, once upon the request of the department chair at Peabody; 990 was his highest score. The faculty petitioned the dean on his behalf, but she was unwilling to see beyond his GRE score. It was her sole basis for disregarding the will of the faculty to admit this applicant. Sadly, the African American assistant professor whom Ian was most interested in working with was denied tenure at Vanderbilt that same year; she was the only faculty member of color in the department. Perhaps it was best that Vanderbilt rejected Ian. He was offered admission to three other doctoral programs, including one at Indiana

University where he had recently completed his master's degree. He chose to stay at Indiana. Three years later, Ian earned a Ph.D. from the fifth-highest-ranked program in his field.

Ian's three-year doctoral journey has several noteworthy features. First was the representation of students of color in his program. The School of Education at Indiana University has a storied history of consistently attracting and enrolling African American students to its Higher Education and Student Affairs (HESA) doctoral program, and Ian's enrollment year was no different. He was never the only person of color in any of his courses. In fact, the year he graduated, so did five other HESA doctoral students of color. Throughout their time in the program, these and other students of color worked collaboratively on research, studied together, read and offered feedback on each other's papers and dissertations, and provided tremendous social and emotional support to each other, all of which was essential in a predominantly White college town. Surprisingly, their time together in Bloomington was fun; lifelong friendships and collaborative relationships were born there.

There was one African American female professor in the HESA program when Ian started; another was hired at the end of Ian's first year. The one Latina assistant professor was denied tenure; she and Ian were close. Every male faculty member in the department was White; there were only two or three Black male faculty members in the entire School of Education. Notwithstanding the shortage of faculty of color, White professors were particularly good at supporting Black HESA students. Faculty members neither dissuaded nor deemed unimportant the pursuit of research topics pertaining to people of color. Put differently, Black students in the Ph.D. program were not told that studying Black things would somehow disadvantage them or undermine their academic credibility. Hence, most students of color conducted research on race and equity-related topics about which they authentically cared. Ian's dissertation was on Black male undergraduates; others wrote about Black cultural centers, desegregation policies at historically Black colleges and universities (HBCUs), African American presidents of predominantly White institutions (PWIs), the intersection of race and gender for tenured Black women professors at PWIs, and a range of other topics.

His speedy time to doctoral degree attainment (three years), eight publications and 25 national conference presentations, and 3.87 GPA are some quantitative indicators of Ian's success in his Ph.D. program. While none of Ian's publications were coauthored with professors in his program, they nevertheless supported him by offering feedback on manuscripts prior to submission and by fostering a culture in which HESA students frequently collaborated with each other on research, conference presentations, and publications. Upon completion of his doctorate, Ian received five job offers and one of the most coveted national dissertation of the year awards. Eight years later, he earned tenure at an Ivy League university, in one of the 10 highest-ranked programs in his field. The Indiana University School of Education presented Ian its Distinguished Alumni Award 11 years after earning his Ph.D. At every juncture in his career, Ian's dissertation chair, a White man (one of the five most-cited higher education researchers), proved to be one of his most reliable advocates and supporters.

Generally speaking, we believe every Black male doctoral student should have the kind of experience Ian had—but unfortunately, most do not. In this chapter we juxtapose aspects of Ian's doctoral journey with statistics from the U.S. Department of Education and the Educational Testing Service (ETS) as well as with insights from published research on the experiences of doctoral students of color. Specifically, we highlight the persistent underrepresentation of Black men among doctoral degree–seeking students and doctoral degree recipients, a range of racialized experiences in Ph.D. programs at PWIs, and the underproduction of Black male professors. We end the chapter with recommendations for replicating the best of Ian's experience among Black men in doctoral programs at universities across the United States. We focus mostly on students in Doctor of Philosophy (Ph.D.) programs, but occasionally include data about Doctor of Medicine (M.D.), Doctor of Dental Surgery (D.D.S.), Doctor of Education (Ed.D.), and a range of other doctoral degree programs.

Enrollment, Testing, and Attainment Trends

Edward Alexander Bouchet graduated from Yale University with a doctorate in physics in 1876; he was the first Black person to attain a doctoral degree from a postsecondary institution in the United States (Felder, 2015). Nineteen years later, W. E. B. Du Bois became the first Black student to earn a Ph.D. from Harvard University. In an 1891 letter to Rutherford B. Hayes, the 19th president of the United States, Du Bois noted,

> I find men willing to help me get thro' cheap theological schools, I find men willing to help me use my hands before I got my brains in working order. . . but I never found a man willing to help me get a Harvard Ph.D. (as cited in Lewis, 1993, p. 126)

Black men have certainly gained more access to doctoral education since Bouchet and Du Bois broke color barriers in the Ivy League. However, they have been disproportionately located in some fields (e.g., education and

Figure 8.1 Enrollments in Postbaccalaureate Degree Programs, 1980–2010

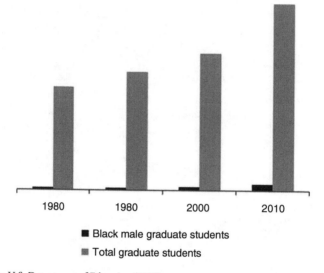

■ Black male graduate students

▧ Total graduate students

Source: U.S. Department of Education (2013).

social services) and persistently underrepresented in others. In 1988, Black men and women comprised less than 2% of doctoral students in history, physics, chemistry, engineering, biological sciences, mathematics, computer sciences, and earth sciences (Bowen & Rudenstine, 1992); these same trends held through the 1990s and into the 2000s (Nettles & Millett, 2006).

Black male student enrollment patterns in graduate programs between 1980 and 2010 are presented in Figure 8.1. They comprised 2.3%, 2.0%, 2.7%, and 3.6% of degree seekers in master's, professional, and doctoral degree programs at the four time points, respectively. Of the 45,260 applicants to doctoral programs in medicine in 2012, only 2.7% were Black men (Association of American Medical Colleges, 2011a). Table 8.1 shows their attainment in doctoral programs (across all fields and disciplines) over those same three decades. As indicated, Black men were 2.3% of doctoral degree recipients in 2011, the same as 30 years prior. Moreover, the sex gap among Black students at other levels of postsecondary education is also found in doctoral education and has widened over time. Women were 43.3% and 64.9% of Black doctoral degree earners in 1981 and 2011, respectively (U.S. Department of Education, 2013). While White men's share of doctoral degrees has dropped slightly, they still drastically outnumber men of color (see Figure 8.2).

TABLE 8.1
Doctoral Degree Attainment, 1981–2011

Year	Total Doctorates Awarded	Doctorates to Black Men	
	N	*n*	*%*
1981	97,281	2,206	2.3
1991	105,547	1,991	1.9
2001	119,585	2,655	2.2
2011	163,765	3,836	2.3

Source: U.S. Department of Education (2013).

Figure 8.2 Doctoral Degree Attainment Among Men by Race, 1981–2011

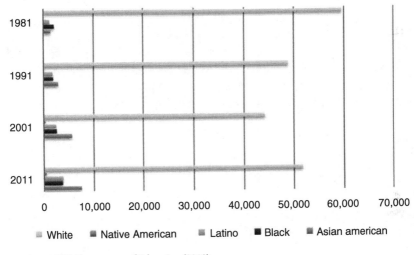

Source: U.S. Department of Education (2013).

The underrepresentation of Black men in doctoral programs is largely attributable to their low attainment rates at earlier junctures in the post-secondary educational pipeline. But among those who endeavor to persist beyond the baccalaureate, the GRE, Medical College Admission Test (MCAT), Graduate Management Admission Test (GMAT), Law School Admission Test (LSAT), and other standardized tests often limit their access to graduate and professional degree programs (Griffin, Muñiz, & Espinosa, 2012; Harper & Porter, 2012; Kidder, 2001; Scott & Shaw, 1985). Michael T. Nettles and Catherine Millett, scholars at the Educational Testing Service (the manufacturer of the GRE), published a book based on data from the largest survey of doctoral students ever conducted. Analyses of GRE scores by race, ethnicity, sex, and field of study raised questions concerning their ability to predict student aptitude in doctoral education. Nettles and Millett therefore concluded the following: "GRE scores might as well be forgotten, because they tend to lose their association with much that matters in the doctoral process, such as research productivity and mentoring relationships" (2006, p. 206). Despite this, the overwhelming majority of U.S. universities rely on them in doctoral admission processes.

Among Black students who aspire to earn degrees beyond the baccalaureate, many have comparatively low GRE scores. In fact, Nettles and Millett (2006) found that Blacks across five broad fields of study — education, engineering, humanities, science and mathematics, and social sciences — scored lowest among all racial groups on the GRE. A 2013 ETS report indicated that Black men accounted for 2.4% of all U.S. citizens who took the GRE that year. Men constituted 29.3% of the 27,388 Black test takers between July 2012 and June 2013 (Educational Testing Service, 2013). Shown in Table 8.2 are racial differences in GRE scores among male examinees; accordingly, Black men scored lowest on the verbal and quantitative sections. In their analyses of data from the 2011 *U.S. News & World Report* ranking of the top 40 schools of education in the United States, Harper and Porter (2012) found that the mean total GRE score at these schools was 322 points higher than the average score ETS reported for Black men.

Similar racial differences exist among applicants to medical doctorate programs. In 2011, Black students' MCAT scores were lowest among all racial/ethnic groups except Puerto Rican examinees (Association of American

TABLE 8.2

Racial Differences in GRE Scores Among Men (U.S. Citizens), 2012–2013

Racial Group	Verbal		Quantitative	
	Mean	*SD*	*Mean*	*SD*
American Indian	152.3	7.5	149.5	7.8
Asian American	153.7	7.8	156.3	8.1
Black	147.4	7.6	144.8	7.4
Mexican American	151.3	7.2	149.4	7.5
Puerto Rican	150.4	7.8	148.1	7.7
Other Latino	151.9	7.5	150.0	7.7
White	155.6	7.0	153.3	7.4

Source: Educational Testing Service (2013).

Medical Colleges, 2011b). Low scores on pointless standardized admission tests, combined with haphazard graduate school recruitment practices, help explain, at least in part, why so few Black male bachelor's degree recipients ultimately attain doctorates. In 2011 the median salary for men with doctorates was $100,800, nearly three times more than men with bachelor's degrees; 25% of male doctoral degree completers earned more than $150,000 annually (Baum, Ma, & Payea, 2013). For myriad reasons (including, but not limited to, the wealth that typically accompanies attainment), attracting more Black men to doctoral programs is imperative. But fostering the conditions to ensure completion and success once they enroll is also important.

Racialized Experiences in Doctoral Education

Palmer, Wood, Dancy, and Strayhorn (2014) synthesized decades of research on Black male students in U.S. higher education. Similarly, Harper (2014) catalogued the scholarship produced on Black male collegians between 1997 and 2012; several research and policy reports, 11 books, and more than 60 peer-reviewed academic journal articles were published during the 15-year period. Literature reviewed in both Palmer et al. (2014) and Harper (2014) focused almost entirely on undergraduates, as very little has been written specifically about the experiences and outcomes of Black male graduate students, especially those in doctoral degree programs. Most research produced over the past two decades has appeared in unpublished doctoral dissertations (see Table 8.3); these studies were conducted in predominantly White university contexts. Despite an 82% increase in doctoral degree attainment among Black graduate students at HBCUs between 1996 and 2006 (Redd, 2008), Palmer, Hilton, and Fountaine (2012) noted, "Research about the experiences of graduate students at HBCUs is basically nonexistent" (p. 2). Notwithstanding the paucity of scholarship specifically pertaining to them across all institution types, it is plausible that much of what has been written broadly about graduate students of color captures certain dimensions of Black men's experiences in doctoral education, particularly at PWIs. Though not the sole focus, Black men are often among the participants in many studies of doctoral students of color.

Harper (2013) defined *onlyness* as "the psychoemotional burden of having to strategically navigate a racially politicized space occupied by few peers, role models, and guardians from one's same racial or ethnic group" (p. 189). Onlyness is an inescapable reality for many doctoral students of color in particular fields, as they are the only or one of very few non-White people in their programs and departments (Adams, 1993; Castellanos, Gloria, & Kamimura, 2006; Cuádraz, 2011; Gasman, Hirschfeld, & Vultaggio,

TABLE 8.3
Dissertations on Black Male Doctoral Students, 1993–2013

Author	Year	University	Dissertation Title
Adrienne Morgan	2013	University of Rochester	*Critical Race Theory: A Counter-narrative of African American Male Medical Students Attending Predominately White Medical Schools*
Herman Horn	2012	Texas State University	*The Stories of Eight Black Males Pursuing Doctoral Degrees Examined Through the Lenses of Critical Race Theory: Don't Believe the Hype; Don't Live the Hype*
Kimberly Matthews	2012	Virginia Commonwealth University	*Persistence to Doctoral Completion of African American Men at Predominately White Universities in One Mid-Atlantic State*
Willette Burnham	2010	University of South Carolina	*Black Males in Medical School: An Exploratory Analysis of Factors Related to Persistence*
Dennis Chambers	2010	Teachers College, Columbia University	*Understanding How African American Males Make Meaning of the Experience of Pursuing Their Doctoral Degree*
Matais D. Pouncil	2009	University of California, Irvine	*Acting Black: Black Men and Doctoral Dissertation Completion*
Denise M. Clay	2008	University of Oklahoma	*A Qualitative Inquiry Into the Motivation of African-American Males to Complete the Doctorate*
Ted N. Ingram	2007	Indiana University	*From Challenged to Triumphant: Factors Contributing to African American Male Doctoral Students' Persistence at Predominantly White Institutions*
Michael Fleming	2005	University of California, Los Angeles	*The Subtlety and Fragility of Educational Achievement: The African-American Male Path to the Ph.D.*
Charles Leonard	1997	Teachers College, Columbia University	*The Black Male Experience in Graduate Education: Declining Participation*
William Respress	1997	East Tennessee State University	*Perceptions of African-American Males Regarding Factors Supporting Doctoral Completion in Colleges of Education*

Source: ProQuest Dissertations and Theses Database (formerly Dissertation Abstracts).

2008; González, 2007; Griffin, Muñiz, & Espinosa, 2012; Solórzano, 1998; Thomas, 1987). This experience often requires Black doctoral students to search beyond their academic disciplines (and often outside of academe) for supportive same-race peers, faculty mentors, and research collaborators (Gay, 2004; Johnson-Bailey, 2004; Patton, 2009; Patton & Harper, 2003). Gay argued that being the only person of color in a graduate program requires emotional energy that could be better invested into academic pursuits. She added that many large research universities are geographically located in contexts that are not racially, culturally, or linguistically diverse, thereby exacerbating feelings of onlyness. The title of Alfredo Miradé's (1988) essay, "I Never Had a Mentor: Reflections of a Chicano Sociologist," conveys an ongoing byproduct of onlyness for many contemporary doctoral students of color.

Researchers (e.g., Felder Thompson, 2008; Lundy-Wagner, Vultaggio, & Gasman, 2013; Perna, 2001; Strayhorn, 2008; Strayhorn, Williams, Tillman-Kelly, & Suddeth, 2013) have documented the important role that HBCUs play in preparing Black undergraduates for doctoral study and subsequent faculty careers, particularly in science, technology, engineering, and mathematics (STEM) fields (Gary, 2008; Palmer, Maramba, Gasman, & Lloyd, 2013; Perna et al., 2009; Perna et al., 2010). According to data from the National Science Foundation, over 40% of Black doctoral degree recipients in the late 1970s earned their bachelor's degrees at HBCUs; that number was approximately 33% in 2006 (Burrelli & Rapoport, 2008). Between 1997 and 2006, HBCUs were 20 of the top 50 baccalaureate degree origin institutions of Black doctoral degree earners. Put differently, 40% of Blacks with doctorates earned their bachelor's degrees from HBCUs. The overwhelming majority of these HBCU alumni attained doctorates from predominantly White research universities. Reportedly, encouragement from and substantive engagement with faculty members at Black colleges greatly influence students' decisions to pursue doctorates in STEM fields (Gary, 2008, 2013; Perna et al., 2009, 2010). McMickens (2011) found that HBCU professors also teach undergraduates to anticipate and effectively respond to racism and assorted racialized experiences (including onlyness) that they are likely to encounter in graduate studies at PWIs.

The literature on racialized experiences in graduate school includes first-hand autobiographical accounts, mostly from women professors of color. For example, in her book *Talking Back: Thinking Feminist, Thinking Black*, bell hooks (1989) devoted a chapter to reflecting on her graduate school experience. hooks reflected on how difficult it was for her and other students of color to find professors who were not racist, as insults on their intelligence were commonplace. Faculty members told racist and sexist jokes, publicly ridiculed students of color whom they believed were stupid (which was just about all of them), and created specialized barriers to doctoral degree attainment for Blacks and Latinos. Gloria Ladson-Billings (1997) wrote about her experience at Stanford, where there were no Black professors in her program. She and other Black students had little support; their research interests in Black topics were often discouraged. "I was not prepared for the sense of alienation I would feel as an African American woman," Ladson-Billings recollected (p. 56). Laura I. Rendón (1992) recalled an encounter with a White graduate student at the University of Michigan who said to her, "You know, Laura, you're pretty smart. I'll have to admit that when I first met you, I thought you were kind of dumb" (p. 61). Rendón also reflected on feeling overwhelmed by the number of White students who had attended undergraduate institutions that were much more prestigious than the one from which she graduated. People also questioned the importance of her interest in studying community colleges, a sector of higher education that provides tremendous access to Latinos and other persons of color. Geneva Gay's (2004) article includes insights from her own graduate school experience, as well as observations of students of color with whom she has interacted as a professor. These and other women of color have offered powerful details about the experiential realities with which many doctoral students of color must contend at PWIs. Interestingly, the literature does not include many firsthand narratives from men of color about their doctoral experiences.

In his study of 66 Chicana/o Ford Foundation predoctoral, dissertation, and postdoctoral fellowship recipients, Solórzano (1998) uncovered several racialized themes from their doctoral experiences. Several comments, classroom interactions, and other encounters made these students feel like they did not belong in their doctoral programs; many felt their professors held low expectations of them. Participants in Solórzano's study reported having their research interests invalidated by faculty and being told that their topics on people/communities of color were too narrow. They also were constantly confronted with racial microaggressions, subtle racial insults that are seemingly innocuous. One example is from a Chicano male who was told, "You're not like the rest of them" (Solórzano, 1998, p. 130). Being presumed to have attended perceivably inferior educational institutions prior to enrolling in graduate school, being constantly mistaken for the other student of color in the program, and being expected to be the spokesperson on all race-related matters are among the many racial microaggressions with which doctoral students of color must routinely contend (Felder & Barker, 2013; Gay, 2004; Gildersleeve, Croom, & Vasquez, 2011; Griffin, Muñiz, & Espinosa, 2012; Solórzano, 1998). Because they are often small, covert comments (as opposed to a more overt, old-fashioned brand of racism), microaggressions can be likened to death by a thousand cuts—an individual one stings, but the cumulative sum of them is quite injurious. Microaggressions and other forms of racism compel many doctoral students of color to ask themselves, "Am I going crazy?" (Gildersleeve et al., 2011, p. 100).

The racialized experiences that doctoral students in Truong and Museus's (2012) study reported extend far beyond microaggressions; the authors characterized their situations as "racial trauma." Participants experienced the following symptoms as a result of the stressful environments created for them at the universities they were attending for doctoral studies:

> Depression, headaches, anxiety, low self-esteem, humiliation, upset stomach, chest pains, tunnel vision, ulcers, back pains, nightmares, loss of appetite or overeating, nausea, shortness of breath, weeping, vomiting, fatigue, increased heart rate and hypertension, anger and frustration, difficulty concentrating, lack of productivity and motivation, sleep deprivation, and recounting specific racist situations days, weeks, months, and years after they occur. (Truong & Museus, 2012, p. 228)

After conducting extensive medical tests, physicians attributed these health issues to stress. Participants said the racism they were experiencing in their doctoral programs was their predominant (sometimes sole) source of stress. Truong's (2010) dissertation is replete with stories of five Black men and 21 other students of color being sexualized and sexually harassed, wrongly accused of theft, yelled at by faculty, and publicly insulted and disregarded in their doctoral programs. Many also had their ideas and actual work stolen by peers and professors. Indeed, these were traumatizing experiences. To protect their sanity and complete their doctorates, these students had to figure out how best to respond to these situations; switching advisers, seeking medical treatment, transferring programs or universities, documenting and filing formal complaints with their institutions, and reconstructing their dissertation committees were among the 17 responses to racial trauma Truong and Museus (2012) highlighted.

In her study of Black doctoral students and Black doctoral degree recipients, Ellis (2001) observed some interesting gender trends. For instance, Black men who had completed doctorates reported the highest level of satisfaction with their experiences. Students who were presently enrolled, regardless of sex, were dissatisfied with the inequitable distribution of research opportunities, support from their faculty advisers, being left on their own to develop teaching competencies, the absence of community in their programs and departments, and toxic racial climates. Despite this, Ellis found that Black men integrated into their doctoral programs with greater ease than did their same-race female counterparts. "The Black males may have been aware of the threat some Whites perceive them to be and, therefore, they may consequently have made more attempts at not being perceived as problem students," Ellis suggested (2011, p. 38). The comparative ease with which Black men integrate into doctoral programs at PWIs does not seem to produce significantly better career outcomes for them. Specifically, there is no evidence that Black men actually profit more from the Ph.D. process in ways that better position them for faculty positions.

Socializing Black Male Ph.D. Students to the Professoriate

Socialization is the process by which a Ph.D. student comes to learn and understand the values, norms, rules, and rewards of academe (Austin, 2002). Austin and McDaniels (2006) suggested that this process occurs on three levels: socialization to the role of becoming a graduate student, socialization to academic life and work, and socialization to one's specific discipline or field. Additionally, Gardner (2007) added that doctoral students are socialized to the culture of the broader institution in which their graduate programs are situated, a context sometimes fraught with racial climate problems that undermine sense of belonging in one's program or department (Griffin, Muñiz, & Espinosa, 2012).

Faculty advisers play the most important role in the doctoral student socialization process, as they possess knowledge about what is required for success in the program and the larger academic discipline or field (Barnes, Williams, & Stassen, 2012; Shore, 2014; Zhao, Golde, & McCormick, 2007). Notwithstanding, women and students of color, in comparison to White doctoral students, report less support, guidance, validation, and mentoring from their advisers (Felder, 2010; Felder & Barker, 2013; Gardner, 2008a; Gasman et al., 2008; Gay, 2004; González, 2006; Noy & Ray, 2012; Patton, 2009; Patton & Harper, 2003). They also tend to be afforded fewer opportunities to collaborate with professors on research and publications. Brown, Davis, and McClendon (1999) asserted that one common myth in graduate education is that only faculty of color can effectively mentor and advise students of color. This myth exacerbates racial and gender disproportionality in service (particularly advising) among professors at PWIs (Griffin, 2012; Griffin & Reddick, 2011; Turner, González, & Wood, 2008), with faculty of color often doing significantly more service than their White colleagues.

Gardner (2008b) highlighted the important role that peers play in the socialization process, as interactions among students can affect sense of belonging, as well as access to information about resources and opportunities. According to Gardner (2008b), doctoral students often spend 60 to 70 hours per week interacting with each other. But given the racial makeup of most doctoral programs and the aforementioned issues of onlyness that many students of color experience at PWIs, White students often profit more from their White peers. Black graduate students in Gasman et al.'s (2008) study characterized their relationships with White peers as cordial, but not close and mutually beneficial. Participants in the Shavers and Moore (2014) study talked about wearing an "academic mask," which entailed having to constantly prove their academic competence to combat negative stereotypes that White peers had about Blacks. These Black female doctoral students "constantly monitored their language, grammar, interactions, and outside appearance to ensure that they always appeared professional. Many also had a heightened awareness of the stereotypes for Black women, and felt a strong need to control how members in their departments perceived them" (Shavers & Moore, 2014, p. 398).

Departmental cultures can enhance or hinder the doctoral students' socialization experiences. Carlone and Johnson (2007) studied successful women of color in science departments from their undergraduate studies through graduate schools and into science careers. Nearly half the participants in their study reported having experienced racialized and gendered moments in which their identities as scientists were disrupted and insufficiently nurtured. Some felt that faculty, teaching assistants, and fellow research group members believed they were only admitted to doctoral programs because they were people of color, not because they were competent scientists. As such, these women did not receive the same opportunities or affirmations as their White peers, and they often felt invisible in their programs. Other studies have found that doctoral students of color generally (Gardner, 2008a) and Blacks in particular (Felder, 2015) often feel like they do not fit the mold of their particular programs and departments. An insufficient sense of belonging helps explain why doctoral students, regardless of race, experience higher levels of stress and depression than do undergraduates (Gardner & Barker, 2015), as well as why approximately half of all students who start doctoral programs never finish (Golde, 2005; Lovitts, 2001).

The socialization process during doctoral study affects career aspirations and helps partly explain why so few Ph.D. recipients of color pursue professorships (Gibbs & Griffin, 2013; Jaeger, Haley, Ampaw, & Levin, 2013). This trend is both raced and gendered, with women of color being most severely affected. But even among men, inequities exist. Table 8.4 presents the distribution of men in tenure-track faculty positions by rank and race at U.S. colleges and universities. The higher the rank, the less represented are Blacks and other men of color.

To be fair, these representation patterns are largely attributable to a complex cocktail of structural forces that disproportionately disadvantage Black

TABLE 8.4

Full-Time Male Faculty at U.S. Colleges and Universities by Race and Rank, 2011

Rank	Racial Group	%
Professor	American Indian	0.3
	Asian American	8.9
	Black	3.1
	Latino	2.7
	White	82.4
Associate Professor	American Indian	0.3
	Asian American	10.2
	Black	4.9
	Latino	3.8
	White	76.3
Assistant Professor	American Indian	0.3
	Asian American	12.3
	Black	5.1
	Latino	4.2
	White	66.4

Note: Percentages do not total 100 due to the exclusion of multiracial faculty, those who are not U.S. citizens, and those for whom race was unreported.

Source: U.S. Department of Education (2013).

male students from preschool through Ph.D. attainment. Hence, Harper and Porter (2012) contend that increasing the number of Black male Ph.D. recipients would create a larger cadre of Black male researchers to study factors, conditions, and policies that undermine Black male student success at all levels of education. They acknowledged the need for more Black male teachers in P–12 schools, but also argued the following: "Often overlooked in efforts to attract more Black men to [classroom teaching] roles is their underrepresentation among scholars who conduct research, publish books and scholarly articles, and are consulted as experts on education policy and practice" (Harper and Porter, 2012, p. 8). The 304 Black undergraduate men in Harper and Davis's (2012) study believed that earning the Ph.D. in education would enable them to research and ultimately fix some of the most vexing equity issues that affect Black communities. They were interested in earning doctorates, most wanted to become professors. In light of these young men's aspirations, several questions are worth considering: How many will encounter onlyness, microaggressions, and racial trauma during doctoral study? How many will enjoy validating interactions with peers and faculty, collaborate with their doctoral advisers on research and publications, and profit from other experiences that effectively socialize them to the professoriate? How many will ultimately become tenure-track assistant professors and persist through promotion to the highest professorial rank?

Replicating the Best of Ian's Doctoral Experience

Ian's experience at Indiana University was not perfect, yet it was substantively better than what the literature consistently reports about Blacks and other doctoral students of color at PWIs. The tenor of Ian's narrative is both hopeful and instructive. We are unconvinced that his is the only positive story to be told. During the 2011–2012 school year, U.S. colleges and universities conferred 4,108 doctorates to Black men (U.S. Department of Education, 2013). Surely, some had experiences that were at least somewhat consistent with Ian's. As researchers and others attempt to explore and document more about Black men's trajectories to and through doctoral degree programs, we caution against the one-sidedness often evidenced in research about Black male students at other levels of education. That is, deficits, disparities, and despair often receive all the attention at the expense of more success-focused narratives. Here are examples of three researchable questions from which much could be learned:

- What compelled 4,108 Black men to apply to doctoral programs?
- What factors enabled these men to persist and ultimately earn their doctorates, despite their encounters with onlyness, racial microaggressions, and other previously documented racial issues?
- Among the 2011–2012 doctoral graduates who have become tenure-track faculty members, how did they manage to compete successfully for professorships?

Ian's narrative proves that questions like these are worthy of pursuit.

Ian's academic performance in his doctoral program and subsequent career success illuminate the flawed predictive ability of standardized admission tests. Nettles and Millett (2006) cautioned against the misuse of the GRE in doctoral admissions; specifically, they argued that the exam should be treated as one of many variables in the process. Moreover, the GRE is only intended to predict grades in one's first year of graduate study. Vanderbilt rejected Ian on the sole basis of his GRE score; the dean's stance was clearly and repeatedly conveyed to him. Like Ian, we know dozens (perhaps hundreds) of Black men who have performed exceptionally in Ph.D. programs at top research universities and achieved impressive levels of career success, despite their low GRE scores. These men are our colleagues, research collaborators, former and current doctoral advisees, role models, and friends; several contributed chapters to this book. We, too, are among them. Given this, we urge faculty members, department chairs, deans, and anyone else who has input in the process to base admission decisions on stronger indicators of academic accomplishment, and less on standardized test scores that "tend to lose their association with much that matters in the doctoral process, such as research productivity and mentoring relationships" (Nettles & Millett, 2006, p. 206).

Peers played a pivotal role in Ian's doctoral journey; having other Black students there greatly enriched his experience. As noted, Indiana University has consistently attracted Black students to its Higher Education and Student Affairs Ph.D. Program. It also has a great reputation for graduating Blacks who move on to rewarding careers as professors, high-level college administrators, and association executives. The College of Education at the University of Illinois has a similar reputation for its record of producing stellar Black Ph.D. recipients. We believe the cultures that produce these outcomes can be replicated elsewhere. Noteworthy is that education is the field in which most Blacks earn doctorates. However, we think that any program at any university in any field can amass a reputation for rigorously recruiting, enrolling, engaging, respectfully treating, effectively socializing, and timely graduating Black students who subsequently go on to prominent positions in their respective fields. Strong partnerships with HBCUs and other minority-serving institutions can help graduate programs at PWIs easily identify talented prospective students. Furthermore, pipeline initiatives like the Grad Prep Academy described in Harper and Porter's (2012) report can help PWIs identify promising Black undergraduate men and strategically prepare them for admission to top graduate schools. Even though two thirds of Black male undergraduates who start college do not graduate (Harper, 2014; Palmer et al., 2014), we know for sure that several among the one third who persist through baccalaureate degree completion could be recruited more aggressively to doctoral programs. PWIs must be willing, though, to look past standardized test scores that reveal little about one's potential for academic success beyond the first year.

Published research repeatedly makes note of doctoral students of color being discouraged from pursuing intellectual interests related to persons and communities of color. These students are routinely told that those topics are devalued in the academy; thus, many fear they will be pigeonholed and otherwise penalized. That was not the case for Ian and other Black Ph.D. students at Indiana. None of them had trouble finding jobs because their dissertations were on topics pertaining to Black education. They all became successful. Our nation needs more scholars who commit themselves to researching and developing sophisticated responses to vexing issues that disproportionately disadvantage communities of color. To be clear, we are not arguing that only Black people can or should study these issues. What we are saying is that our society will be stronger if a larger supply of Black Ph.D. recipients were available to research inequities that have affected them, their families, and their communities. Faculty members across all fields should spend more time teaching Ph.D. students how to conduct methodologically rigorous research that will ultimately reduce inequities, instead of investing energies into dissuading smart people of color from pursuing topics that inspired many of them to pursue doctorates.

There are too few faculty members of color at PWIs across all ranks, especially at the full professor level (the power epicenter of the professoriate). More were needed when Ian applied to Vanderbilt and enrolled at Indiana. More are presently needed at these two universities and other PWIs across the nation. Recruiting more Black men and other students of color to Ph.D. programs and effectively socializing them to faculty roles will help expand the pool of professors of color. On its own, diversifying the faculty is an insufficient approach to increasing sense of belonging, enhancing academic success, and facilitating productive career transitions among students of color. Also needed are more efforts to increase the cultural competence of White professors given that they constitute the overwhelming majority of faculty members across all ranks. Supporting students of color, collaborating with them on research projects, publishing articles with them, and so on cannot be the sole responsibility of faculty of color. Moreover, raising consciousness among White faculty about their stereotypes, communication of low expectations, inequitable distribution of collaborative opportunities, and use of racial microaggressions is also essential. Ian's faculty mentor and dissertation chair was a White man. More White professors should assume responsibility for the success and career development of students of color in doctoral programs.

While Ian is not the only Black man to have ever positively experienced doctoral study, a substantial body of evidence confirms that his experience is less common than it should be. In light of the barriers experienced at every juncture of education—from preschool through postsecondary education—we think it unfortunate that some Black male students persist to Ph.D. programs only to be met with suspicion concerning their academic aptitude, stereotypes about who they are, discouragement of their research interests, and insufficient investment into their personal, academic, and professional development. Also appalling to us is that an otherwise extraordinary Black man who might discover some breakthrough that revolutionizes our world will be denied the opportunity to pursue a doctorate simply because his standardized test scores are low. Had Vanderbilt been the only university to which Ian applied, who knows if our nation would have ever benefitted from his important scholarly contributions? Fortunately, faculty at Indiana University did not misuse Ian's GRE scores in the admission process. They fostered conditions that enabled him and other Black students to succeed in the HESA Ph.D. program and beyond.

References

Adams, H. G. (1993). *Focusing on the campus milieu: A guide for enhancing the graduate school climate*. South Bend, IN: University of Notre Dame, National Consortium for Graduate Degrees for Minorities in Engineering and Science.

Association of American Medical Colleges. (2011a). *Table 16: Applicants to U.S. medical schools by race and ethnicity, selected combinations within sex, 2003–2012*. Retrieved from https://www.aamc.org/download/321492/data/2012factstable16.pdf

Association of American Medical Colleges. (2011b). *Table 19: MCAT scores and GPAs for applicants and matriculants to U.S. medical schools by race and ethnicity, 2011*. Retrieved from https://www.aamc.org/download/161696/data/table19.pdf

Austin, A. E. (2002). Preparing the next generation of faculty: Graduate school as socialization to the academic career. *Journal of Higher Education, 73*(1), 94–122.

Austin, A. E., & McDaniels, M. (2006). Preparing the professoriate of the future: Graduate student socialization for faculty roles. In J. C. Smart (Ed.), *Higher education: Handbook of theory and research* (vol. 21, pp. 397–456). Netherlands: Springer.

Barnes, B. J., Williams, E. A., & Stassen, M. L. A. (2012). Dissecting doctoral advising: A comparison of students' experiences across disciplines. *Journal of Further and Higher Education, 36*(3), 309–331.

Baum, S., Ma, J., & Payea, K. (2013). *Education pays, 2013: The benefits of higher education for individuals and society*. New York: College Board.

Bowen, W. G., & Rudenstine, N. L. (1992). *In pursuit of the Ph.D.* Princeton, NJ: Princeton University Press.

Brown, M. C., II, Davis, G. L., & McClendon, S. A. (1999). Mentoring graduate students of color: Myths, models, and modes. *Peabody Journal of Education, 74*(2), 105–118.

Burrelli, J., & Rapoport, A. (2008). *Role of HBCUs as baccalaureate-origin institutions of Black S&E doctorate recipients*. Washington, DC: National Science Foundation.

Carlone, H. B., & Johnson, A. (2007). Understanding the science experiences of successful women of color: Science identity as an analytic lens. *Journal of Research in Science Teaching, 44*(8), 1187–1218.

Castellanos, J., Gloria, A. M., & Kamimura, M. (Eds.). (2006). *The Latina/o pathway to the Ph.D.: Abriendo caminos.* Sterling, VA: Stylus.

Cuádraz, G. H. (2011). From doctoral students to faculty: Chicanas' articulation with trauma in academe. In G. Jean-Marie & Lloyd-Jones (Eds.), *Women of color in higher education: Turbulent past, promising future* (pp. 195–216). Bingley, UK: Emerald.

Educational Testing Service. (2013). *A snapshot of the individuals who took the GRE revised general test, July 2012–June 2013.* Princeton, NJ: Author.

Ellis, E. M. (2001). The impact of race and gender on graduate school socialization, satisfaction with doctoral study, and commitment to degree completion. *Western Journal of Black Studies, 25*(1), 30–45.

Felder, P. (2010). On doctoral student development: Exploring faculty mentoring in the shaping of African American doctoral student success. *Qualitative Report, 15*(2), 455–474.

Felder, P. P. (2015). Edward A. Bouchet: A model for understanding African Americans and their doctoral experience. *Journal of African American Studies, 19*(1), 3–17.

Felder, P. P., & Barker, M. J. (2013). Extending Bell's concept of interest convergence: A framework for understanding the African American doctoral student experience. *International Journal of Doctoral Studies, 8*, 1–20.

Felder Thompson, P. (2008). On firm foundations: African American Black college graduates and their doctoral student development in the Ivy League. In M. Gasman & C. L. Tudico (Eds.), *Historically Black colleges and universities: Triumphs, troubles, and taboos* (pp. 27–40). New York: Palgrave MacMillan.

Gardner, S. K. (2007). "I heard it through the grapevine": Doctoral student socialization in chemistry and history. *Higher Education, 54*(5), 723–740.

Gardner, S. K. (2008a). Fitting the mold of graduate school: A qualitative study of socialization in doctoral education. *Innovative Higher Education, 33*(2), 125–138.

Gardner, S. K. (2008b). "What's too much and what's too little?" The process of becoming an independent researcher in doctoral education. *Journal of Higher Education, 79*(3), 326–350.

Gardner, S. K., & Barker, M. J. (2015). Engaging graduate and professional students. In S. J. Quaye & S. R. Harper (Eds.), *Student engagement in higher education: Theoretical perspectives and practical approaches for diverse populations* (pp. 339–354). New York: Routledge.

Gary, S. (2008). Bennett and Spelman Colleges: Creating Black female Ph.D.s in the sciences. In M. Gasman & C. L. Tudico (Eds.), *Historically Black colleges and universities: Triumphs, troubles, and taboos* (pp. 41–52). New York: Palgrave MacMillan.

Gary, S. (2013). Supporting the dream: The role of faculty members at historically Black colleges and universities in promoting STEM Ph.D. education. In R. T.

Palmer, D. C. Maramba, & M. Gasman (Eds.), *Fostering success of ethnic and racial minorities in STEM: The role of minority-serving institutions* (pp. 86–101). New York: Routledge.

Gasman, M., Hirschfeld, A., & Vultaggio, J. (2008). "Difficult yet rewarding": The experiences of African American graduate students in education at an Ivy League institution. *Journal of Diversity in Higher Education, 1*(2), 126–138.

Gay, G. (2004). Navigating marginality en route to the professoriate: Graduate students of color learning and living in academia. *International Journal of Qualitative Studies in Education, 17*(2), 265–288.

Gibbs, K. D., & Griffin, K. A. (2013). What do I want to be with my Ph.D.? The roles of personal values and structural dynamics in shaping the career interests of recent biomedical science Ph.D. graduates. *CBE-Life Sciences Education, 12*(4), 711–723.

Gildersleeve, R. E., Croom, N. N., & Vasquez, P. L. (2011). "Am I going crazy?!": A critical race analysis of doctoral education. *Equity & Excellence in Education, 44*(1), 93–114.

Golde, C. M. (2005). The role of the department and discipline in doctoral student attrition: Lessons from four departments. *Journal of Higher Education, 76*(6), 669–700.

González, J. C. (2006). Academic socialization experiences of Latina doctoral students: A qualitative understanding of support systems that aid and challenges that hinder the process. *Journal of Hispanic Higher Education, 5*(4), 347–365.

González, J. C. (2007). Surviving the doctorate and thriving as faculty: Latina junior faculty reflecting on their doctoral studies experiences. *Equity & Excellence in Education, 40*(4), 291–300.

Griffin, K. A. (2012). Black professors managing mentorship: Implications of applying social exchange frameworks to analyses of student interactions and their influence on scholarly productivity. *Teachers College Record, 114*(5), 1–37.

Griffin, K. A., Muñiz, M. M., & Espinosa, L. (2012). The influence of campus racial climate on diversity in graduate education. *Review of Higher Education, 35*(4), 535–566.

Griffin, K. A., & Reddick, R. J. (2011). Surveillance and sacrifice: Gender differences in the mentoring patterns of Black professors at predominantly white research universities. *American Educational Research Journal, 48*(5), 1032–1057.

Harper, S. R. (2013). Am I my brother's teacher? Black undergraduates, peer pedagogies, and racial socialization in predominantly white postsecondary contexts. *Review of Research in Education, 37*(1), 183–211.

Harper, S. R. (2014). (Re)setting the agenda for college men of color: Lessons learned from a 15-year movement to improve Black male student success. In R. A. Williams (Ed.), *Men of color in higher education: New foundations for developing models for success* (pp. 116–143). Sterling, VA: Stylus.

Harper, S. R., & Davis, C. H. F., III. (2012). They (don't) care about education: A counternarrative on Black male students' responses to inequitable schooling. *Educational Foundations, 26*(1), 103–120.

Harper, S. R., & Porter, A. C. (2012). *Attracting Black male students to research careers in education: A report from the Grad Prep Academy Project.* Philadelphia: University of Pennsylvania, Center for the Study of Race and Equity in Education.

hooks, b. (1989). *Talking back: Thinking feminist, thinking Black.* Cambridge, MA: South End Press.

Jaeger, A. J., Haley, K. J., Ampaw, F., & Levin, J. S. (2013). Understanding the career choice for underrepresented minority doctoral students in science and engineering. *Journal of Women and Minorities in Science and Engineering, 19*(1), 1–16.

Johnson-Bailey, J. (2004). Hitting and climbing the proverbial wall: Participation and retention issues for Black graduate women. *Race, Ethnicity, and Education, 7*(4), 331–349.

Kidder, W. C. (2001). Does the LSAT mirror or magnify racial and ethnic differences in educational attainment? A study of equally achieving "elite" college students. *California Law Review, 89*(4), 1055–1124.

Ladson-Billings, G. (1997). For colored girls who have considered suicide when the academy's not enough: Reflections of an African American woman scholar. In A. Neumann & P. L. Peterson (Eds.), *Learning from our lives: Women, research, and autobiography in education* (pp. 52–70). New York: Teachers College Press.

Lewis, D. L. (1993). *W. E. B. Du Bois: Biography of a race, 1868–1919.* New York: Henry Holt.

Lovitts, B. E. (2001). *Leaving the ivory tower: The causes and consequences of departure from doctoral study.* Lanham, MD: Rowman & Littlefield.

Lundy-Wagner, V., Vultaggio, J., & Gasman, M. (2013). Preparing underrepresented students of color for doctoral success: The role of undergraduate institutions. *International Journal of Doctoral Studies, 8*, 151–172.

McMickens, T. L. (2011). *Racism readiness as an educational outcome for graduates of historically Black colleges and universities: A multi-campus grounded theory study* (Unpublished doctoral dissertation). University of Pennsylvania, Philadelphia.

Miradé, A. (1988). I never had a mentor: Reflections of a Chicano sociologist. *American Sociologist, 19*(4), 355–362.

Nettles, M. T., & Millett, C. M. (2006). *Three magic letters: Getting to Ph.D.* Baltimore, MD: Johns Hopkins University Press.

Noy, S., & Ray, R. (2012). Graduate students' perceptions of their advisors: Is there systematic disadvantage in mentorship? *Journal of Higher Education, 83*(6), 876–914.

Palmer, R. T., Hilton, A. A., & Fountaine, T. P. (2012). Black graduate education at historically Black colleges and universities: Trends, experiences, and outcomes. In R. T. Palmer, A. A. Hilton, & T. P. Fountaine (Eds.), *Black graduate education at historically Black colleges and universities: Trends, experiences, and outcomes* (pp. 1–8). Charlotte, NC: Information Age.

Palmer, R. T., Maramba, D. C., Gasman, M., & Lloyd, K. D. J. (2013). Charting the course: The role of minority-serving institutions in facilitating the success of underrepresented racial minority students in STEM. In R. T. Palmer, D. C. Maramba, & M. Gasman (Eds.), *Fostering success of ethnic and racial minorities in STEM: The role of minority-serving institutions* (pp. 1–15). New York: Routledge.

Palmer, R. T., Wood, J. L., Dancy, T. E., & Strayhorn, T. L. (2014). *Black male collegians: Increasing access, retention, and persistence in higher education.* ASHE Higher Education Report (vol. 40, no. 3). San Francisco: Jossey-Bass.

Patton, L. D. (2009). My sister's keeper: A qualitative examination of mentoring experiences among African American women in graduate and professional schools. *Journal of Higher Education, 80*(5), 510–537.

Patton, L. D., & Harper, S. R. (2003). Mentoring relationships among African American women in graduate and professional schools. In M. F. Howard-Hamilton (Ed.), *Meeting the needs of African American women.* New Directions for Student Services (no. 104, pp. 67–78). San Francisco: Jossey-Bass.

Perna, L. W. (2001). The contribution of historically Black colleges and universities to the preparation of African Americans for faculty careers. *Research in Higher Education, 42*(3), 267–294.

Perna, L. W., Gasman, M., Gary, S., Lundy-Wagner, V., & Drezner, N. D. (2010). Identifying strategies for increasing degree attainment in STEM: Lessons from minority-serving institutions. In S. R. Harper & C. B. Newman (Eds.), *Students of color in STEM.* New Directions for Institutional Research (no. 148, pp. 41–51). San Francisco: Jossey-Bass.

Perna, L. W., Lundy-Wagner, V., Drezner, N. D., Gasman, M., Yoon, S., Bose, E., & Gary, S. (2009). The contribution of HBCUs to the preparation of African American women for STEM careers: A case study. *Research in Higher Education, 50*(1), 1–23.

Redd, K. E. (2008). *Data sources: Trends in graduate enrollment and doctoral degrees at historically Black colleges and universities, 1996 to 2006.* Retrieved from http://www.cgsnet.org/ckfinder/userfiles/files/DataSources_2008_03.pdf

Rendón, L. I. (1992). From the barrio to the academy: Revelations of a Mexican American "scholarship girl." In L. S. Zwerling & H. B. London (Eds.), *First-generation students: Confronting the cultural issues.* New Directions for Community Colleges (no. 80, pp. 55–64). San Francisco: Jossey-Bass.

Scott, R. R., & Shaw, M. E. (1985). Black and white performance in graduate school and policy implications of the use of Graduate Record Examination scores in admissions. *Journal of Negro Education, 54*(1), 14–23.

Shavers, M. C., & Moore, J. L. (2014). Black female voices: Self-presentation strategies in doctoral programs at predominately white institutions. *Journal of College Student Development, 55*(4), 391–407.

Shore, B. H. (2014). *The graduate advisor handbook: A student-centered approach.* Chicago: University of Chicago Press.

Solórzano, D. G. (1998). Critical race theory, race and gender microaggressions, and the experience of Chicana and Chicano scholars. *International Journal of Qualitative Studies in Education, 11*(1), 121–136.

Strayhorn, T. L. (2008). Influences on labor market outcomes of African American college graduates: A national study. *Journal of Higher Education, 79*(1), 28–57.

Strayhorn, T. L., Williams, M. S., Tillman-Kelly, D., & Suddeth, T. (2013). Sex differences in graduate school choice for Black HBCU bachelor's degree recipients: A national analysis. *Journal of African American Studies, 17*(2), 174–188.

Thomas, G. E. (1987). Black students in U.S. graduate and professional schools in the 1980s: A national and institutional assessment. *Harvard Educational Review, 57*(3), 261–282.

Truong, K. A. (2010). *Racism and racial trauma in doctoral study: How students of color experience and negotiate the political complexities of racist encounters* (Unpublished doctoral dissertation). University of Pennsylvania, Philadelphia.

Truong, K. A., & Museus, S. D. (2012). Responding to racism and racial trauma in doctoral study: An inventory for coping and mediating relationships. *Harvard Educational Review, 82*(2), 226–254.

Turner, C. S. V., González, J. C., & Wood, J. L. (2008). Faculty of color in academe: What 20 years of literature tells us. *Journal of Diversity in Higher Education, 1*(3), 139–168.

U.S. Department of Education. (2013). *Digest of education statistics, 2012.* Washington, DC: National Center for Education Statistics, Institute of Education Sciences.

Zhao, C., Golde, C. M., & McCormick, A. C. (2007). More than a signature: How advisor choice and advisor behaviour affect doctoral student satisfaction. *Journal of Further and Higher Education, 31*(3), 263–281.

Joint Response From Leading Educational Research Centers to My Brother's Keeper Task Force Report

In response to a recent task force report to President Barack Obama on My Brother's Keeper, an initiative that brings together private sector and philanthropic organizations to improve the lives and outcomes of boys and young men of color in the United States, seven university-based research centers have jointly issued a statement.

The Center for the Study of Race and Equity in Education (University of Pennsylvania), Minority Male Community College Collaborative (San Diego State University), Morehouse Research Institute (Morehouse College), Project MALES and the Texas Education Consortium for Male Students of Color (University of Texas at Austin), Todd Anthony Bell National Resource Center on the African American Male (The Ohio State University), UCLA Black Male Institute (University of California, Los Angeles), and Wisconsin's Equity and Inclusion Laboratory (University of Wisconsin–Madison) are all research enterprises that rigorously and routinely study factors that enable and limit educational, social, and occupational opportunities for boys and young men of color.

Leaders of the seven centers emphasize the importance of effective research-based interventions and are jointly issuing the following statement in response to the task force report:

> As Black and Latino male professors and research center directors, we salute President Obama as well as the many philanthropic and private sector funders for their commitment to improving the conditions of our nation's boys and young men of color.

The task force report offers a commendable articulation of challenges and opportunities for young men of color and various agents who play some role in their life outcomes. Recommendations offered therein are appropriately informed by research from a range of academic disciplines.

As our nation prepares to enact recommendations from the task force, we call for programs, policies, and services that are guided by research and documented effectiveness. We caution, for example, against the widespread replication of mentoring programs that haphazardly match young men with adults, as evidence concerning the outcomes of such programs is mixed. Moreover, we believe interventions should focus on better understanding and remedying systemic inequities in policies, schooling and social practices, and structures that persistently undermine the success of boys and men of color. More significant investment in the dissemination of existing research on what works, as well as funding new studies on promising policies and practices, would help ensure the success of My Brother's Keeper and the Americans it aims to effectively serve.

We urge private foundations, federal funding agencies (i.e., the Institute of Education Sciences, the National Science Foundation, and the National Institutes of Health), and other entities that invest in projects associated with My Brother's Keeper to take seriously the evidence base of initiatives that are proposed, as well as rigorous evaluations of newly funded projects. Funds are needed to facilitate productive collaborations among research centers such as ours, and to connect researchers with agents who lead organizations and initiatives for young men of color across our nation. The success of My Brother's Keeper depends heavily on the quality of research produced about its effectiveness. Ultimately, strong cultures of evidence and efficacy should guide all programs, services, and interventions associated with the initiative.

My Brother's Keeper affords our country an important opportunity to reframe hopeless, deficit-oriented narratives about boys and young men of color, schools that educate them, and communities in which they live. We are hopeful that the initiative will produce replicable models of success, but doing so requires more investment in studies of what works. To ensure the success of My Brother's Keeper, our research centers stand ready to serve as resources to its funders and the Obama administration.

Shaun R. Harper, University of Pennsylvania
J. Luke Wood, San Diego State University
Frank Harris III, San Diego State University
Bryant T. Marks, Morehouse College
Victor B. Sáenz, University of Texas at Austin
Luis Ponjuan, Texas A&M University
James L. Moore III, The Ohio State University
Tyrone C. Howard, University of California, Los Angeles
Jerlando F.L. Jackson, University of Wisconsin–Madison

ABOUT THE EDITORS AND CONTRIBUTORS

Editors

Shaun R. Harper is on the faculty in the Graduate School of Education, Africana Studies, and Gender Studies at the University of Pennsylvania. He is founder and executive director of the Center for the Study of Race and Equity in Education, codirector of RISE for Boys and Men of Color, and an advisory council member of President Barack Obama's My Brother's Keeper Alliance. Professor Harper's research examines race and gender in education, equity trends and racial climates on college campuses, Black and Latino male student success in high school and higher education, and college student engagement. He has authored more than 90 peer-reviewed journal articles and other academic publications. *Review of Research in Education, Journal of Higher Education, Journal of College Student Development, Review of Higher Education, Harvard Educational Review,* and *Teachers College Record* are some journals in which Dr. Harper's research is published. His 12 books include *Student Engagement in Higher Education* (2015), *College Men and Masculinities* (2010), and the fifth edition of *Student Services: A Handbook for the Profession* (2011). Professor Harper has received over $11.4 million in grants to fund his research on boys and men of color. The American Educational Research Association presented him its 2010 Early Career Award and 2014 Relating Research to Practice Award. He also received the 2008 Association for the Study of Higher Education Early Career Award, the 2012 National Association of Student Personnel Administrators Robert H. Shaffer Award for Faculty Excellence, and the 2014 American College Personnel Association Contribution to Knowledge Award. The *New York Times, Los Angeles Times, Washington Post, USA Today, Wall Street Journal, Sports Illustrated, Chronicle of Higher Education, Inside Higher Ed,* and over 400 other media outlets have quoted Dr. Harper and featured his research. He has appeared on CNN, ESPN, CSPAN, and NPR. In 2015, he was recognized in *Education Week* as one of the 50 most influential professors in the field of education. Professor Harper earned his bachelor's degree from Albany State, a historically Black university in Georgia, and his Ph.D. from Indiana University.

J. Luke Wood is an associate professor of administration, rehabilitation, and postsecondary education at San Diego State University. He is also codirector of the Minority Male Community College Collaborative (M2C3), a national project that partners with community colleges across the United States to enhance access, achievement, and success among minority male community college students. He is also the founder and current editor of the *Journal of African American Males in Education*, chair of the Multicultural and Multiethnic Education Special Interest Group of the American Educational Research Association, and chair-elect for the Association for the Study of Higher Education (ASHE) Council on Ethnic Participation (CEP). Dr. Wood has authored over 80 publications, including five coauthored books, four edited books, and 40 peer-reviewed journal articles. He is coauthor of five textbooks: *Community College Leadership & Administration: Theory, Practice, and Change* (2010); *Leadership Theory in the Community College: Applying Theory to Practice* (2013); *Ethical Leadership and the Community College: Paradigms, Decision-Making, and Praxis* (2014); *Black Male Collegians: Increasing Access, Retention, and Persistence in Higher Education* (2014); and *Black Men in Higher Education: A Guide to Ensuring Student Success* (2015). He is also coeditor of the books *Black Men in College: Implications for HBCUs and Beyond* (2012); *Black Males in Postsecondary Education: Examining Their Experiences in Diverse Institutional Contexts* (2012); *Community Colleges and STEM: Examining Underrepresented Racial and Ethnic Minorities* (2013); and *STEM Models of Success: Programs, Policies, and Practices in the Community College* (2014). Dr. Wood received the 2013 Barbara K. Townsend Emerging Scholar Award from the Council for the Study of Community Colleges and the 2010 ASHE CEP Mildred Garcia Award for Exemplary Scholarship. He earned his Ph.D. in educational leadership and policy studies from Arizona State University.

Contributors

Mauriell H. Amechi is director of the Community Outreach, Retention and Engagement (CORE) Program at the University of Minnesota. He also is a Ph.D. candidate in educational leadership and policy analysis at the University of Wisconsin–Madison. His research interests are primarily centered on the access, experiences, and outcomes of underrepresented communities in higher education, with a special emphasis on foster care youth and their college transitions. He earned his bachelor's degree in communication from the University of Illinois at Urbana-Champaign and his master's degree in higher education and student affairs from The Ohio State University.

Jonathan Berhanu is a Ph.D. student in educational policy studies and gender and women studies at the University of Wisconsin–Madison. His research agenda centers on the experiences of Black college men at predominantly

White institutions, specifically examining how college environments influence gender performance. He has worked in urban youth development, with particular emphases on college readiness and preparedness, since 2002. Berhanu previously worked at the Posse Foundation as a senior trainer, preparing Posse Scholars for their enrollment and transition into college through an intensive, eight-month precollegiate training program. His bachelor's degree in business administration is from Adelphi University, and his master's degree in higher education is from the University of Pennsylvania.

Edward Bush received his bachelor's degree in political science from University of California, Riverside; his master's degree in public administration from California State University–San Bernardino; and his doctorate in urban educational leadership from Claremont Graduate University. Dr. Bush's research has focused on African American male achievement in California Community College. His publications have appeared in *Black Issues in Higher Education, Community College Week, Educational Horizons*, and the *Community College Journal*. Dr. Bush is coauthor of *The Plan: A Guide for Women Raising African American Boys from Conception to College*. He has over 20 years experience in higher education and currently serves as vice president of student services at Riverside City College.

Dorinda Carter Andrews is an associate professor in the Department of Teacher Education at Michigan State University, where she teaches courses on racial identity development, urban education, critical multiculturalism, and critical race theory. Her research is broadly focused on race and equity in education. She studies issues of educational equity in suburban and urban schools, urban teacher preparation and identity development, and critical race praxis with K–12 educators. Dr. Carter Andrews is a former industrial engineer, kindergarten teacher, and high school math teacher. She regularly conducts professional development for in-service educators on addressing the academic and social needs of culturally diverse learners in various educational contexts and engaging in courageous conversations about the implications of race and bias in schools. Her work has been published in top-tier journals such as *Harvard Educational Review, Teachers College Record, Journal of Negro Education,* and *Anthropology & Education Quarterly*, among others.

Jonathan M. Cox is a Ph.D. candidate in sociology at the University of Maryland, College Park. His research focuses on new operationalizations of Black racial identity, the experiences of Black students at historically Black and predominantly White institutions, and the intersection of race and gender for collegiate men. Cox previously served as assistant director for multicultural affairs at Wake Forest University. He holds a master's degree in sociology from the University of Maryland, a master's degree in college student affairs from The Pennsylvania State University, and a bachelor's degree in education from Hampton University.

Terry K. Flennaugh is an assistant professor in the Department of Teacher Education at Michigan State University. He is also a core faculty member in the African American and African Studies Program and the Center for Gender in Global Context. Dr. Flennaugh's research focuses broadly on race, culture, and equity in education, with a particular emphasis on the educational experiences of Black males and other students of color in urban contexts. Utilizing both qualitative and quantitative methodologies, he examines the sense-making processes involved in constructing identities that lead to high academic performance in urban schools. He also studies issues of educational access and equity for communities of color as well as single-sex educational spaces for urban youth. His bachelor's degree in psychology and Ph.D. in urban schooling are from the University of California, Los Angeles.

Terence Hicks is dean of the Whitlowe R. Green College of Education at Prairie View A&M University in Texas. Dr. Hicks has conducted research on self-efficacy, teacher education, college retention, and the psychological well-being of college students. He has published four books, has presented and published over 75 research papers, and has been cited over 200 times. He has served as a principal or coprincipal investigator on federal and state grants totaling more than $1.4 million. Dr. Hicks holds bachelor's and master's degrees from Virginia State University. He earned an Ed.D. from Wilmington University and a Ph.D. from North Carolina State University.

David J. Johns is an educator, advocate, policy expert, and community organizer. He currently serves as the executive director of the White House Initiative on Educational Excellence for African Americans. With work experience ranging from the halls of Congress to urban elementary schools, Johns has worked on issues affecting low-income and minority students, neglected youth and early childhood education, and workforce development and postsecondary education. His research as an Andrew W. Mellon Fellow served as a catalyst to identify, disrupt, and supplant deleterious stereotypes of African American males in academia and society. Johns earned a master's degree in sociology and education policy from Teachers College, Columbia University, where he graduated with honors while simultaneously teaching elementary school in New York City. His bachelor's degree in English, creative writing, and African American studies is also from Columbia University.

Hassiem A. Kambui is an assistant professor of counseling at Florida Agricultural and Mechanical University. Dr. Kambui received a bachelor's degree in physics at North Carolina State University, a master's degree in school counseling from North Carolina Central University, and a Ph.D. in counseling and counselor education from North Carolina State University. He authored the book *Africentric Education: Public Schools Versus Charter Schools*, published in 2014. For over 10 years he worked at the North Carolina State Counseling Center. Professor Kambui has also worked as a professional counselor in public schools and other diverse settings.

Keon M. McGuire is an assistant professor of higher education in the Mary Lou Fulton Teachers College at Arizona State University. Dr. McGuire previously worked for the Center for the Study of Race and Equity in Education at the University of Pennsylvania, the College Board Advocacy and Policy Center, and Complete College America. His research interests include the development, experiences, and outcomes of students of color at predominantly White colleges and universities; race and racism in U.S. higher education; and the intersections of race, gender, and spiritual identities among Black undergraduates. His bachelor's degree in history is from Wake Forest University. Professor McGuire earned his Ph.D. in higher education and Africana studies from the University of Pennsylvania.

Demetri L. Morgan is a Ph.D. candidate at the University of Pennsylvania, where he serves as a research associate in the Center for the Study of Race and Equity in Education and a predoctoral fellow with the Penn Alliance for Higher Education and Democracy. Morgan's research agenda centers on the roles and purposes of higher education institutions in a diverse democracy. Specifically, he is concerned with student political development and engagement, as well as the nexus among diversity, inclusion, and equity and democratic engagement. Morgan earned his bachelor's degree in political science from the University of Florida and his master's degree in higher education and student affairs from Indiana University.

Robert T. Palmer is associate professor and program coordinator in the Department of Educational Leadership and Policy Studies at Howard University. His research examines issues of access, equity, retention, persistence, and the college experience of racial and ethnic minorities, particularly Black men as well as other student groups at historically Black colleges and universities. Dr. Palmer's work has been published in national refereed journals, and he has authored or coauthored well over 85 academic publications and produced nine books. In 2011 Dr. Palmer was named an ACPA Emerging Scholar, and in 2012 he received the Carlos J. Vallejo Award of Emerging Scholarship from the American Education Research Association. Furthermore, in 2012 he received the Association for the Study of Higher Education's Mildred García Junior Exemplary Scholarship Award.

Terrell L. Strayhorn is professor of higher education at The Ohio State University, where he also serves as director of the Center for Higher Education Enterprise. He has authored seven books and monographs and over 120 refereed journal articles, book chapters, and scholarly publications. Strayhorn has presented over 150 research papers and workshops at state, national, and international conferences. His research focuses on vulnerable populations in education, social psychological determinants of student success, and the science of broadening participation in STEM. The *Journal of Blacks in Higher Education* named him "one of the most highly visible new scholars in his field." Professor Strayhorn has received numerous awards and honors, including the Association for the Study of Higher Education Early Career Award. His bachelor's and master's degrees are from the University of Virginia, and his Ph.D. is from Virginia Tech.

Chezare A. Warren is an assistant professor in the Department of Teacher Education at Michigan State University. In 2014 he completed a postdoctoral research fellowship at the University of Pennsylvania's Graduate School of Education in the Division of Applied Psychology and Human Development and the Center for the Study of Race and Equity in Education. He has over a decade of professional experience as a Chicago Public Schools math teacher and school administrator. Dr. Warren's research interests include urban teacher education, culturally responsive teaching, and critical race theory in education. His work has been published in peer-reviewed journals such as *Teachers College Record, Urban Education,* the *Urban Review,* the *Interdisciplinary Journal of Teaching and Learning,* and the *Journal of Negro Education.*

Collin D. Williams Jr. is a senior research associate in the Center for the Study of Race and Equity in Education at the University of Pennsylvania, where he also teaches a graduate-level course on diversity issues in the United States. His research explores how undergraduates' social experiences and participation in intercollegiate athletics influence engagement, academic performance, and postcollege outcomes, especially for students from low-income, first-generation college, and underrepresented minority backgrounds. Williams earned his bachelor's degree in sociology and Africana studies and his Ph.D. in higher education from the University of Pennsylvania.

Michael Steven Williams is on the faculty in School of Public Affairs at Baruch College, City University of New York. His research broadly explores equity and diversity, the social psychological development of students, and institutional diversity in American postsecondary education. Specifically, he centers his inquiry on two aspects of higher education: *the student*, particularly student socialization and mentoring, and *the institution*, with focus on specialized institutions such as historically Black colleges and universities. To date he has authored over 15 scholarly publications, including peer-reviewed journal articles and other academic publications. He earned his bachelor's degree from Villanova University, his master's degree from the University of Pennsylvania, and his Ph.D. from The Ohio State University.